THE
MARINO
MISSION

THE
MARINO
MISSION

One Girl, One Mission,
One Thousand Words

1,000 Need-to-Know
*SAT Vocabulary Words

Karen B. Chapman

Published by Wiley Publishing, Inc., Hoboken, New Jersey

For general information on our other products and services or to obtain technical support please contact our Customer Care Department within the U.S. at (800) 762-2974, outside the U.S. at (317) 572-3993 or fax (317) 572-4002.

Wiley also publishes its books in a variety of electronic formats. Some content that appears in print may not be available in electronic books. For more information about Wiley products, please visit our web site at www.wiley.com.

Library of Congress Cataloging-in-Publication Data available from publisher upon request.

ISBN: 0-7645-7831-6

Printed in the United States of America

10 9 8 7 6 5

Book design by Kathie Rickard

Cover design by José Almaguer

Book production by Wiley Publishing, Inc. Composition Services

Table of Contents

About the Author

Karen B. Chapman, Ph.D., grew up in upstate New York and graduated from Cornell University with a B.S. in Biology. She received a Ph.D. in Molecular Biology and Genetics from John Hopkins University School of Medicine and went on to complete postdoctoral fellowships at both the Pasteur Institute in Paris and at Harvard Medical School. Currently, she resides in Northern California with her husband and four young children.

1

A Futile Request

Alexa waited at the school entryway, anxiously scanning the line of cars jostling for position at the curb. It was five after 3:00 on Friday and the school week was mercifully over. Today Alexa's father was scheduled to pick her up along with Doug and Caroline, the two other kids in her carpool. Alexa was fervently hoping that her dad wouldn't be late. It was so awkward to wait when Doug and Caroline were impatient to leave.

"Is your mom coming?" Doug asked pointedly.

Alexa shifted uncomfortably and adjusted the wayward straps of her backpack. Doug was the star of both the junior varsity soccer team and the lacrosse team. In the social hierarchy[1] of Ithaca High School, Doug reigned with a status and popularity unmatched by his classmates. Alexa was far too shy to pursue a friendship with a boy like Doug, but the proximity of their houses made it natural for them to carpool together. Caroline was the third member of their group, and her picture-perfect

---

[1] Hierarchy: the classification of a group of people according to ability or to economic, social, or professional standing; pecking order, chain of command

appearance and popularity made her a more natural counterpart for Doug. "My dad's coming today," Alexa answered, as she stood on her tiptoes to catch a glimpse of the end of the line. "There he is!" Alexa couldn't hide the relief in her voice as she spotted her father's red Chevy Suburban.

Alexa slid into the front seat next to her father while Doug and Caroline hopped into the back. They must have been sharing a private joke—Caroline was giggling incessantly.[2] Alexa silently speculated[3] that the two would probably begin dating this summer and would end up being homecoming king and queen. The two of them just seemed to emulate[4] the conventional[5] image of popularity-contest winners, she thought with disdain.

Alexa greeted her father with a quick kiss on the cheek. She was genuinely happy to see him because she hadn't seen him since last weekend. Her parents had separated recently, and the process of finalizing the divorce was currently underway. It was still a fresh and painful wound for Alexa, exacerbated[6] by this shuttling back and forth from her childhood house to her father's apartment.

After dropping off Doug, they continued on in silence to the exclusive[7] cul-de-sac where Caroline lived in a large, pretentious[8] Tudor-style mansion. Caroline left with a quick "thanks" and Alexa breathed a sigh of relief. Caroline's haughty[9] attitude and disdainful[10] glances were tiring. It wasn't that she felt jealous of Doug and Caroline, nor did she feel

---

[2] Incessantly: non-stop, never ending
[3] Speculate: to review something idly or casually and often inconclusively
[4] Emulate: try to be like, imitate
[5] Conventional: according with, sanctioned by, or based on convention (a principle or procedure accepted as true or correct); ordinary, conformist, predictable
[6] Exacerbate: to make more violent, bitter, or severe
[7] Exclusive: restricted in distribution, use, or appeal because of expense
[8] Pretentious: making usually unjustified or excessive claims (as of value or standing); showy, ostentatious
[9] Haughty: blatantly and disdainfully proud; snooty, conceited
[10] Disdainful: full of a feeling of contempt for what is beneath one; scornful

particularly miffed[11] that the two of them often didn't include her in their conversations. It just seemed that they perpetuated[12] an aura of superiority that Alexa didn't aspire to.

Alexa pulled the visor down and flipped open the mirror, studying her reflection. She pulled the rubber band out of her ponytail and her shiny, shoulder-length brown hair came tumbling down, covering her green eyes. Growing up, Alexa had always been a bit of a tomboy—she was not inclined[13] to obsess about her looks the way so many of her contemporaries[14] did. Her attitude had begun to change only recently, when she realized that it was not incongruous[15] to be both athletic and concerned with your appearance. This past year, Alexa's first year of high school, was really the first time that she started feeling good about the way she looked. She had started running on the track team and it was as if she had undergone a transformation[16] from an awkward, shy tomboy to an attractive and confident 16-year-old.

Alexa took her hairbrush out of her backpack and fixed her ponytail as they drove past Alexa's house high on the hill overlooking Cayuga Lake. "It looks like the lawn could use a little work," Alexa's father noted as he glanced at the house the three of them had shared up until two months ago, when he took a modest[17] apartment in downtown Ithaca. Alexa maintained her silence as she wondered what her father was thinking. His demeanor[18] didn't reveal anything, but Alexa wondered if he could really feel that detached[19] from the house they had all shared for so many years.

---

[11] Miff: to put into ill humor; offend
[12] Perpetuate: to make perpetual or to cause to last indefinitely
[13] Incline: to lean, tend, or become drawn toward an opinion or course of conduct
[14] Contemporaries: one of the same age or nearly the same age as another
[15] Incongruous: lacking congruity, not harmonious, incompatible
[16] Transformation: the act, process, or instance of transforming (to change in composition or structure)
[17] Modest: unassuming, unpretentious; limited in size, amount, or scope
[18] Demeanor: behavior toward others, outward manner; conduct
[19] Detached: exhibiting an aloof objectivity; disconnected, removed

Alexa's father, David McCurry, was a venerated[20] professor of molecular biology at Cornell University. He taught the rudiments[21] of DNA technology to lecture halls filled with aspiring pre-med students. "The Inner Machinations[22] of the Cell" was the title of his popular graduate-level seminar, attended by scores of serious-minded scientists in the making. He was highly regarded by his colleagues in the research community for being at the forefront of emergent[23] technologies in the rapidly evolving field of genetics.

Alexa was proud of her father and treasured the time they spent together during her childhood, as brief as these interludes[24] were. Alexa's father was also busy running a molecular biology laboratory, where he and his graduate students studied DNA in endless detail. He studied the DNA of a worm called a nematode, which was so tiny you needed a microscope to see it. Alexa would often go to the laboratory with her father on weekends, where he would inevitably become embroiled[25] in deep and lengthy discussions with the graduate students who, it seemed to her, appeared to live in the laboratory.

It was Alexa's mom, Helen, who was always there for her with abundant time and an unswerving[26] devotion to managing the details of her daughter's life. Helen was also a scientist, but as she liked to characterize it when the subject of vocation[27] came up, she was an "unemployed marine biologist, landlocked in the middle of upstate New York." Helen had forgone a scientific career, citing the fact that it was next to impossible to have a career in marine biology so far from the ocean.

---

[20] Venerate: to regard with reverential respect or with admiring deference
[21] Rudiment: a basic principle, element, or fundamental skill
[22] Machination: a scheming or crafty action or artful design intended to accomplish some usually evil end
[23] Emergent: newly formed or prominent
[24] Interlude: an intervening or interruptive period, space or event; interval
[25] Embroil: to involve in conflict or difficulties
[26] Unswerving: not swerving or turning aside; steady
[27] Vocation: the work in which a person is regularly employed; career, occupation, profession

Meanwhile, Alexa's father had a burgeoning[28] scientific career and he had successfully climbed the academic ladder. Alexa had begun to suspect that the chasm[29] between her parents had something to do with the conflicting requirements of their careers. Alexa's mother wanted to move to an academic setting near the ocean, while her father was reluctant to move away from the successful laboratory he had created at Cornell.

Alexa and her dad arrived at the small apartment that he now called home. She followed him inside and settled in at the desk in front of a giant-screen computer. Her father was clearly inept[30] at decorating, Alexa thought as she looked at the lurid[31] green curtains that the previous occupants had left. Or maybe he was just indifferent[32] to the aesthetics[33] of his surroundings. Alexa reconsidered and thought that was probably it. To Alexa, her father seemed adept[34] at everything he put his mind to. But he abhorred[35] spending time thinking about such mundane[36] things as decorating. Her father was an archetypal[37] professor—his mind was always on his studies.

"Do you want a soda?" her father asked.

"Sure," Alexa replied, sensing her father was making an effort to make her happy in this awkward new routine.

"What do you say we go to Zeus' for pizza tonight?" her father asked as he set the can of soda down next to the mouse pad.

"OK, but I'm supposed to go to Laurie's tonight to watch a movie with my friends," Alexa said as she typed in her e-mail password.

"No problem, I'll drop you off there after dinner."

---

[28] Burgeoning: growing and expanding rapidly
[29] Chasm: a marked division, separation, or difference
[30] Inept: generally incompetent; bungling
[31] Lurid: causing horror or revulsion; ghastly
[32] Indifferent: apathetic, unconcerned
[33] Aesthetics: a pleasing appearance or effect; beauty
[34] Adept: thoroughly proficient; skillful
[35] Abhor: to regard with extreme repugnance; loathe
[36] Mundane: characterized by the practical, transitory, and ordinary; commonplace
[37] Archetypal: classic example, model example

"Can I stay there until 11:30?" Alexa asked in her sweetest tone, which she hoped wasn't too cloying.[38] She had gotten her driver's permit when she turned sixteen last month, but she was still unable to drive unaccompanied by an adult.

Her father made an exaggerated pained expression. He liked to be in bed by 11:00, but Alexa could plainly see by his smile that he would let her.

Alexa saw a message from Laurie in her inbox. This past year they had become best friends, and this had changed Alexa's life immeasurably for the better. All throughout junior high, Alexa had felt like she didn't have a close group of friends. It wasn't like she was totally bereft[39] of friends, but she hadn't formed any friendships that felt particularly meaningful and enduring.[40]

This past year, everything had changed when Alexa entered Ithaca High School and met Laurie. Laurie was editor of the school newspaper. She was bright, funny, and gregarious.[41] Alexa had joined the school newspaper this past year and her easy camaraderie[42] with Laurie had grown into a deep friendship. It was so easy to talk to her—Alexa confided everything to Laurie. Laurie, in turn, was a solid friend. She always included Alexa in her close circle of friends, a group of girls Alexa really liked. It was as if Laurie's endorsement[43] opened up a whole new existence for Alexa. It felt so good to finally find a group of friends she liked and trusted—friends she cherished[44] and wanted to keep forever.

Alexa opened the message from Laurie, which read:

---

[38] Cloying: excessively sweet or sentimental
[39] Bereft: deprived or robbed of possession of something
[40] Enduring: lasting
[41] Gregarious: marked by or indicating a liking for companionship; sociable
[42] Camaraderie: a spirit of friendly good fellowship
[43] Endorsement: backing, sanction, approval
[44] Cherished: to hold dear; feel or show affection for

"Hi Lexxie!

Are you home yet?? Call me ASAP! You're not going to believe my unbelievable luck! I got an internship with CNN this summer! Can't wait to tell you all about it. I'm going to be the assistant to the reporter who works right in downtown Ithaca. I'm soooo excited!! Are you coming over tonight? Call me! :-) Laurie

Alexa smiled at the thought of Laurie's elation.[45] Laurie was such a go-getter. She had an easygoing demeanor, yet she approached challenges with enthusiasm and ardor.[46] Even when she faced imminent[47] failure, Laurie persevered[48] with her positive attitude. After receiving a stack of rejection letters, she had scored the internship of her dreams. Her persistence had paid off spectacularly.

While Alexa was happy for Laurie and her great summer job, she had been brooding[49] about her own uncertain plans for the summer. She desperately wanted to stay in Ithaca and spend her vacation with Laurie. However, Alexa was cognizant[50] of her mother's plans to spend the summer in Nicaragua, and Alexa had the perception[51] that she was expected to go with her. But since the final decision had not yet been made, Alexa hoped that she could cajole[52] her father into letting her stay in Ithaca with him.

---

[45] Elation: marked by high spirits; exultant
[46] Ardor: extreme vigor or energy; intensity
[47] Imminent: ready to take place; looming, about to happen
[48] Persevere: to persist in a state, enterprise, or undertaking in spite of challenges
[49] Brooding: to dwell gloomily on a subject, worrying
[50] Cognizant: knowledgeable about something, especially through personal experience; mindful
[51] Perception: the effect or product or perceiving (to come aware of through the senses)
[52] Cajole: to persuade with flattery or gentle urging, especially in the face of reluctance

CRO CRO

Zeus' pizza house was the best of several excellent pizza places in the college town of Ithaca. It was always busy, and this being Friday night, was even more chaotic than usual. The clientele[53] was largely made up of students, one of whom waved a greeting to Professor McCurry as he and Alexa entered the restaurant. Another group of students was eyeing the esteemed[54] professor with reverence.[55] He was a minor celebrity in town, and Alexa beamed with pride. Her father waited until the pizza arrived at the table, piping hot, thick, and cheesy, to bring up the topic she'd been dreading. Without preamble,[56] he delved into the dreaded subject.

"You know about the new job offer your mother got for this summer." Alexa took a bite of pizza as her father spoke gingerly.[57] Helen had been offered a consulting position at a marine biology facility called Puerto Marino, which was located on a Caribbean island off of the coast of Nicaragua in Central America. "This would be a really great opportunity for you," her father continued. "You could work on your Spanish, see a new place, get to..."

"I don't want to go to Nicaragua for the summer!" Alexa cut him off. "I want to stay here in Ithaca! Can't I stay here with you?" Alexa pleaded volubly.[58] "All my friends are here, we're going to go swimming in the gorge every day, and Laurie's brother has a boat on the lake, and I applied for a job at Hansen's Department Store!" The words were tumbling out of Alexa's mouth, but she could already sense it was a losing battle.

---

[53] Clientele: customers, patrons
[54] Esteem: to regard highly
[55] Reverence: honor or respect felt or shown; deference; especially profound or adoring awed respect
[56] Preamble: an introductory statement
[57] Gingerly: very cautiously or carefully
[58] Volubly: marked by a ready flow of speech

"A department store?" Alexa's father repeated in a disparaging[59] tone of voice. "Why would you want to sell clothes all summer when you could work in a lab? They have a fully equipped molecular biology lab at Puerto Marino and your mother has already arranged for you to work there. It would be a great opportunity for you to have a project of your own, not to mention the fact that it may very well help you get into a good school. Colleges invariably[60] look for this type of thing—an interesting and educational summer experience."

"I don't think that spending a whole summer locked up in a laboratory sounds very interesting!" Alexa exclaimed. She was in no mood for her dad's rhetoric[61] about college admissions. It wasn't that she didn't want to go to college. It was that her parents unending discourse[62] about "what you should be doing if you want to go to a good college" was truly tiring and left Alexa feeling ambivalent[63] about the whole subject.

Alexa's father raised his eyebrows in a tacit[64] response. Her flippancy[65] had clearly struck a sour note with him. Alexa looked down at her pizza, seeing it was futile[66] to argue. Her father was resolute.[67] She was going to Nicaragua for the summer.

---

[59] Disparaging: to speak slightingly about; decry

[60] Invariably: not changing or capable of change; constant

[61] Rhetoric: a type or mode of language or speech; also insincere or lofty language

[62] Discourse: talk, converse

[63] Ambivalent: simultaneous and contradictory feelings (as attraction and repulsion) toward an object, person, or action

[64] Tacit: expressed or carried on without words or speech

[65] Flippancy: unbecoming levity or pertness, especially in respect to grave or sacred matters

[66] Futile: serving no useful purpose; completely ineffective

[67] Resolute: marked by firm determination; resolved

2

Captivating Creatures

Alexa pressed her forehead to the glass window of the airplane to get a better view of the spectacular scenery below. The crystal clear blue water and sandy white beaches looked so inviting, especially after such a long and exhausting journey. The day had started painfully early for Alexa and her mom, with an hour-and-a-half drive to the Syracuse Airport to catch the first flight to New York City. In New York, they boarded a jet for Managua, the capital of Nicaragua. Then they boarded the twin-engine prop plane destined for an island off of the east coast of Nicaragua called the Isla del Maize Grande.

Alexa had barely conversed with her mother at all during the journey. At first, she felt in a bit of a daze from waking up so early. Later in the day, as the journey continued endlessly, she simply didn't feel like making the effort to be genial.[1] To be affable[2] now would imply that she

---

[1] Genial: marked by sympathy or friendliness; kindly
[2] Affable: being pleasant and at ease talking to others

was happy to go along with her parents' plans for her summer vacation. In reality, Alexa still harbored[3] a lot of resentment because she didn't get to choose where she would be spending her summer and what she would be doing.

Now they were descending over this spectacular island in this small plane that afforded an amazing view, and despite her lingering resentment, Alexa's curiosity was piqued[4] with the exotic beauty of her surroundings. Helen held out her hand for Alexa to hold as the plane initiated a steep descent, punctuated[5] with bumps from air turbulence. Alexa felt too old to be holding her mother's hand like this, but this was an extenuating[6] circumstance. When she turned to see her mother's face, she could see the nervousness etched into the lines around her eyes and mouth. Alexa squeezed her hand and smiled bravely.

Alexa had sensed that her mother's forsaken career had been an issue between her parents over the years. Although she was devastated by her parents' divorce, she was glad her mother was finally getting out of the house and exploring her options. However, Alexa had never seen her mother so nervous before. She knew it wasn't just the airplane's descent that was evoking[7] her anxiety, but the new job ahead of her.

Helen was a marine biologist who specialized in mammals that live in the ocean, such as dolphins, whales, and sea lions. In the past, her research had focused on dolphins and their innate[8] ability to use sonar for underwater navigation. Alexa loved listening to stories of her mother's work with dolphins in San Diego. They had traveled to San Diego several times when Alexa was growing up, and Alexa was always amazed

---

[3] Harbor: to hold a thought or feeling of
[4] Pique: to excite or arouse by a provocation, challenge, or rebuff
[5] Punctuate: to break into or interrupt at intervals
[6] Extenuating: to mitigate; to lessen or try to lessen the seriousness or extent of by making partial excuses
[7] Evoke: to call forth or up; conjure
[8] Innate: existing in, belonging to, or determined by factors present in an individual from birth

to see the special rapport[9] her mother had with the dolphins that she studied.

As the airplane touched down on the tarmac, Helen breathed an audible sigh of relief. They disembarked from the small airplane right onto the landing strip. One of the two pilots assisted the eleven passengers down the stairs while the other pilot procured[10] the luggage from the cargo hold. When Alexa approached the door of the airplane to disembark, the heat and humidity hit her face like a smothering warm blanket. The steamy jungle air was so different from the arid[11] heat that Alexa had experienced during a childhood trip to the desert in New Mexico.

"Wow, is it ever hot!" Alexa turned to inform her mother.

"Don't worry, as soon as you change into your summer clothes you're going to like it." Alexa's mother had a look of satisfaction on her face as she absorbed the warm gentle breeze and the view of the swaying palm trees in the distance. Helen hated the harsh winters of upstate New York, so for her the warm climate of Central America was a tropical utopia.[12]

"This is an impressive airport!" Alexa said sarcastically. "Look at that color!" The terminal consisted of a single shack-like building that was painted a garish[13] shade of turquoise. A single bright red Coca-Cola machine stood under the sagging awning.

"Well, maybe the color is a little crass,[14] but I think this little terminal is charmingly unpretentious!" Helen replied. The two of them headed to the small building, struggling with their voluminous[15] belongings.

"Where are we going?" Alexa inquired as they entered the building. She realized that she hadn't even asked her mother anything about her

---

9   Rapport: relation marked by harmony, conformity, accord, or affinity
10   Procure: to get possession of; obtain by particular care and effort
11   Arid: excessively dry
12   Utopia: a place of ideal perfection
13   Garish: offensively or distressingly bright; glaring
14   Crass: having or indicating such grossness of mind as precludes delicacy and discrimination
15   Voluminous: having or marked by great volume or bulk

job here in Nicaragua. She'd been so preoccupied trying to think of a way to stay in Ithaca that she was oblivious[16] to her mother's plans. Once her parents decided she was going to Nicaragua, Alexa didn't even ask her mother for any details. She was so embittered[17] at having the decision made for her that for the last two weeks she had stubbornly acted indifferent to the whole subject.

"Someone is supposed to meet us here—an emissary[18] from Puerto Marino. He'll show us to the boat. We'll be taking a boat to another island where Puerto Marino is located." Helen scanned the small room, but no one was waiting for them.

Alexa picked up the Nicaragua guide book in her mother's bag and began scanning. "I don't see any island called Puerto Marino, Mom."

"Puerto Marino isn't the name of the island, it's the name of the marine biology facility. It's owned by an American company called the Marino Enterprise. I have a different map in the yellow folder in my black bag over there." She gestured toward a bag on top of their pile of luggage. "You're welcome to take a look."

"OK," Alexa replied. She pulled out the yellow folder and flipped through the papers. The map was printed on pale blue paper and it had the word "CONFIDENTIAL" stamped in vivid[19] red block letters at the top. On this map it was easy to locate Puerto Marino. There it was, on a small, unnamed island off of the east coast of Nicaragua, about twenty miles from the Isla del Maize Grande, the island that they were on now.

Alexa was surprised that she hadn't been able to locate the island on the map in the guide book. She reached for the original map and put the two side by side. "Mom, the island isn't even on this map—it looks like

---

[16] Oblivious: lacking active conscious knowledge or awareness
[17] Embittered: having bitter feelings
[18] Emissary: one designated as the agent of another
[19] Vivid: producing a strong or clear impression on the senses; sharp, intense

there's nothing around that area at all. It's only on your blue map." Alexa's brow furrowed in thought. Had the cartographer[20] purposefully omitted the island from the tourist map?

Alexa rechecked the blue map. It was just then that she noticed the insignia of the U.S. Navy in the bottom right-hand corner.

"Mom, why do you have a map from the U.S. Navy?" Alexa asked with a sense of foreboding.[21] She racked her memory trying to recall what she'd learned in history class. There had been a civil war in Nicaragua in the 1980s, but Alexa couldn't remember any of the details. That whole affair had happened such a long time ago—right around the time she was born. This map looked new.

"Oh, I think they do some work with Puerto Marino and the dolphins there," Helen replied absentmindedly as she rummaged through her purse for a moist towelette. Her expression turned quizzical as she reconsidered what she had just said. "To be completely honest, I don't know exactly what the relationship is between the Navy and Puerto Marino. I know that the Navy has been interested in dolphins for decades. Maybe they're sponsoring some of the work there. Who knows? But we're about to find out, aren't we?" She smiled with anticipation.

Alexa smiled weakly in response. She simply didn't feel like showing too much enthusiasm for her mother's agenda.

"They have a big project there studying sonar in marine mammals. They're interested in the work I did years ago on echolocation. Puerto Marino is quite big, from what I understand—apparently the compound encompasses[22] a significant portion of the island. It's like a small city on

---

[20] Cartographer: one who makes maps
[21] Foreboding: to have an inward conviction of (as coming ill or misfortune)
[22] Encompasses: to form a circle about, enclose

an island that is otherwise fairly undeveloped. I think there's a small town—a local fishing community—but not much else." Her mother continued, "We'll be staying at an apartment right on the compound."

"Really?" Alexa answered. She was a bit perplexed[23] by this turn of events. She hadn't expected they would stay at a five-star resort, but she had never anticipated they would be on such a remote island for the whole summer.

"Alexa," her mother began her oration[24] softly, "this is a really important opportunity for me. You know how difficult it is to find a job as a marine biologist. I haven't worked in *so* long, and this is only a temporary position. But if it goes well, it'll be great for my résumé and hopefully lead to more opportunities down the line."

"I know, Mom. I want it to go well for you too." Alexa reached for her mother's hand and gave it a squeeze. She felt a tinge of remorse at her own unyielding[25] selfishness. She didn't want to undermine[26] her mother's optimism with continual strife.[27] Her mother had always been there for her. Alexa silently vowed to improve her attitude and try to be more agreeable for her mother's sake.

The one-room terminal emptied out quickly as the rest of the eleven passengers from the airplane departed. Alexa and her mother waited on the only bench in the room. The airplane they had arrived on had quickly left again, and now they were the only people in the airport.

A young man burst into the terminal, breathless from exertion. He was holding a sign that read "Dr. Helen McCurry."

Alexa burst out laughing. It was so funny for him to be holding a sign when they were the only ones in the entire airport!

---

[23] Perplexed: filled with uncertainty; puzzled

[24] Oration: speech; an elaborate discourse delivered in a formal and dignified manner

[25] Unyielding: not yielding (to surrender or relinquish to the control of another)

[26] Undermine: to weaken or ruin by degrees

[27] Strife: an act of contention; fight, struggle

Their guide was eager to converse with them but he spoke only Spanish, and both Alexa and Helen were too rusty in Spanish to be active interlocutors,[28] so they continued their journey in silence. Their guide had a car waiting for them that brought them to the island's marina.

∾ ∾

Everything about the marina was in a state of disrepair. The old wooden dock was dilapidated and creaked portentously[29] as they walked on it. All of the boats moored to the ramshackle dock looked only marginally seaworthy, except for one. A shiny new white yacht looked awkwardly out of place in the modest marina. On its stern, the words "Puerto Marino" were printed in bold block letters. They hopped aboard for the final phase of their interminable[30] journey.

The sun was setting as they approached their destination. Alexa felt invigorated by the boat ride and spectacular scenery. Now she was insatiably curious about her surroundings, but it was difficult to make out many details about their new island home, which was now enveloped[31] in darkness. They docked the boat at an empty pier and climbed aboard a waiting Jeep. Now they were on a remote,[32] unpaved road riddled with potholes and flanked by verdant[33] jungle.

"Where are we?" Alexa whispered to her mother, who sat next to her in the back seat.

"We're almost there," her mother answered, with excitement in her voice. They were approaching a gated entryway, guarded by two armed men. As they pulled up to the gate, one of the men approached the Jeep as the other spoke into a walkie-talkie in the small booth flanking the gate.

---

[28] Interlocutor: someone who takes part in a dialogue or conversation
[29] Portentously: something that foreshadows a coming event
[30] Interminable: having or seeming to have no end
[31] Enveloped: to enclose or enfold completely with or as if with a covering
[32] Remote: isolated, secluded, far from activity
[33] Verdant: green with growing plants

The guard exchanged words with their guide in Spanish and then turned to Helen and spoke in English. "Do you have your security clearance papers?" the guard prompted.[34]

"Yes, I think they're right in this folder." Helen scrambled through the pile of papers, pulled out the appropriate one, and handed it to the guard.

"I'll also need to see your passports," the guard added as he perused[35] the legitimacy[36] of the documents.

The guard looked carefully at the passport photos and at the two women in the backseat, then walked to the guardhouse, where he disappeared with their passports. In a few moments he returned and leaned his head through the open window to talk to Helen.

"Welcome to Puerto Marino, Dr. McCurry," the guard said with a wide smile. It appeared that with the perfunctory[37] security measures taken care of, the guard's demeanor changed profoundly.[38] "I'll escort you to security headquarters to check in and get your identification badges. After we've taken care of these necessities, you'll be meeting with Dr. Villeponce in the main building. Please follow me."

"OK," Helen agreed as their driver put the car in gear. The guard hopped on a motorcycle and waved for them to follow. The road ahead became a cloud of dust as the motorcycle agitated the dry, packed mud road into clouds of billowing dust.

"Well, this looks like a fun place to spend the summer!" Alexa said sarcastically.[39] The security was so tight, it appeared to be run like a prison. As soon as the words were out of her mouth, she felt a tinge of

---

[34] Prompt: to move to action; incite

[35] Peruse: to examine or consider with attention and in detail; study

[36] Legitimacy: the quality or state of being legitimate (being exactly as purposed, neither spurious nor false)

[37] Perfunctory: characterized by routine or superficiality

[38] Profoundly: characterized by intensity of feeling or quality

[39] Sarcastically: having the character of sarcasm (a mode of satirical wit depending for its effect on bitter, caustic, and often ironic language that is usually directed against an individual)

regret in her stomach as she saw the hurt look in her mother's face. Alexa chided herself silently.

"Alexa, we haven't even had a chance to settle in. Don't be so quick to judge."

"I'm sorry, Mom." Alex renewed her vow to improve her attitude. She could clearly see that her mother needed her support.

The guard on the motorcycle pulled up in front of a small gray building. Alexa and her mother climbed out of the Jeep, which immediately took off. The guard ushered them inside, where they had their pictures taken. Minutes later they were handed two photo IDs, each hanging from a circular chain designed to wear as a necklace.

"You must wear your identification badges at all times—security is maintained at a high level," the guard admonished.[40] "I can take you to meet Dr. Villeponce now, if you'll come with me."

The two women walked with the guard down the dusty road to a large circular cul-de-sac surrounded by several gray, nondescript[41] buildings that were illuminated by powerful floodlights mounted on the walls. The largest, on the right, looked like a colossal[42] domed warehouse. It was several stories high and nearly windowless, except for several small windows clustered near the door. All of the buildings were made of the same gray material, Alexa noticed. An absence of any kind of landscaping added to the austere[43] tone of the compound.

They followed the guard through the entryway of the large domed building. Flashing their newly minted photo IDs to the security desk, they waited in the foyer for Dr. Villeponce, who had been summoned by telephone.

---

[40] Admonish: to express warning or disapproval especially in a gentle, earnest, or solicitous manner
[41] Nondescript: lacking distinctive or interesting qualities; dull
[42] Colossal: of a bulk, extent, power, or effect approaching the stupendous or incredible
[43] Austere: stern and cold in appearance or manner

"Welcome to Puerto Marino! You must be Dr. McCurry. I'm Gavin Villeponce." A sturdy-looking man with a crew cut offered his hand enthusiastically to Helen. He seemed delighted to meet his new collaborator.[44]

"Hi. Yes, I'm Helen McCurry—please just call me Helen. And this is my daughter Alexa." Alexa dutifully shook the hand that was outstretched to her.

"Well, if you're not too tired from your trip, I'm anxious to show you around. Would you like to see the dolphins?" He looked expectantly at Helen and Alexa.

Alexa nodded mutely while Helen couldn't contain her burgeoning enthusiasm. "Oh, yes, let's go!"

They headed down a long windowless corridor ending in a wide double-door entryway. The doors were shut tight.

"This is a card key for you, Helen. It gives you access to the areas that you'll be using. Why don't we make sure it works." He handed Helen the card and motioned toward the device mounted on the wall. Helen swiped the card and the device responded with a mechanical click. They all looked toward the portal[45] as the immense double doors opened.

Alexa's senses were heightened as she crossed the threshold. It was like another world, alive with activity. The room was a vast[46] open space, like an enormous gymnasium with lofty high ceilings. The far side of the room was open to the outside and Alexa realized that they were situated right on the ocean. Large, deep pools of water nearly covered the floor space and Alexa was delighted to see that there were dozens of dolphins swimming in the water!

---

[44] Collaborator: co-worker, colleague; a person working jointly with others, especially in an intellectual endeavor

[45] Portal: a door or entrance, especially a grand or imposing one

[46] Vast: very great in size, amount, degree, or intensity, especially in extent or range

Dr. Villeponce led them onto a walkway between two of the pools and it was there that they paused to take in the incredible scene. There were dolphins everywhere, engaged in a multitude of activities. The air was alive with their high-pitched squeaks and the water below was teeming with activity. Several were clustered around a man in a wetsuit who was tossing small fish into their open mouths. A few of the dolphins looked to be doing nothing at all—they appeared torpid[47] as they floated motionless near the surface.

One dolphin surfaced near them and looked right at them. Alexa was mesmerized by the dolphin's face. It looked like it was smiling at her. She was surprised at the flood of emotions she felt rising up in her. She wanted to touch this charismatic[48] dolphin, to know it and to talk to it. With a start, she realized why her mother was so passionate about her work. She looked over at her mother, who had a sparkle of excitement in her eyes that Alexa had rarely seen.

"This is Speckle," Dr. Villeponce introduced the dolphin. "She's been with us for the longest amount of time—she's our oldest dolphin and quite a leader. She's the potentate[49] of the pool!" he chuckled. "All of the other dolphins treat her with respect," he added as he tossed her a fish. Speckle's head rose from the water just in time to catch the fish in midair. It was swallowed instantly. Speckle dove headfirst underwater and her sleek, supple[50] body disappeared from view.

As they continued along the walkway between the pools, Alexa couldn't help but watch the smooth, streamlined forms of the dolphins swimming underwater. They appeared so well adapted to their underwater

---

[47] Torpid: lacking in energy or vigor

[48] Charismatic: having, exhibiting, or based on charisma (a special magnetic charm or appeal)

[49] Potentate: one who has the power and position to rule over others; a monarch

[50] Supple: able to perform bending or twisting movements with ease and grace

habitat. Alexa had to consciously remind herself to watch where she was going—the walkway between the pools was only two feet wide and there was no railing to hold onto. She was captivated[51] with the vision of the dolphins swimming below, but she tried to remain cognizant of her precarious[52] position.

Dr. Villeponce continued talking as he led them to the outer pool, which was actually outdoors. "We have forty-two dolphins in our program, housed in these four interconnecting pools." He gestured toward the outer pool. "This one is contiguous[53] with the ocean, so that fresh ocean water bathes the facility." Bright floodlights mounted on the exterior of the building lit the walkway as the group continued around the periphery[54] of the outer pool. "There's a retractable gate over here that we can open so that we can release particular animals out into the bay periodically[55] for open water exercises." A sturdy ocean vessel was moored next to the gate.

Dr. Villeponce continued his oration in a commanding tone; he obviously enjoyed presiding[56] over the dolphin facility. As he rambled[57] on, Alexa barely heard his voice, she was so entranced with the scene unfolding beneath the surface of the water below. A dolphin had found a leaf floating on the surface of the water, deftly picked the leaf up in its mouth, and then dove under the surface. When the dolphin resurfaced, it released the leaf right in front of a very small dolphin, which appeared to be a baby. The larger dolphin goaded the youngster with some loud squeaking noises, clearly enticing the little one to play with its rousing[58] banter. The baby dolphin grabbed the leaf in its mouth and dove underwater. It swam all of the way down to the end of the pool underwater,

---

51 Captivate: to influence and dominate by some special charm, art, or trait and with an irresistible appeal
52 Precarious: characterized by a lack or security or stability that threatens with danger
53 Contiguous: touching or connected throughout in an unbroken sequence
54 Periphery: the external boundary or surface of a body
55 Periodically: occurring or recurring at regular intervals
56 Presiding: occupying a place of authority, acting as president, chairman, or moderator
57 Rambled: to talk or write in a long-winded, wandering fashion
58 Rousing: giving rise to excitement; stirring

then circled back and resurfaced right next to Alexa. It looked like the baby dolphin was trying to hand the leaf to her, as if to say "Your turn now!"

"Oh my gosh, it looks like he wants to play!" Alexa gushed.

"It's a 'she.' This is Coco. She's our youngest recruit—around one year old."

"Was she born in captivity?" Helen asked.

"No, she was obtained from the wild about two weeks ago."

Helen's face momentarily clouded over, obscuring her earlier enthusiasm. Dr. Villeponce reached down to take the leaf from Coco, putting an end to the game by depositing the soggy leaf in a nearby trash container.

"Let's go down to the observation level," Dr. Villeponce directed, as he led them to a stairway descending to a lower level. They followed him down into the darkness.

Alexa couldn't help but to gasp as she saw the immense windows on either side of her, allowing her to see all of the action underwater in both tanks. It felt like she was in a tunnel underwater. She couldn't help but marvel at the effortless way the dolphins maneuvered their streamlined bodies through the water. One of the dolphins paused at the window to look at the visitors, who in turn were looking at it. This vantage point made Alexa feel as if she could really be a part of the dolphins' world. It was intoxicating.

"How about if we stop by our molecular biology lab to show you where you'll be working on your project, Alexa?" Dr Villeponce looked at her expectantly.

"OK," Alexa nodded absently, her reverie preempted[59] with his question. A laboratory seemed comparatively[60] dull after the compelling[61] visit with the dolphins.

"Then I'll show you where the cafeteria is, and of course, the apartment where you'll be staying."

"Sounds good," Helen agreed.

As they returned to the doorway, Dr. Villeponce paused at a desk to pick up a thick yellow folder, which he handed to Helen. "Here's some background information for you on our sonar project. It would be great if you could familiarize yourself with it before our staff meeting tomorrow morning. We begin at 8 A.M. sharp." Dr. Villeponce smiled warmly at Helen as he handed her the arduous[62] assignment. He seemed like a nice person, Alexa thought.

Alexa looked at the formidable[63] thick folder her mother now carried. She knew that her mother would tackle her assignment assiduously.[64] It would probably take her most of the night to get through it all, but her enthusiasm for her new job would give her fortitude.[65] Alexa noticed that the front of the folder was stamped with another "CONFIDENTIAL," in red block letters. There sure were a lot of secrets around here, she thought.

❧   ❧

As Alexa walked to the molecular biology lab with Dr. Villeponce and her mother, she couldn't stop thinking about the dolphins—she was awestruck[66] at the sight of so many dolphins in the same place. It was difficult to show any interest in the laboratory, but Alexa tried to be cordial[67] as she was introduced to Janine, the laboratory technician. Alexa

---

[59] Preempted: to take the place of
[60] Comparatively: considered as if in comparison to something else; relatively
[61] Compelling: demanding attention
[62] Arduous: hard to accomplish or achieve
[63] Formidable: causing fear, dread, or apprehension
[64] Assiduous: marked by careful unremitting attention or persistent application
[65] Fortitude: strength of mind that enables a person to encounter danger or adversity with courage
[66] Awestruck: filled with wonder
[67] Cordial: warmly and genially affable

dutifully agreed that she would report to the lab at 8:00 in the morning to begin her project.

"Why don't I take you to your apartment now." Dr. Villeponce suggested. "You both must be exhausted from your trip."

Alexa nodded silently, but in reality she didn't feel the least bit tired. The amazing sight of the dolphins had heightened her senses. While they walked the short distance to the apartment, Alexa formulated her plan. She simply *had* to find a way to spend the coming weeks in the dolphin facility, rather than toiling away in a stuffy laboratory.

As soon as Dr. Villeponce left them alone in their new apartment, Alexa articulated[68] her yearning[69] to work with the dolphins.

"Mom, can't I work with you and the dolphins this summer instead of in the lab?" Alexa pleaded.

"Oh, Alexa," her mother began compassionately,[70] "I would love to have you work with me too. But it's just not possible right now. All of the people working with the dolphins need a special security clearance, a process they refused to conduct for a high school student. I tried, but I couldn't coerce[71] them into bending the rules."

"But it just doesn't seem fair to be here where there are so many dolphins and not be able to see them!" Alexa was exasperated.[72]

"I know it doesn't seem fair." Her mother was empathetic,[73] but only to a point. "When I was younger, I had to wait eons before I was allowed to work with dolphins. Not only did I have to finish college, I had to complete two years of graduate coursework as well."

Alexa looked forlorn[74] and on the verge of tears. She was bitterly disappointed. It seemed so unfair to be so close to creatures that were so

---

[68] Articulate: expressing oneself readily, clearly, or effectively

[69] Yearning: to long persistently, wistfully, or sadly

[70] Compassionately: having or showing compassion (sympathetic consciousness of others' distress, together with a desire to alleviate it)

[71] Coerce: to compel to an act or choice

[72] Exasperated: irritated or annoyed

[73] Empathetic: being understanding of, aware of, and sensitive to the feelings, thoughts, and experiences of another

[74] Forlorn: being in poor condition; miserable

captivating and not be able to spend time with them. In fact, she couldn't even go into the dolphin building without her mother because she didn't have a card key.

"Alexa, I know it seems difficult to accept. I would feel the same way if I were in your shoes. I promise you that I will do everything I can to get you a position in the dolphin facility. But I just need to foster[75] a more secure relationship with the management before I press for a big favor."

"OK, Mom," Alexa replied in a defeated tone. Her mother gave her a redeeming[76] hug. At least her mother was understanding of her grievances,[77] Alexa thought. She was grateful for that.

---

[75] Foster: to promote the growth or development of
[76] Redeeming: to release from blame or debt
[77] Grievance: a cause of distress (as an unsatisfactory working condition) felt to afford reason for complaint

3

A Serendipitous Find

Alexa awoke to the sound of a multitude of birds singing and chirping loudly outside the window. She slowly regained consciousness and remembered the events of yesterday. It had been such a full day and there was so much to think about. Alexa couldn't get the image of the dolphins out of her mind. In her dreams, she was playing in the water with little Coco, swimming with the ease and grace of these beautiful, animated[1] creatures.

Alexa looked over at her mother, who was still sleeping peacefully in the adjacent bed. They were sharing a small one-bedroom apartment that had a tiny kitchenette and small living room, which consisted of a couch and a small television on a pedestal. The cramped kitchen didn't bother Alexa because she was not particularly domestic,[2] but the television predicament certainly did. There was no cable TV and the reception, as she'd found out last night, was terrible. They could only get one channel

---

[1] Animated: full of movement and activity
[2] Domestic: devoted to home duties and pleasures

clearly, and because everything was in Spanish, it didn't seem worth watching.

Thankfully, they had access to the Internet. Alexa's mother had brought her laptop and it was plugged in on the kitchen counter. Alexa logged on and checked her e-mail. She couldn't wait to see if Laurie had written to her. But her inbox was empty. Alexa sighed. It was hard to keep her attitude upbeat when she felt so isolated on this secluded island, away from her friends. Furthermore, they couldn't even make outgoing calls on their telephone without a phone card to cover the very expensive long-distance fees. With all of these limitations[3] on communication with her friends back home, Alexa felt like her coveted[4] friendships were slipping away.

Alexa deliberated[5] and decided that she would send an e-mail to Laurie every day. If they could keep in touch by cultivating[6] an e-mail relationship, Alexa wouldn't feel so desolate.[7] Truthfully, she admitted to herself, she was wary[8] of this long absence from Laurie because she didn't want her role as Laurie's best friend to be usurped[9] by someone else in her absence. Alexa consigned[10] herself to write to Laurie diligently.

Time: 6:54 A.M.
To: "Laurie"
From: "Alexa"
Subject: *Hola!*

Dear Laurie,

Hola! That's Spanish for hi! How are you doing? I miss you! Did you start your job at CNN yet? I am doing OK. We arrived here

---

3 Limitation: something that limits; restraint
4 Covet: to wish for enviously
5 Deliberate: characterized by or resulting from careful and thorough consideration
6 Cultivating: fostering, furthering, encouraging
7 Desolate: deserted, isolated
8 Wary: marked by keen caution
9 Usurp: to take the place of by or as if by force; supplant
10 Consign: commit, especially to a final destination or fate

yesterday and got a tour of the place. They have over 40 dolphins here—they are so amazing! The only problem is that my job is in the laboratory. I'm so disappointed about that. I really wanted to work with the dolphins this summer. So far, I've only seen one person my age here. Her name is Charlotte and she is the daughter of Colonel Brandt—a very important Navy colonel who is visiting Puerto Marino. I was introduced to her last night when we ate dinner at the cafeteria. I'm not going to be spending much time with her, though—it's not even debatable.[11] She reminds me of Caroline—she is very pretty and very conceited. Just what I need!! Well, I have to go now and get ready for my first day at work—yuk! Write to me soon!!

Your best friend and comrade,[12]
Alexa

Alexa hit Send with a flourish[13] and almost immediately felt a tinge of regret. Perhaps this e-mail was too negative, Alexa thought. Alexa reread it and realized that she had denounced[14] virtually everything. Next time, she thought, instead of writing from such a disgruntled[15] perspective, she would try to find the positive and make her letters more upbeat.

Alexa realized she forgot to tell Laurie about the best part of their living arrangements—a motorbike! Dr. Villeponce had shown them the small motorbike parked outside of their apartment and told them it was theirs to use to get around the compound if they found walking tiresome. Alexa's mother, who was not a fan of any type of motorcycle, had told Alexa that she could use it as long as she wore the helmet at all times.

---

[11] Debatable: arguable, worthy of debate or consideration
[12] Comrade: an intimate friend or associate; companion
[13] Flourish: grand gesture, display (also has another meaning, to thrive)
[14] Denounce: to pronounce (especially publicly) to be bad, blameworthy, or evil
[15] Disgruntled: discontent, unhappy

Alexa's mother awoke and they shared tea and toast in the kitchenette. They took turns taking a brief shower, and then it was time to go. They walked outside and Alexa prepared to get on the motorbike.

"I hope you have a good day. You have my pager number if you need me. Be careful in the lab! And be especially careful on that bike!" Alexa's mother added emphatically[16] as she gave her an affirming[17] hug.

"Don't worry, Mom. I'll be fine," Alexa asserted,[18] reassuring her mother. But inside her stomach felt a little queasy from nervousness. It always seemed a challenge to start something new and be the young upstart[19] in an unfamiliar place.

"Let's meet back here at five. We can go to the cafeteria together for dinner." "OK, Mom. See you then." Alexa put on the helmet and started the motorbike. She pulled out onto the road with her mother watching nervously. Alexa waved as she pulled away for the short ride to the molecular biology lab.

It was exhilarating to ride the motorbike, and Alexa was disappointed that the ride was so short. She pulled up in front of the small building that housed the laboratory and reluctantly went inside.

Janine noticed her immediately and greeted her enthusiastically. "Good morning, Alexa! Are you ready to begin?"

Alexa managed a weak smile and an affirmative nod. She appreciated Janine's hospitable[20] welcome. She followed Janine over to the lab bench and took a seat next to her on one of the tall stools that laboratory workers use while conducting experiments.

Janine arranged the papers on top of the lab bench to show Alexa. "I know you have some molecular biology experience, is that right?"

---

[16] Emphatically: with emphasis, forcefully
[17] Affirming: expressing dedication
[18] Asserted: to declare forcefully
[19] Upstart: unknown, insignificant person, low on the totem pole
[20] Hospitable: promising or suggesting generous and cordial welcome

"Yes," Alexa replied. "My father is a molecular biologist and I've done a few experiments with DNA in his laboratory at Cornell." Alexa didn't elaborate[21] with any details.

"Terrific. I have a project I think will be very appropriate for your skills. We would like to have DNA from each of the dolphins here at Puerto Marino so that we can carry out some genetic studies. It will also be useful to have their DNA so that we can positively identify individuals in any circumstances that may arise. We already have cells from all 42 animals, so I thought you could work on preparing DNA from each of these samples. Sound good?"

"Yes," Alexa nodded. "I've extracted DNA from worms before, so if this is similar, I already know how to do it."

"I'm sure the protocol[22] is very similar. Here is the protocol we're using for dolphin cells." Janine handed her a paper with the instructions printed on it. "I'm hoping you can work independently on this, if possible. I have a daily 9 A.M. meeting and lots of fieldwork to do. Of course, I'll be available if you have any questions."

"I don't mind working independently," Alexa replied. In fact, she quite liked it. Alexa knew from her previous experience in the lab that it felt empowering[23] to complete an experiment independently.

"Terrific. The first thing you'll need to do is to make up all of the solutions on this list. Once you're done with that, come find me and I'll show you where the dolphin cells are kept in the liquid nitrogen."

Alexa nodded as Janine started gathering her things to leave. She seemed to be in such a hurry. Alexa looked around the windowless room. There was nobody else there. I wonder if it's going to be this quiet all

---

[21] Elaborate: give details, expand upon a subject
[22] Protocol: the plan of a scientific experiment
[23] Empowering: yielding power or authority

summer long, Alexa mused. If only I had gotten a really great summer job in Ithaca, like Laurie, my parents would have let me stay home.

Alexa looked down at the list of solutions: 5M $NaCl_2$, TE, 70% Ethanol... I'd better get started, Alexa thought reluctantly. She headed over to the scale and the chemical supplies and got down the big bottle of $NaCl_2$.

The work proceeded quickly and soon she had finished making the five solutions on the list. Alexa looked around for Janine, but the lab was still empty and so was the adjacent office. She looked at her watch. It was only 9:15 A.M. Alexa opened the door and looked outside, but Janine was nowhere in sight. She thought about paging her mother, but thought better of it. It was her mother's first day on the job, and Alexa vowed to handle her own problems, at least for today. The sight of her motorbike beckoned.

"What harm would it do if I just went for a ride to take a look around this island?" Alexa thought impulsively.[24] She pulled on her helmet and swung her leg over the bike. She looked over her shoulder one last time to see if Janine was around. Nobody. Alexa started the motorbike and took off.

She rode leisurely past their apartment, then past the cafeteria building, and the big dolphin building where her mother was now working. Alexa continued past the security building and then she could see the main gate with the two omnipresent[25] guards looming in the distance.

I wonder if they'd mind if I leave the compound for awhile, she mused. She was steadily approaching the security checkpoint. The guard, posted authoritatively[26] at the gate, had clearly seen her. He didn't look

---

[24] Impulsively: spontaneously, on a whim
[25] Omnipresent: present in all places at all times
[26] Authoritatively: with authority, commandingly, convincingly

alarmed, Alexa thought. Nor was he motioning for her to stop. He nodded, a tacit acknowledgement, and Alexa kept going and rode right out of the compound! She felt a tingle of excitement at her impetuous[27] escape.

The bumpy dirt road continued for about a mile and then ended at the intersection of another dirt road, which looked to be in better condition. Alexa didn't remember this part from her journey here; it had been dark when they drove to the compound. She looked right and left, searching for a signal that might indicate which way to go. The answer was not obvious. Both directions looked equally nondescript.

Alexa went left. There appeared to be a void of trees in the distance. Could it be the ocean? After a mile or so there was another intersection and what looked like the rudiments of a small town. She passed by a few small, dilapidated houses and a small general store. A little boy in bare feet was sweeping the doorway of the store. He looked at her curiously with big brown eyes.

A fruit stand was adjacent to the store. Piles of oranges, bananas, pineapples, and some unfamiliar fruits beckoned. Alexa realized she had not brought anything to drink with her and she was already parched.[28] Maybe I'll stop on the way back, she thought.

Alexa continued in the same direction. There was little commercial activity in this small town—the ubiquitous[29] McDonalds' franchise[30] had yet to penetrate this isolated island. The houses lining the street became more numerous and a few people were going about their activities. The ramshackle houses looked like they could barely stand up. It looked more like a threadbare encampment[31] than a neighborhood of sturdy houses. She felt a wave of emotion for the people who lived in

---

[27] Impetuous: marked by impulsive vehemence or passion
[28] Parched: very dry, dehydrated (can also mean very thirsty)
[29] Ubiquitous: existing or being everywhere at the same time
[30] Franchise: the license granted to an individual or group to market a company's goods or services in a particular territory
[31] Encampment: the state of being encamped (to place or establish in a camp)

houses like this. From her perspective,[32] it appeared so miserable and deprived.[33] An elderly mendicant[34] sitting in front of the general store held out his cup to her, beseeching[35] her to contribute. Feeling uncomfortable, she avoided eye contact and continued on. But she couldn't help but ponder what it must be like to subsist[36] on a handful of coins like that which was in the beggar's cup.

I wonder what it's like to live here, she thought as she watched a woman hang her laundry out to dry on a short rope draped between two houses. The woman returned her gaze with a disapproving look. Apparently she did not enjoy being the subject of Alexa's anthropological musings. The children, however, seemed oblivious to their penurious[37] circumstances. They were running around playing and eyeing Alexa on her motorbike with curious, if cautious, brown eyes. The patrons[38] sitting outdoors at an open-air café eyed her suspiciously. Alexa felt so conspicuous—not only was she a different ethnicity[39] than the townspeople, she was an outsider. She had the distinct sense of feeling ostracized[40] by their direct gaze.

It looked as if the road ended up ahead in a dense grove of palm trees. As Alexa approached, she could see that there was a wide path leading through the trees. She caught a glimpse of water ahead. She continued on the path, and suddenly the dense canopy of trees opened up onto a spectacular expanse of sandy beach!

"Oh, my gosh!" Alexa exclaimed softly to herself. "This is spectacular!" The sand was so white and pristine. Alexa parked her motorbike by a tree and kicked off her shoes. Her bare feet hit the warm sand and it felt

---

[32] Perspective: point of view
[33] Deprived: marked by deprivation, especially a lack of the necessities of life or of healthful environmental influences
[34] Mendicant: beggar
[35] Beseech: to beg for urgently or anxiously
[36] Subsist: to have or acquire the necessities of life (such as food and clothing)
[37] Penurious: marked by a cramping and oppressive lack of resources (as in money)
[38] Patrons: customers
[39] Ethnicity: ethnic quality or affiliation
[40] Ostracized: to exclude from a group by common consent

great. Delighted, she scurried[41] toward the translucent[42] water, which was a beautiful shade of turquoise. It was a spectacularly beautiful cove that she had discovered serendipitously.[43] On the right, there was a long pier with several dilapidated fishing vessels tied to the posts. To her left, the cove was bordered by a long, rocky outcrop jutting into the bay.

Alexa felt herself drawn to the water, where a gentle surf was breaking. She stepped gingerly over broken bits of seashells and touched the water with her toes. The sensation was decadent[44]—the water was warm and refreshing. It appeared quite shallow as well. It was so inviting, she wished that she had brought a bathing suit.

Maybe I'll just wade out in the water a bit, she thought. The beach was nearly deserted, except for a couple of grizzled old fishermen on the pier who looked to be unloading the day's catch. Alexa rolled up the bottom of her pants up to her knees and waded out a bit farther. "I'm definitely coming back tomorrow with my bathing suit," she vowed out loud. The sunshine felt so hot on her hair that she contemplated diving right in with her clothes on. She thought this through and decided she could probably take a quick swim, drive back to the apartment, and change her clothes quickly before heading back to the lab.

Just as she was about to take the plunge, she noticed a small, archaic[45] boat motoring its way toward the pier. It was a dingy[46] metal rowboat with an outboard engine, operated by a young man seated in the back of the boat. He appeared to be alone but he was talking quite loudly in Spanish over the noise of the motor. Even though she had taken one year of Spanish, his words were unintelligible.[47] Who was he talking to? Alexa was puzzled.

---

[41] Scurried: scampered; to move in or as if in a brisk, rapidly alternating step

[42] Translucent: clear, transparent

[43] Serendipitously: obtained by serendipity (the faculty of finding valuable or agreeable things accidentally)

[44] Decadent: self-indulgent

[45] Archaic: characteristic of an earlier or more primitive time

[46] Dingy: dirty, discolored

[47] Unintelligible: incomprehensible, making no sense

Then she saw it. It was a dolphin leaping out of the water near the bow of the boat! Alexa put her hand above her eyes like a visor to deflect[48] the blinding sunshine. The boat was heading toward the pier and it looked like the dolphin was coming with it. The dolphin was surfing in the bow's wake, periodically leaping out of the water.

Alexa was so mesmerized by the dolphin that she didn't realize that the boy driving the boat was waving to her. As he pulled in closer to the pier he yelled out to her.

"*Hola!*" he called, waving his arm in a friendly greeting.

Alexa finally took notice of him. He looked to be about sixteen. His black hair was long, almost to his shoulders, and his body deeply tanned and lithe.[49] He was smiling at her. All of a sudden she felt exorbitantly[50] self-conscious—and very glad she hadn't plunged into the water a moment ago. She managed a weak wave.

The boy was concentrating on docking the boat now, so Alexa continued to watch. She couldn't see the dolphin. Maybe it was on the other side of the boat. The boy unloaded several buckets of fish onto the dock and then climbed up the ladder to the pier. The dolphin surfaced right when the boy stood up on the dock. The dolphin was making some squeaking noises. The boy tossed it a fish, which the dolphin appeared to catch and swallow in the same instant. The boy tossed the dolphin two more fish as he talked to the animal in Spanish.

Now it looked as if the conversation was over. The dolphin had disappeared in an instant and the boy was now walking down the pier. He smiled again at Alexa as he headed her way.

---

[48] Deflect: to turn from a straight course or fixed direction; bend
[49] Lithe: characterized by easy flexibility and grace
[50] Exorbitantly: excessively; exceedingly

What if he was coming over to talk to her? The thought of it made Alexa a little nervous. She decided it was time to extricate[51] herself from this situation. She immediately turned around and headed for her motorbike. If I walk fast, Alexa thought, I can be off the beach before he reaches the end of the pier. She walked swiftly over the hot sand and tossed her shoes into the basket on the back of the bike. She started the bike in her bare feet and took off without looking back.

The ride back to Puerto Marino was quick and Alexa regained her composure as she rode along. It was so foolish to have left the cove in such a hurry, she thought. The boy obviously wanted to talk to her. And I want to talk to him too, she realized. It's just silly to evade[52] precisely the person you want to get to know, she thought. This is exactly why I've never had a real boyfriend. Alexa knew that whenever she liked a boy, she studiously avoided any interaction with him. But, having the perspicacity[53] to realize that her actions were silly, she vowed emphatically that next time, she would be braver.

As she approached the proximity[54] of the Puerto Marino compound, she again had a nervous feeling in her stomach. What if they don't let me back in? she thought. Or worse, what if they call her mother? Alexa held her breath as the security gate loomed closer.

The guard looked at her and waved her in! That was easy, she thought as she sped back to the lab. She parked her motorbike, slipped her shoes back on, and raced into the lab. It was still empty! Alexa breathed a sigh of relief as she returned to her lab bench. Everything was as it was when she left it. She looked at her watch. She had only been gone 45 minutes.

---

[51] Extricate: to release from entanglement or difficulty
[52] Evade: avoid, dodge
[53] Perspicacity: having acute mental vision or discernment; clear-sighted; shrewd
[54] Proximity: nearness, closeness

"Hi, Alexa! How is everything going?" Janine breezed into the lab.

"Fine. I've made all five of the solutions and I'm ready to start the DNA extractions," Alexa replied calmly. It looked as if Janine didn't even know she'd been gone. Alexa decided that she would not divulge[55] her indiscretion[56] to her. There was no reason Janine needed to know that Alexa had gone to the beach when she was supposed to be working. It was discretionary[57] information.

"Wow! You're efficient," Janine complimented.

"Oh, it wasn't that difficult." Alexa feigned[58] a smile.

"Good. I'm glad you're able to work both independently and efficaciously.[59] What do you say we do the first DNA extraction together as a practice run, and then you can work on all of the other extractions independently. It'll essentially be a repetitive task, and it would be great if you could do it all on your own. I am just inundated[60] with field work."

"That's fine with me," Alexa replied.

"Great. Then let's get started."

Janine led Alexa to a big tank of liquid nitrogen, where she donned thick gloves to protect her hands from the ultra-cold solution. Each dolphin at Puerto Marino had several vials of cells frozen away in this tank. Janine lifted a rack of boxes out of the liquid nitrogen and foraged[61] among the boxes with heavily gloved hands. She found what she was looking for—one vial of cells from dolphin 36 (each dolphin had a number assigned to it as well as a nickname that was used by the trainers)—and placed it in a bucket of crushed ice to thaw.

Alexa looked at the orange-capped vial. It was smaller than her little finger, but Janine assured her the vial had over 10 million cells in it!

---

[55] Divulge: reveal, tell

[56] Indiscretion: something (an act or a remark) marked by a lack of discretion (cautious reserve)

57 Discretionary: left to discretion, exercised at one's own discretion (the quality of being discreet; cautious reserve in speech)

58 Feigned: fictitious, faked; artificial

59 Efficaciously: effective; having the power to achieve the desired effect

60 Inundate: to overwhelm with abundance; as if with a flood

Next they added a buffer solution so that the cells were suspended in a milliliter (about a fifth of a teaspoon) of solution. Then they donned protective gloves and glasses to add a mixture of phenol and chloroform, the corrosive[62] chemicals that are used to break open the cells and release the DNA. The mixture was shaken vigorously and then centrifuged. When Alexa carefully lifted the tube out of the centrifuge, there were two layers of solution, similar to oil on water. Janine explained that the bottom layer was the organic solution containing the debris of the broken cells. The top layer was what they wanted—this was the aqueous solution containing the soluble[63] DNA. Alexa carefully lifted the top layer out using a micropipette and placed it in a fresh clear plastic test tube.

"Now for the dénouement!"[64] Janine declared dramatically.

Alexa added an ethanol solution to the tube, snapped the lid on tight, and slowly inverted the tube several times to gently mix the solutions. There was a lull[65] in the conversation as Alexa held the tube up to the light as both women peered intently through the test tube. A delicate and thin white string had coalesced[66] in the tube. It looked a bit like the delicate fibers of a spider's web, except that the white DNA in the tube had a hint of a translucent blue color to it, which only added to its enigmatic[67] aura.

"There it is! Good job! I think you have some DNA there," Janine declared triumphantly.

Alexa felt a tingle of excitement at visualizing the DNA. It is such an elusive and mysterious molecule, she thought. It's in control of virtually everything about us—our eye color, our hair color, even our propensity[68]

---

61 Foraged: searched; rummaged
62 Corrosive: having the power to break down or eat away at something (can also mean very sarcastic)
63 Soluble: able to dissolve in a liquid
64 Dénouement: finale, conclusion
65 Lull: quiet period
66 Coalesce: to arise from the combination of distinct elements; to unite into a whole
67 Enigmatic: something hard to understand or explain; mysterious
68 Propensity: an often intense natural inclination or preference

to succumb to debilitating[69] diseases. DNA is like a silent and elusive dictator, bequeathing[70] the characteristics that make us who we are. It was a thrill to see it and hold it in her hands, Alexa thought as she studied the potent molecule in the tube.

"This needs to sit on ice for awhile. What do you say we go get lunch at the cafeteria and we can finish with the DNA prep after?" Janine suggested.

"Sounds good," Alexa replied, suddenly realizing that she was famished. It had been an invigorating[71] morning of science and adventure.

As they strolled toward the cafeteria, Alexa found herself thinking about her mother and wondering how she was doing on her first day at work. It had to be exciting to work with the dolphins, Alexa thought, as her mind wandered to images of the immense dolphin tanks she had seen the night before. She recalled that feeling of connection when she made eye contact with Speckle and when little Coco brought her a leaf, enticing her to play.

"Which dolphin is number 36? I mean, do you know its nickname?" Alexa asked. It would be so interesting to know which dolphin's DNA was in the tube, she thought.

"Why, I think that's Coco," Janine replied. "She's just a youngster."

"Yes, I know," Alexa replied thoughtfully. "I met her yesterday."

---

69 Debilitating: impairing the strength of
70 Bequeathing: handing down, transmitting
71 Invigorating: stimulating, energizing

4

An Old Maxim

"So tell me, how was your day?" Alexa's mother asked her eagerly as the two of them walked to the cafeteria for dinner.

"It was good. I extracted DNA from Coco!" Alexa replied enthusiastically. She had to admit to herself that her day in the laboratory was far from stifling,[1] as she had feared it would be earlier. In fact, she found her work in the lab to be compelling and uplifting.[2] "We're going to make DNA from all of the dolphins." Alexa thought for a moment about telling her mother about her foray to the beach that morning, but then thought better of it. Alexa had a feeling that her mother, with her protective and maternal sensibilities,[3] might not approve of her leaving the Puerto Marino compound, although she hadn't explicitly[4] forbade it.

"Wow, that sounds great. Say, I talked to Dr. Villeponce and he said that you can come out on the boat with us when we do our field work with the dolphins next week. Sound good?"

"Sounds great!" Alexa replied with a smile as they each picked up a tray in the cafeteria. It looked like it was going to be burritos for dinner

---

[1] Stifling: to withhold from circulation or expression; repressing
[2] Uplifting: improving the spiritual, social, or intellectual condition of; inspiring, enriching
[3] Sensibilities: sensitivities; awareness of and responsiveness to something
[4] Explicitly: clearly, unambiguously

tonight. Alexa was surveying the salad bar when she sensed someone looking at her. It was the boy from the fishing boat that morning! He was standing behind the counter in the kitchen wearing a white kitchen uniform and was absentmindedly wiping the counters as he looked at her with a big smile. Alexa felt herself blush as she looked down.

But she couldn't resist looking back at him again. Running into him twice in the same day seemed like some sort of prophetic[5] sign that they were destined to meet. Remembering how she had vowed to be braver when it came to interacting with boys, she managed to give him a shy smile. Alexa glanced at her mother, who was busy foraging among the vegetables at the salad bar. It didn't seem that she had noticed anything. But Alexa had a moment of panic. What if the boy came over to say hello right here in the cafeteria? Then she would surely have to explain to her mother how she had met this boy earlier on the beach.

Alexa surreptitiously[6] put her finger to her lips as if to signal "shhh" as she looked at him. She then ever so discreetly pointed to her mother. Would he understand what she meant? She fervently[7] hoped so!

The boy nodded and made a motion like he was zipping his lips together. The universal[8] signal for "don't worry, I'll keep your secret." Alexa breathed a sigh of relief.

He was still looking at Alexa with a big smile as he started walking... right into a wall! Alexa burst out laughing. It almost seemed like he did it on purpose just to make her laugh. He seemed both funny and perceptive, Alexa thought.

"What's so funny?" Helen asked curiously.

---

5 Prophetic: foretelling events; predictive
6 Surreptitiously: done, made, or acquired by stealth; secretly, slyly
7 Fervently: exhibited or marked by great intensity of feeling; zealously
8 Universal: worldwide, general, common

"Oh, nothing, really. It was just someone in the kitchen bumping into a wall," Alexa replied as they carried their trays into the sitting area. They sat down at a small round table near the window.

"How's your burrito?" Helen asked.

"Not bad," Alexa replied in an upbeat manner. Actually, the burrito was surprisingly good, she thought, even though the salad was rather anemic.[9]

Helen, who was a true gourmand,[10] picked fussily at her salad, looking as if she didn't want to eat at all. For her, cafeteria-style food was an affront[11] to the palate. "Oh, look! There's Charlotte Brandt sitting over there with her younger brother. Why don't you go over there and say hello? She's just your age and it would be nice for you to have a friend here!" she prompted.

"Yes, she seems like just the kind of person I want to spend my time with," Alexa replied with great sarcasm. She had no intention of saying hello to Charlotte. Although Alexa had only briefly met Charlotte last night and hadn't had a real conversation with her yet, she just envisioned[12] Charlotte as the type of person who would be pretentious. She reminded her of Caroline and her conceited affectations[13] when she saw Charlotte adjusting her perfect black bow in her perfect long blond hair. She couldn't help but notice that Charlotte was wearing a stylish—not to mention expensive—Juicy Couture sweat suit with a matching t-shirt. Alexa's parents were much too frugal[14] to indulge her with such a trendy ensemble.[15] They thought buying her such materialistic things would vitiate[16] her wholesome morals. They were academics and thus it seemed

---

[9] Anemic: lackluster, insipid (can also refer to the medical condition caused by the disease anemia)
[10] Gourmand: one who is heartily interested in good food and drink
[11] Affront: to insult especially to the face by behavior or language
[12] Envision: to picture to oneself
[13] Affectation: mannerisms, especially pretentious ones
[14] Frugal: characterized by economy in the expenditure of resources
[15] Ensemble: a complete costume of harmonizing or complementary clothing and accessories
[16] Vitiate: to make faulty or defective, often by the addition of something that impairs

unavoidable that they would have a haughty intellectual perspective on bourgeois[17] materialism.

As a result of her parents' parsimony,[18] Alexa's wardrobe was an eclectic[19] mix of styles, but all of the pieces were affordable. Alexa tended to eye those girls who wore expensive clothes with a bit of suspicion, although she had to admit that she fantasized[20] about wearing some of the chic outfits herself.

"Oh, Alexa, don't judge a book by its cover," Helen repeated the well-known maxim.[21] "You don't even know her yet. You shouldn't put people into pigeonholes.[22] Everybody has hidden dimensions[23] that you simply don't see when you first meet them. You may find that she's quite nice and has a lot to offer."

Alexa didn't reply, hoping her mother would drop the subject. Instead, she looked around the room as she munched on her burrito. The cafeteria was filling up. Dr. Villeponce and two other men sat at the table next to them. They appeared to be in a heated discussion. Alexa recognized one of the men as Al Janowitz, the CEO of Puerto Marino. The other man was wearing a military uniform.

They were so embroiled in their querulous[24] discussion that they didn't seem to notice Alexa or her mother. The words among them were flying rapidly as their voices rose. Alexa couldn't understand what they were talking about, although she knew that it had something to do with the dolphins.

Alexa leaned in toward her mother and asked softly, "What are they arguing about?"

---

[17] Bourgeois: marked by a concern for material interests and respectability and a tendency toward mediocrity; usually used disparagingly

[18] Parsimony: the quality of being careful with money or resources; thrift

[19] Eclectic: composed of elements drawn from different sources

[20] Fantasize: to indulge in fantasy or reverie; daydream

[21] Maxim: a saying of a proverbial nature; adage

[22] Pigeonhole: a neat category that usually fails to reflect actual complexities

[23] Dimension: one of the elements or factors making up a complete personality or entity

[24] Querulous: argumentative

Alexa's mother looked concerned and she hesitated, as if she wasn't quite sure how to phrase her answer. "Well...Dr. Villeponce is a scientist and Mr. Janowitz is a businessman. Sometimes peoples' interests clash." Helen paused as she watched the argument heat up. "I think it has something to do with a project that Mr. Janowitz wants to do. And Colonel Brandt—well, he has his own agenda."

"That's Charlotte's father?"

"Yes," her mother nodded.

Alexa was silent as she listened to their confrontation,[25] which had escalated dramatically.

"I just don't think that that maneuver has enough mechanisms[26] to ensure the safety of the dolphins!" Dr. Villeponce argued logically and coherently,[27] but the expression on his face revealed that he was livid.[28]

"Dr. Villeponce," Al Janowitz replied in an inappropriately loud voice that turned heads throughout the cafeteria, "we have a mission to carry out here at Puerto Marino, and as the CEO, I intend to see that we fulfill that mission. The decision has been made." Apparently oblivious of his indecorous[29] vocalizations, Janowitz stood up and left the room without touching his tray. Colonel Brandt politely excused himself, and Dr. Villeponce was left alone. He looked deflated and miserable.

Alexa wondered what Al Janowitz could possibly want to do that might be unsafe for the dolphins. And what was Colonel Brandt's role here at Puerto Marino? Helen looked concerned and immediately rose from her chair to talk with Dr. Villeponce. Alexa wanted to ask her mother so many questions, but it didn't look like she was going to have the

---

[25] Confrontation: the clashing of forces or ideas; conflict
[26] Mechanisms: a process or technique for achieving a result
[27] Coherently: logically or aesthetically ordered or integrated
[28] Livid: very angry; enraged
[29] Indecorous: not decorous; conflicting with accepted standards of good conduct or good taste

opportunity now. Dr. Villeponce was probably joining them for dinner, now that his quarrel had dissipated.[30] Alexa knew that it would be impolite to bring up his very public argument. She would just have to ask her mother later.

Dr. Villeponce was very cordial over dinner as the conversation turned to the echolocation project that Alexa's mother was helping to design and carry out. The conversation began to get quite technical as the two scientists talked about their favorite topic. Alexa couldn't follow all of the details, but her mother looked so animated and engaged. She appeared to have a lot in common with Dr. Villeponce and he, in turn, had many compliments for Alexa's mother.

"As I'm sure you already know, Alexa," Dr. Villeponce momentarily digressed,[31] "the dolphin has a sixth sense of sorts. It can locate objects by emitting a series of clicks and then receiving and interpreting the sound waves that bounce back. Essentially, they can 'see' things via echolocation that they can't see with their eyes. Your mother here has designed a study to determine to what extent dolphins can detect objects buried beneath the ocean floor." He smiled at Helen. "I think it's going to be fabulous."

Alexa watched as her mother beamed with the praise that was showered on her. She had always thought that her mother was not the type to like someone who behaved like a toady,[32] but here she was enjoying the abundant flattery of Dr. Villeponce. Actually, Alexa admitted to herself, what seemed so untenable[33] about this situation was that her mother was clearly enjoying the company of a man other than her father.

---

[30] Dissipated: to cause to spread thin or scatter and gradually vanish
[31] Digress: to turn aside, especially from the main subject of attention or course of argument
[32] Toady: one who flatters in hope of gaining favors
[33] Untenable: not able to be defended or occupied

She felt a twinge of sadness as she realized it would probably take a long time for her to come to grips with the unalterable[34] fact that her parents were now divorced.

---

[34] Unalterable: not capable of being altered or changed

5

A Surprising Revelation

The next morning Alexa returned to the lab at 8:00, where Janine was waiting for her to resume their experiment. Today they were going to analyze the dolphin DNA that they had made yesterday.

"Each individual has a unique pattern of bands when the DNA is cut, and then the pieces are separated on a gel," Janine explained, as she pointed to a column of bands on the computer screen. "The results of this experiment look sort of like a bar code, and just like a bar code, each one is unique and can be used to unambiguously[1] identify an individual."

"Kind of like a fingerprint," Alexa concluded.

"Exactly," Janine replied.

Janine showed Alexa the instructions for this phase of the experiment and pointed to the first two steps. "Do you think you can handle this part on your own? I have a 9:00 A.M. meeting I need to attend."

---

[1] Unambiguously: without ambiguity or uncertainty; clearly, precisely

"No problem," Alexa replied. "I've done this before."

"Terrific. I'll be back around eleven and we'll go on to step three."

Alexa looked around the empty lab and started to feel a bit lonely. It didn't help that Laurie hadn't returned any of her e-mails, and Alexa had already written to her three times. She arbitrarily[2] concluded that Laurie must be too busy with her new job to check her e-mail. It pained her to think that Laurie might be apathetic[3] about writing to her all summer.

Alexa decided that to alleviate[4] her woes, she would make another trip to the beach. In fact, she had been anticipating[5] this opportunity eagerly. She had her bathing suit on under her clothes and a towel and sunscreen packed in her backpack. She saw her opportunity after she completed the first step of her experiment—it needed to incubate for an hour. She grabbed her backpack and was out the door.

If anything, the beach was more beautiful than she remembered from yesterday. It looked like a utopian paradise, resplendent[6] with glistening white sand. Alexa took a walk along the shore and collected a few seashells. It was hard to find a shell intact, but even the broken ones were interesting. The colors, textures, and shapes were so diverse.

Alexa decided to walk out to the end of the rocky outcrop that jutted into the bay. It looked like a good place to take a swim without being in direct view of the fishermen who were unloading their catch on the dock. There was a well-worn path leading out to the end of the point, and Alexa traversed it quickly.

The morning sun was becoming more intense every minute and Alexa surveyed the area for a place to set her backpack and clothes while she took a swim. This area appeared to be well used by the fishermen and

---

2 Arbitrarily: based on or determined by individual preference or convenience rather than by necessity or the intrinsic nature of something

3 Apathetic: having little or no interest or concern; indifferent

4 Alleviate: to make (as suffering) more bearable

5 Anticipating: to look forward to as certain; expect

6 Resplendent: shining brilliantly; characterized by a glowing splendor

others. There was a flat-topped rock that looked like it was used as a table for cleaning fish and a fire pit for cooking. It also looked like a perfect place to take a swim. The large boulders at the very tip of the peninsula provided a natural staircase of sorts leading down to the clear blue water. The shadows on the water created by the large rocks wavered[7] hypnotically in the gentle swells. Alexa couldn't wait to get in—it looked so inviting.

The rocks were a bit slippery, but the water was warm and refreshing. Alexa immersed[8] herself in the transparent[9] water and resurfaced several yards out. The bottom was sandy and it seemed relatively shallow in the area around the rocks. It was only about four feet deep and perfect for swimming. The water was so amazingly clear that it was easy to see the underwater activity—there were schools of fish swimming by her feet. The colors of the tropical fish were spectacular—vivid blue, orange, and iridescent[10] silver.

This is truly a place of idealistic[11] beauty, Alexa thought as she floated on her back languidly.[12] The ocean waves were so mild in the cove that she felt relaxed by their gentle motion. It felt so restorative[13] to take a refreshing swim after having spent endless hours in the stagnating[14] environment of airplanes two days earlier.

A high-pitched squeak startled her out of her reverie. Alexa let out an involuntary gasp as she turned around toward the source of the noise. It was a dolphin! The dolphin dove underwater with a graceful arch of its back just as she turned around. "Oh, I hope it doesn't disappear!" she said out loud.

Whoosh! Alexa felt the water swirl around her legs as the dolphin swam by underwater. She felt a tingle of excitement go down her spine.

---

[7] Wavered: to weave or sway unsteadily to and fro

[8] Immerse: to plunge into something that surrounds or covers; especially to plunge or dip into a fluid

[9] Transparent: fine or sheer enough to be seen through

[10] Iridescent: a lustrous rainbowlike play of color caused by differential refraction of light waves (as from an oil slick, soap bubble, or fish scales) that tends to change as the angle of view changes

[11] Idealistic: characteristic of idealism (the practice of forming ideals or living under their influence)

[12] Languidly: lacking force or quickness of movement; slow

[13] Restorative: something that serves to restore to consciousness, vigor, or health

[14] Stagnating: remaining stale (usually from lack of circulation or flow)

She was only a little bit frightened. She knew that dolphins were, for the most part, very friendly.

Finally the dolphin surfaced, making a gurgling noise as it cleared the water from its blowhole. Now the dolphin was looking right at Alexa, and it was only about three feet away! The dolphin appeared to be trying to communicate something to her. It was making noises that sounded like a cacophony[15] of chirps, gurgles, and squeaks. The dolphin seemed to be smiling at her, and Alexa couldn't help but notice the rows of sharp teeth.

"Hi there. What are you saying?" Alexa murmured softly. She felt compelled to talk and further the growing sense of kinship[16] she felt with this animal. "I'm Alexa. What's your name?" Alexa continued a bit louder.

The dolphin replied with a squeak and a big toothy grin, legitimating[17] Alexa's attempt to have a conversation.

"It looks like you have freckles!" Alexa noted. Indeed, the dolphin's bulbous forehead had several dark spots on it. "I think I'll call you Freckles. Would you like that name? Of course, I don't know if you're a girl or a boy, but I think the name Freckles would work for either one."

The dolphin dove underwater and swam in a big circle circumscribing[18] Alexa. Alexa started swimming too, but it was hopeless to try to keep up with this graceful sea creature. The dolphin appeared to enjoy the chase, however mismatched it was. Alexa was thrilled as the lithe dolphin swam by her at a fast pace, almost brushing her as she swam. It was like they were playing a game and nobody had to explain the rules. They didn't need conventional linguistic[19] communication—they understood each

---

[15] Cacophony: harsh or discordant sound; dissonance
[16] Kinship: the quality or state of being kin; relationship
[17] Legitimating: to show or affirm to be justified
[18] Circumscribe: to surround by or as if by a boundary
[19] Linguistic: of or relating to language

other without words. Somehow, Alexa felt like she had made a visceral[20] connection with this charismatic creature.

Alexa felt a powerful urge to actually touch the dolphin. She held her arm out to touch the beautiful animal as she swam by. Freckles seemed to understand what Alexa was doing and didn't seem to mind at all. In fact, the dolphin swam right by Alexa's outstretched arm and Alexa stroked its back as it swam by. The dolphin's skin felt smooth and slippery.

"*Hola!*" Alexa heard a young man's voice from behind her.

Alexa turned around to see that it was the same boy from yesterday in his fishing boat.

"Hi! I'm José. How are you?" he continued in nearly perfect English with a just a trace of a Spanish accent. He was standing on the seat in his small fishing boat, which was bobbing about in the gentle swells.

"I'm Alexa." Before she had a chance to say another word, an unusually big swell caused José's boat to pitch and he was fighting for his balance, his arms flailing comically.

Splash! He hit the water and resurfaced with a sheepish look on his tanned face. "It's nice to meet you," he added with a grin.

Alexa couldn't help but burst out laughing. "That's quite an introduction!" José was smiling at her, apparently aware of little else. "Should we grab your boat so it doesn't float away?" Alexa inquired.

"No, it's fine. I dropped the anchor." José started swimming toward Freckles.

Alexa wondered if he truly was a lummox[21] or if he had fallen in the water on purpose. She guessed it was the latter, seeing as though he had

---

[20] Visceral: dealing with crude or elemental emotions; instinctive
[21] Lummox: clumsy person

the foresight to anchor the boat before he fell out. Well, at least he's got a sense of humor, she thought with a smile. He seemed to have a penchant[22] for breaking the ice and making her laugh with his jovial[23] antics.

The dolphin appeared to recognize José and swam up beside him. José grabbed hold of its dorsal fin (the triangular-shaped fin on the dolphin's back) with his strong, tanned arms and hitched a ride through the water. José had a big smile on his face as he enjoyed being propelled[24] through the water by the dolphin. He let go when he was close to Alexa and stroked the dolphin's side as if to bid it farewell. "*Adios*, Pecas!" he said softly as she swam away.

"I didn't know the dolphin already had a name—I was calling it Freckles," Alexa said.

"That's what we call her too! *Pecas* is Spanish for 'Freckles'!"

"I like the name Pecas! I'll call her that too! Do you know that it's a 'she'?"

"Yes, Pecas is definitely a girl. She had a baby last year, and up until last week the calf was always at her side."

"What happened to the baby dolphin?" Alexa asked.

"I don't know—I feel so much sadness for her. She seems so distressed since the baby disappeared." José's face momentarily clouded over with sentiment[25] for the lost baby dolphin. They could see Pecas swimming off in the distance. José abruptly changed the subject. "I can tell you are American, but where in America are you from?"

"Ithaca, New York. My dad is a professor at Cornell University."

---

[22] Penchant: a strong and continued inclination; liking
[23] Jovial: markedly good-humored, especially as evidenced by jollity and conviviality
[24] Propelled: to drive forward or onward by or as if by means of a force that imparts motion; pushed
[25] Sentiment: an attitude, thought, or judgment prompted by feeling

"I know of Cornell. It is such a good school. It is my dream to go to University in America. I am trying to save some money so that I can go, but it is very difficult. I need to help my mother and my sisters. But I will go someday," José added fiercely, his indomitable[26] spirit revealing itself. "Do you go to University there?"

"Not yet. I'm still deciding where I will apply for college. I might go to Cornell—my parents really want me to go there—but I might go somewhere else."

"Wow, you are very lucky," José said admiringly.

"Yes, I guess so." Alexa felt a tinge of guilt. She hadn't really thought of herself as financially or socially privileged before. Not surprisingly, she found that this juxtaposition[27] with someone from a different background made her more introspective.[28] She had always just thought of her parents as members of the intelligentsia[29] rather than the social elite. Although she knew that she would go to college someday, Alexa had never really thought of it as an elusive[30] privilege. It seemed more like a predetermined[31] rite of passage in her family.

José, by contrast, was working very hard to save money for school. Not only was he working in the kitchen at Puerto Marino, he was also supplementing his income by fishing. And it was not at all clear if he would have the opportunity to go to college. It didn't appear that his parents would be able to subsidize[32] his education. The disparity[33] in their backgrounds was immense. Alexa hoped that he didn't assume that she

---

[26] Indomitable: incapable of being subdued; unconquerable
[27] Juxtaposition: the act or an instance of placing two or more things side by side
[28] Introspective: a reflective looking inward; an examination of one's own thoughts and feelings
[29] Intelligentsia: intellectuals who form an artistic, social, or political vanguard or elite
[30] Elusive: tending to elude, as in tending to evade grasp or pursuit
[31] Predetermined: to determine beforehand
[32] Subsidize: to furnish with a subsidy (a grant or gift of money)
[33] Disparity: containing or made up of fundamentally different and often incongruous elements

was an elitist[34]—because in reality, she considered herself to be very open-minded and egalitarian.[35]

"How about you—do you live right around here?" Alexa probed gently.

"Yes I live in the village—you probably passed right by my house on the way here. I live there with my mother and father and my two sisters. Maybe you can come to my house to meet them!" José's hospitality was undeterred by his modest dwellings.

"Maybe sometime, but I'm supposed to be working right now," Alexa said with a laugh. "That's why I didn't want you to say anything last night at the cafeteria."

"I understood," José said, his brown eyes connecting with hers for a moment. "I have two jobs—besides the fishing, I mean. I work at Puerto Marino during the afternoons and evenings, and then I work at the library sometimes on the weekends. They have a computer that I can use at the library. I love computers!"

"Me too," Alexa added, although she wasn't sure if she really liked them as much as José did. Distracted by his intense gaze, she wasn't quite sure what to say and "me too" just came out.

Off in the distance, it looked like Pecas was joined by two other dolphins that Alexa hadn't noticed earlier. "I think they are going to the Coconut Bay," José explained. "The dolphins like it there. I can show you if you like." He motioned toward his boat.

"Oh, thanks, but I need to get back to work." Alexa was starting to feel a bit like a malinger[36]—she had skipped out on work now two mornings in a row.

---

[34] Elitist: consciousness of being or belonging to an elite (a socially superior group)

[35] Egalitarian: one who believes in human equality, especially with respect to social, economic, and political rights

[36] Malinger: to pretend incapacity (as illness) so as to avoid duty or work; shirk

"Are you sure you don't want to come for just a little while?" José reiterated[37] his invitation.

"I really better get back before they know I'm gone." She smiled at José's handsome dark face.

"Maybe tomorrow I can show you Coconut Bay?" he asked hopefully.

"Maybe! See you later!"

"Wait! Do you like ping-pong? There is a ping-pong table in the recreation room next to the cafeteria. Sometimes I go there after work. Maybe I will see you there tonight?" José asked.

"Maybe. I'll try to go there after dinner," Alexa replied tentatively.[38]

"Great! See you then!" he replied enthusiastically.

Alexa waved goodbye as she started swimming toward the outcrop and José waved back as he swam in the opposite direction back to his boat. She toweled off quickly and pulled her clothes on over her wet bathing suit. Her shoulder-length brown hair was already starting to dry in the hot sun. As she scurried over the rocks to her motorbike, she looked over her shoulder at José. He was busy unloading his catch of fish onto the dock and didn't see her. Alexa hopped on the bike and sped toward Puerto Marino. She would need to stop at the apartment to change clothes before returning to the lab.

Alexa burst into the lab, ignited[39] with the excitement of her morning exploit.[40] She glanced quickly at the clock on the wall—it was 10:42. She had been gone for well over an hour on her illicit[41] adventure. Fortunately, Janine was not back yet. Alexa breathed a sigh of relief as she rushed to resume her experiment in the tranquility[42] of the empty lab.

---

[37] Reiterate: to state or do over again or repeatedly, sometimes with wearying effect
[38] Tentatively: hesitantly
[39] Ignite: to heat up; excite
[40] Exploit: a deed or an act
[41] Illicit: not permitted; against the rules or law
[42] Tranquility: the quality or state of being tranquil (free from disturbance or turmoil)

This afternoon, they were going to complete the analysis of the DNA they made yesterday. The first step was to cut the DNA into fragments using a special enzyme that clipped the DNA in specific locations. They had already completed that step this morning. The second step was to separate the pieces of DNA in a gel so that the fragments could form the characteristic bar-code pattern. Preparing the gel for the experiment seemed somewhat akin to making Jell-O, Alexa thought. First the gelatinous material is heated and then it is poured into the rectangular mold. Alexa watched her flask containing the "Jell-O" as it started to boil in the microwave oven, then deftly[43] removed the flask and gave it a gentle swirl.

Alexa cooled the boiling liquid by swirling the flask in a warm-water bath, and then she carefully poured the gel into the mold. She reflected silently in the quiet lab as the gel hardened in the apparatus.[44] I'm actually really interested to see the results of this experiment, she thought. It was a surprisingly fulfilling and exciting process to take cells from an animal, make DNA from the cells, and finally to actually visualize the DNA. Alexa had a surprising revelation[45]—maybe her father was right, about this one thing at least. Perhaps it *was* better to spend the summer doing something meaningful in a laboratory rather than frittering[46] away the time at the shopping mall back home.

It seemed that despite the inauspicious[47] beginning, the summer was turning out to be rather interesting after all. Alexa couldn't wait to e-mail Laurie with a surfeit[48] of details about the dolphins, the lab, the beach—and, of course, José.

---

[43] Deftly: characterized by facility and skill
[44] Apparatus: an instrument or appliance designed for a specific operation
[45] Revelation: the act of revealing an enlightening or divine truth
[46] Fritter: to spend or waste bit by bit on trifles, or without commensurate return
[47] Inauspicious: not auspicious or favorable; ominous
[48] Surfeit: an overabundant supply; excess

6

Pecas' Plea

The recreation room at Puerto Marino was exceedingly simple, almost ascetic[1] in its décor. It was as if aesthetic concerns had been set aside, and in their place, a utilitarian[2] theme prevailed. The walls were unadorned and the floor was bare cement. On one side of the room there was a reading corner, with several plain gray chairs clustered around a low table and a rack of magazines and newspapers. On the other side, two computer terminals faced the wall. In the middle, there was the ping-pong table, which looked new and virtually unused.

Alexa barely noticed anything about the sparsely[3] adorned room— she quickly scanned the area to see if José was there. The room was empty except for one person sitting in the reading corner. To her dismay, that person was not José—it was Charlotte! She was sitting there quietly read-ing a fashion magazine and didn't notice Alexa's entrance.

Alexa decided to avoid Charlotte and instead to sit down at one of the computers and wait for José. She logged on to check her e-mail yet again. There was still no reply from Laurie! But there was a very sweet

---

[1] Ascetic: plain, stark, simple; austere in appearance, manner, or attitude [not to be confused with aesthetic, which means pleasing in appearance or effect; beauty]
[2] Utilitarian: no-frills, practical and functional as opposed to decorative
[3] Sparsely: of few and scattered elements; especially not thickly grown or settled

note from her father, who was eager to hear about her project in the lab. He also said that he missed her very much, which gave Alexa a nice warm glow inside.

Alexa started to compose a reply when someone sat down beside her.

"*Hola!*" José smiled brightly. "I hope you weren't waiting long—I just got out of work." José spoke very quietly, almost in a whisper.

"No, I just got here," Alexa replied in a conspiratorial whisper.

"So, are you any good at ping-pong?" José asked.

"Hardly!"

"Oh, I'll bet you are a virtuoso[4] ping-pong player!"

"You'll see!" Alexa replied, laughing at José's pronouncement.[5] In reality, she had only played the game three times before, and that was several years ago.

As they picked out their paddles, José continued talking in a hushed voice. "Why are we whispering?" Alexa finally asked.

"Well, I am not really supposed to be using this recreation room. Usually it's not a problem. I am friends with most of the people who work here and they don't mind at all. There's just one guard who found me in here before, and he was very strict—he threatened to get me fired. So, hopefully, he's not working tonight!"

"Yikes! Maybe we shouldn't play," Alexa said with concern.

"It will be fine, don't worry." José picked up the ping-pong ball and beckoned to Alexa, who relented and took her position at the end of the table opposite José. They started hitting the ball back and forth. Neither one of them was very skillful at the game, but this only seemed to fuel their laughter and fun.

---

4   Virtuoso: expert, incredibly skillful and masterful
5   Pronouncement: a usually formal declaration of opinion

Alexa could see Charlotte in the background, pretending to be pre-occupied[6] with her magazine. But instead she was watching Alexa and José have a good time, laughing and being silly. It looked like she wanted to join them. Alexa felt a bit discourteous[7] ignoring Charlotte this way, but truthfully, she didn't want Charlotte encroaching[8] on her special friendship with José.

But she couldn't ignore her indefinitely. When Alexa inadvertently hit the ball a little too hard, it went flying over José's head and landed right at Charlotte's feet! Alexa cringed as José went over to retrieve the ball.

"I'm sorry!" José apologized to Charlotte as he picked up the ball.

"Don't worry about it. It looks like fun," Charlotte said demurely.

"Did you want to play with us?" José was unfailingly polite.

Charlotte looked over at Alexa expectantly. It looked like Charlotte wanted to join them, but she didn't want to intrude if Alexa didn't want her to. Alexa, however, didn't really want Charlotte to join them. She knew it would be polite to reiterate José's invitation and make Charlotte feel welcome, but instead she remained silent.

"Oh, no thanks—I was just leaving anyway," Charlotte replied politely as she got up and started to leave.

Just as Alexa was breathing a sigh of relief, a uniformed security guard walked into the room, his gaze focused on José. Alexa could tell by the look on José's face that this was the guard he would rather avoid.

"What are you doing in here?" the guard asked José sternly. "I thought I told you this room is only for the resident staff and their children—not for the locals who work in the kitchen!"

---

[6] Preoccupied: engrossed, busy or occupied with thought
[7] Discourteous: lacking courtesy; rude, impolite
[8] Encroaching: to enter by gradual steps or by stealth into the possessions or rights of another

Alexa felt her stomach sink. She would feel so terrible if José lost his job. There was an awkward silence as José faced the wrath[9] of the guard without a response. He was indefensible[10] in the face of the guard's charges, and he instinctively knew that combativeness[11] would only worsen his situation.

"It's quite all right, Mr. Jamison," Charlotte said sweetly but authoritatively. "He's my guest—I invited him." Charlotte smiled coyly at the guard, placating[12] his anger. It was clear who was in control of the situation. Charlotte, being the daughter of the Colonel Brandt, was used to getting her way around Puerto Marino. Alexa wasn't sure exactly what sort of role Colonel Brandt played at Puerto Marino, but it was clearly an important one because he and his family were treated like VIPs by the staff.

"I do apologize, Miss Brandt." Mr. Jamison immediately tried to rectify[13] the situation. "Sorry to have interrupted," he added, hastily departing.

"Thank you so much!" José said gratefully.

"That was really nice of you," Alexa added.

"Don't mention it—it was nothing, really," Charlotte replied, brushing off their praise. "Enjoy your game," Charlotte added politely as she too departed.

"Whew!" José said in relief after Charlotte departed. Alexa was also immensely relieved. The two continued playing ping-pong, but Alexa couldn't help but think about Charlotte's surprising actions. She never expected Charlotte to be her advocate[14]—in fact, Alexa had viewed her as more of an adversary.[15] Even after Alexa neglected to invite her to join

---

[9] Wrath: strong vengeful anger or indignation

[10] Indefensible: incapable of being justified or excused; inexcusable

[11] Combativeness: marked by eagerness to fight or contend

[12] Placating: to soothe or mollify especially by concessions; appease

[13] Rectify: to set right; remedy, correct

[14] Advocate: one who pleads the cause of another; specifically one who pleads the cause of another before a tribunal or judicial court

[15] Adversary: one who contends with, opposes, or resists; opponent, rival

their game, Charlotte was not at all vindictive.[16] Quite the contrary, she had generously wielded her influence to exculpate[17] José. Alexa realized that perhaps her preconceptions[18] about Charlotte were wrong. Maybe she *was* worth getting to know a little bit better.

❧   ☙

Alexa's first experiment at Puerto Marino was an unmitigated[19] failure. Janine looked over her shoulder at the computer screen the next morning and said some encouraging words. Janine was being very graceful with her solicitous[20] attention, but Alexa could plainly see that the experiment was botched.[21] The image should have been showing crisp bands forming a characteristic bar code, but instead there was an amorphous[22] smear.

"I'm not quite sure what went wrong here," Janine analyzed. "It looks like something might have gone wrong with the gel."

"I followed the instructions," Alexa replied, looking a bit forlorn.

"Yes, but sometimes mistakes just happen. Don't fret about it. Just try it again today." Janine started to leave for her daily 9:00 A.M. meeting, but the expression on Alexa's face revealed that she needed further assurance.[23]

"Anything worthwhile requires a lot of perseverance. Wasn't it Thomas Edison who said genius is 1% inspiration and 99% perspiration?" Janine smiled warmly at Alexa and continued her speech. "All successful scientists have a large number of botched experiments under their belts. The thing that makes them successful is that they use their minds to figure out what they need to fix and they keep trying. It's analogous[24]

---

[16] Vindictive: disposed to seek revenge; spiteful
[17] Exculpate: to clear from alleged fault or guilt
[18] Preconceptions: opinions that are formed prior to actual knowledge or experience
[19] Unmitigated: not lessened; unrelieved
[20] Solicitous: manifesting or expressing solicitude (attentive care and protectiveness)
[21] Botched: to foul up hopelessly; failed, spoiled
[22] Amorphous: without shape or form
[23] Assurance: something that inspires or tends to inspire confidence
[24] Analogous: showing an analogy or a likeness that permits one to draw an analogy

to learning how to ride a bike. When you fall off, you need to get back on and try again."

"Yes, but doesn't the saying go that once you learn how to ride a bike you never forget? Does that mean that my experiments will always work now?" Alexa asked, her eyebrows raised to emphasize the cynicism[25] of her retort.

Janine laughed heartily. "You are too smart for your own good! This is just what I need to brighten my morning—satire[26] and spunk from my summer student!"

The two of them shared a good laugh. Janine looked at her watch and then hurriedly gathered her things to leave for her meeting. As she breezed out the door, she cheerfully yelled goodbye and good luck to Alexa.

Once again, the lab was quiet and Alexa set her mind to the task before her, resolving to make it work. This time she would follow the instructions meticulously.[27] She carefully and methodically[28] poured the gel again.

While the molten gel was setting in its mold, Alexa couldn't resist taking another trip to the beach. She was anxious to see the dolphins again and admittedly, to see José as well.

It was another beautiful, sunny day and the wind rushing by her felt great as she drove to the beach on her motorbike. She hurried to the end of the rocky outcrop to see if Pecas was there, but there was no sign of the dolphin.

Off in the distance she could see a boat. It looked like José! He was waving to her and it looked like he had altered his course to come her way.

---

[25] Cynicism: having or showing the attitude or temper of a cynic (a faultfinding captious critic)
[26] Satire: wit, irony, or sarcasm used to expose and discredit vice or folly
[27] Meticulously: extremely carefully, painstakingly
[28] Methodically: habitually proceeding according to method; systematically

"Hola!" José yelled over the noise of the motor. His boat was almost to the large rock where Alexa was standing when he cut the motor. He scurried to the front of the boat, where he nimbly seated himself on the bow with his legs dangling off the front end of the boat. He deftly stepped onto the rock and quickly turned and caught the boat to prevent it from hitting the outcrop.

"How are you?" José asked as he stood next to her on the large boulder.

"I'm fine," Alexa managed to say. She couldn't think of what to say next. Even though they had talked quite a bit last night playing ping-pong, Alexa felt shy all over again. She hadn't noticed how tall José was until he was standing right next to her like this. And really, really cute, she couldn't help thinking. An awkward silence ensued.

"I saw Pecas and the other dolphins over at Coconut Bay. Do you want to come with me to see?" José looked down at her and saw her hesitation. "It's only a few minutes from here," he added persuasively.

"OK," she gave in with a smile. "But I have to be back in a half an hour to get back to work."

"No problem," José replied confidently as he held the boat with one hand and reached the other hand out for her to hold as she stepped into the boat.

Alexa sat in the middle of the old rowboat as José ran the outboard motor from the back seat. She looked at the ripped cushions and well-worn fishing equipment. While the boat seemed marginally seaworthy, it certainly could use some refurbishing.[29] Nevertheless, she couldn't help

---

[29] Refurbish: to brighten or freshen up; renovate

but think that it felt really great to be out on the clear blue water with the fresh salty air rushing by.

"There's Puerto Marino," José pointed out, raising his voice over the loud motor.

"Wow! I didn't realize that it was so close!" Alexa replied, surprised to see that Puerto Marino was actually adjacent to the bay where she was swimming. She could see the exterior of the enormous dolphin facility with the sturdy white boat moored to the dock. The road must have wound around the town in a circuitous[30] fashion, only to end up at the beach right next to the compound, she realized.

"And the next bay is Coconut Bay," José added as they went around the peninsula that delineated[31] the border between Puerto Marino and Coconut Bay. "This is the best fishing area around. That's why the dolphins like it here, too." José smiled and pointed to the middle of the bay where a group of four dolphins were jumping out of the water.

The bay was deserted except for two fishing boats. From a distance they could see a scuba diver climb up onto the boat. The diver was bringing something out of the water, but Alexa couldn't make out what it was. She watched curiously.

"They are diving for lobsters," José explained.

"Diving for lobsters?" Alexa repeated with disbelief. "Don't they catch the lobsters in traps?"

"Not around here. It is so much more efficient to dive down and get them by hand. And it pays well. It's one of the few ways that anyone can make any money around here. But it is extremely dangerous."

---

[30] Circuitous: having a circular or winding course; roundabout, indirect
[31] Delineated: to mark the outline of; demarcated

"Why is it dangerous? I didn't think that scuba diving was that dangerous," Alexa asked curiously.

"It is very dangerous if you don't have the proper training and equipment. My father got the bends diving for lobsters. Now he is in a wheelchair—he probably won't be able to walk again. He made me promise that I would never do it!"

"I hope you don't go diving for lobsters either!"

"Well, unfortunately, conventional fishing isn't nearly as profitable. I was lucky to find the job at Puerto Marino. I need to help my family and hopefully, save some money to go to college someday."

"I'm really amazed at all you do. I feel like I've had it so easy by comparison."

"Did you want to go swimming?" José inquired, shrugging off her compliments. The beautiful sandy beach rimmed with coconut palms beckoned invitingly. He pulled the boat up to shore and again held his hand out to Alexa to help her out of the boat.

"Yes! I can't wait. I wonder if Pecas will recognize me?" Alexa was thankful she had worn her bathing suit under her clothes again today. She started wading into the water and José was quick to follow. Alexa could hardly contain her excitement as she walked on the sandy ocean bottom toward deeper water.

One of the dolphins approached, and Alexa stood still as José caught up to her. He stood by her side as they both waited quietly for the dolphin to come closer. In this minute of silence between them—a moment that didn't feel the least bit awkward—Alexa couldn't help but feel that she and José had begun a special friendship.

"Pecas!" Alexa exclaimed. "It's you! How are you?" Alexa talked to the dolphin as it surfaced in front of them. "I'm so happy to see you."

Pecas appeared to be attempting a squeaky reply.

"How come Pecas is so friendly and the other dolphins are keeping their distance?" Alexa asked José curiously. In the distance, three other feral[32] dolphins hovered, reticent[33] to join Pecas in her folly[34] with the humans.

"Several dolphins are friendly with the fishermen around here. Some don't seem to like to interact with people and some do." José shrugged as he gestured toward the dolphins in the distance. "The ones that like people—we give them fish when we have some extra. It's been going on for generations. My grandfather fished in these waters, and he has many stories to tell about the dolphins."

"My mom told me you're not supposed to feed dolphins in the wild. It's not ethical."[35]

"Why not?" José asked, puzzled. He hardly saw feeding a dolphin as a heinous[36] act. As far as he could tell, it appeared to be inconsequential.[37]

"Well, I think that it interferes with their normal routine of hunting for their food. They might forget how to catch fish if people keep giving fish to them," Alexa said, trying not to sound too confrontational.

"That's absurd!" José replied, indignant[38] at the suggestion that his actions would cause the dolphins harm. "They still catch fish—I see them do it!" José pointed out why, from his perspective, Alexa's argument was illogical.[39]

"Well, they look fine to me, too. Look at Pecas jump!" Alexa changed the subject, backing off her earlier assertion. She hadn't meant to incriminate

---

32 Feral: not domesticated or cultivated; wild
33 Reticent: restrained in expression, presentation, or appearance
34 Folly: lack of good sense or normal prudence and foresight; foolishness
35 Ethical: involving or expressing moral approval or disapproval
36 Heinous: hatefully or shockingly evil
37 Inconsequential: of no significance or importance
38 Indignant: filled with or marked by indignation (anger aroused by something unjust, unworthy, or mean)
39 Illogical: not observing the principles of logic; not reasonable or sound

José or to be antagonistic;[40] she had only been trying to make conversation. She decided that in order to avoid getting entangled[41] in an argument with José she would try to find a topic that didn't generate so much friction.[42] He was a very passionate person, she realized, as she began to analyze his actions in her mind. On the one hand, his impassioned[43] love for life was incredibly attractive. He was so full of positive energy that he simply radiated enthusiasm. On the other hand, he tended to see things as black or white. If he were to have a fault, this would be it, she thought. But on the whole, Alexa concluded, he was simply wonderful.

José also seemed eager to get past the awkward moment and showed her how to hold her arms out so that Pecas could swim next to their outstretched hands. Alexa was thrilled when Pecas swam right in between her and José. They both stroked the dolphin's side. Even though she had already touched Pecas yesterday, it still felt unimaginably exciting to swim with this wild dolphin and especially to touch it. Alexa tried to figure out why she felt so intensely emotional about these encounters with Pecas. It must be that the dolphins seem so similar to us, and yet so different, she thought. Communicating with them seemed somehow profound in a way that was hard to put her finger on.

It appeared that Pecas also had communication on her mind. Although her face appeared fixed in a permanent smile, her tone of voice suggested otherwise. It looked like Pecas was trying to tell her human friends something upsetting in her series of high-pitched squeaks. She swam out a ways and then turned back to face Alexa and José, only to "speak" again.

---

[40] Antagonistic: marked by or resulting from antagonism (actively expressed opposition or hostility)
[41] Entangled: to involve in a perplexing or troublesome situation
[42] Friction: the clashing between two persons or parties of opposed views
[43] Impassion: to arouse the feelings or passions of

"I wonder what she's trying to tell us?" Alexa asked José, puzzled at the dolphin's erratic[44] behavior.

"I don't know. She's been acting this way ever since her baby disappeared last week," José replied in a voice filled with concern.

Pecas swam out farther and repeated her urgent cry, goading[45] them to do something.

"I wonder if she wants us to follow her?" Alexa asked.

"Yes! Let's go!" José replied, without wasting a second. He took her hand as they raced through the water with great alacrity[46] back to the boat. Alexa grabbed her backpack off the beach and tossed it into the boat. José had already pulled the boat off of the beach and was standing next to it in shallow water holding his hand out for Alexa. He helped Alexa into the boat, pushed the boat into deeper water, and quickly hopped in himself, anxious to begin their urgent quest.[47]

"Do you think she'll be afraid of the motor?" Alexa inquired over the noise of the outboard engine.

"I don't think so. The dolphins here are used to the fishing boats. In fact, they like to ride in the bow waves. You'll see," José answered confidently.

Sure enough, Pecas joined them by leading the way in front of the boat. She swam right in the wake of the bow, periodically jumping clear out of the water. Alexa was impressed by how effortlessly Pecas swam at a fast clip.

It wasn't long, however, before Pecas broke away and turned to "talk" to them once again. She seemed to be leading them to go in a new direction.

---

[44] Erratic: characterized by lack of consistency, regularity, or uniformity; deviating from what is ordinary or standard

[45] Goading: to incite or rouse as if with a goad; provoking, prodding

[46] Alacrity: promptness in response; cheerful readiness

[47] Quest: an act or instance of seeking; pursuit, search

Alexa turned to José. They were silent for a moment. They knew they couldn't possibly follow Pecas where she wanted to go. She was headed straight for Puerto Marino!

"We can't go there!" Alexa voiced the obvious.

"It looks like she's headed straight for the dolphin facility. I wonder why she would want to go near there?" José asked, puzzled. He prided himself in his uncanny[48] ability to understand these animals.

"Maybe she wants to see one of the dolphins that's living in there," Alexa offered.

"But she has lots of dolphin friends out here in the bay. If her cries are symptomatic[49] of her loneliness, why wouldn't she be heading out into the bay to play with the other dolphins?"

"Didn't you say her baby is missing? What if her baby is in there?" Alexa theorized.[50] It was a horrifying thought—the specter[51] of such a tragedy made her sick to her stomach.

"Do they have such young dolphins in there?" José asked incredulously. Although he worked at Puerto Marino, he had never been inside the dolphin facility.

"I know they have at least one dolphin that's only around twelve months old," Alexa replied, thinking of little Coco.

"How could they possibly take a baby dolphin from its mother! *That* is really unethical!" José quickly condemned[52] the reprehensible[53] act. He could barely contain his anger. "It's also illegal! The government hasn't given out any permits to catch the dolphins here. In fact, they promulgated[54] a law two years ago that made it illegal for anyone to catch a wild dolphin in these waters. There's a statute[55] that specifically protects

---

[48] Uncanny: being beyond what is normal or expected, suggesting superhuman or supernatural powers
[49] Symptomatic: characteristic, indicative
[50] Theorized: to form a theory about; speculate
[51] Specter: a haunting or disturbing image or prospect (can also refer to a ghost or apparition)
[52] Condemn: to declare to be bad, wrong, or evil
[53] Reprehensible: deserving criticism
[54] Promulgate: to put (a law) into action or force
[55] Statute: a law enacted by the legislative branch of a government

these dolphins! That dolphin facility should be razed[56] to the ground and all of the dolphins set free!"

"We don't know for sure that Pecas' baby is in there," Alexa said, hoping to calm José. But inside, she felt a sense of dread. Obviously, Puerto Marino had to get its dolphins from somewhere, and what better source than the waters right outside the facility? If no one saw them actually catching the dolphin, who would ever know? How could anyone ever figure out where the dolphins came from?

"We have to do something about this!" José was adamant. In his mind, it was incumbent[57] upon them to find a solution to this dilemma.

"First we need to figure out if Pecas' baby is in Puerto Marino," Alexa said, her mind churning and beginning to formulate[58] an idea. She knew they needed to be calm and rational[59] about this.

"How are we going to do that?" José asked, his voice laden with emotion. "We can't even get into the dolphin facility, the security is so tight!"

"I think I have an idea," Alexa replied thoughtfully.

---

[56] Razed: demolished, destroyed to the ground

[57] Incumbent: obligatory, imposed as a duty (is also commonly used to refer to a politician who is currently in office)

[58] Formulate: to reduce to or express in a formula

[59] Rational: relating to, based on, or agreeable to reason; lucid

7

The Clandestine Mission

Alexa looked at her watch—it was 9:15 A.M. She waited impatiently at the water's edge at the end of the rocky outcrop for José to pick her up in his boat. They had settled into a routine during the past week of meeting each other every day between 9:15 and 10:15. They had a mission to carry out and they were determined to see it through to the end.

Like clockwork, José's boat approached from the distance, right on time. Alexa was much more agile[1] hopping into the boat now, having practiced this maneuver every day for the past week. But José still held his hand out for her to hold when she jumped aboard and Alexa always took it, even though at this point, she really didn't need to. The past week had strengthened the bond between them. Not only were they friends, they were now collaborators on a clandestine[2] mission.

---

[1] Agile: marked by a ready ability to move with a quick, easy grace
[2] Clandestine: marked by, held in, or conducted with secrecy

"I think Pecas is out in the open water near Coconut Bay," José said, pointing off in the distance. He always had some idea where the dolphins were from his early morning fishing expedition.

"Let's go!" Alexa replied with enthusiasm. "We don't have much time!" She began unpacking her backpack. She got out her sterile swab, still covered in its plastic wrapping, and her sterile, capped test tube and got them ready for their endeavor.[3]

Last week, Alexa had gone back to the molecular biology lab with a newfound sense of purpose when she realized she had figured out a way to determine if Coco or one of the other captive dolphins at Puerto Marino was actually Pecas' baby. She had burst back into the laboratory that fateful day to excitedly ask Janine a question: "Can the DNA analysis that we're doing be used to figure out if two dolphins are related?"

"Of course," Janine replied. "That's how paternity tests are done."

At that moment, a plan crystallized[4] in her mind. If DNA analysis could be used to determine paternity, it seemed reasonable to assume it could be used to test maternity as well. Alexa was thrilled to have figured out such a cunning[5] way to determine if Pecas' baby was one of the dolphins at Puerto Marino.

Alexa's father had been even more helpful. When Alexa told him she wanted to determine the relationship between two dolphins by analyzing their DNA, he was ecstatic[6] that she had taken an interest in molecular biology. To help feed her curiosity, he faxed several papers to her that described how to compare two DNA samples and determine if they are related. Then he lectured her on how to formulate and test a hypothesis.[7]

---

[3] Endeavor: to attempt (as the fulfillment of an obligation) by exertion of effort
[4] Crystallize: to cause to take a definite form
[5] Cunning: displaying keen insight
[6] Ecstatic: of, relating to, or marked by ecstasy (a state of overwhelming emotion, especially rapturous delight)
[7] Hypothesis: a tentative assumption made in order to draw out and test its logical or empirical consequences; theory

Alexa assured him she harbored no preconceived[8] notions[9] of the out-come of the experiment—she intended to be scrupulous[10] and unbiased in her interpretation of the data.

But in order to get started, they needed to get some DNA from Pecas. This was proving to be a real challenge. They needed to swab some cells from the inside of Pecas' mouth in a manner similar to the way a doctor would take a throat culture.

It was José's idea that they could probably do this while feeding Pecas fish. He had been feeding Pecas on occasion for years, so the dolphin trusted him. The only problem was that Pecas ate the fish so quickly—it looked like she was swallowing them whole—that they could never even get near her mouth with the swab. This time José was planning on hold-ing the fish very close to the boat to see if Pecas would come up to him and take it right out of his hand. Today he had three buckets full of fish. Yesterday, they had gone through all of the fish that he had caught in the morning without successfully getting the cells from Pecas.

Alexa was pleasantly surprised to see how dedicated José was to their undertaking. Initially, Alexa had been concerned that José was going to do something radical[11] out of vengeance[12]—he was so emotional about this issue. Alexa's scheme,[13] however, was a persuasive one. She convinced him that by using DNA from the dolphins, their conjecture[14] was easily verifiable.[15] Now they shared a bond of solidarity[16] in their passion for the dolphins and the search for Pecas' baby. José also seemed fascinated with Alexa's work in the laboratory. Not only did he share her reverence for the power of DNA, he was anxious to help with the experiment she

---

[8] Preconceived: to form (as an opinion) prior to actual knowledge or experience
[9] Notions: a theory or belief held by a person or group
[10] Scrupulous: punctiliously exact; painstaking
[11] Radical: tending or disposed to make extreme changes in existing views, habits, conditions, or institutions
[12] Vengeance: punishment inflicted in retaliation for an injury or offense
[13] Scheme: a plan or program of action, especially a crafty or secret one
[14] Conjecture: a conclusion deduced by surmise or guesswork
[15] Verifiable: capable of being verified (to establish the truth, accuracy, or reality of)
[16] Solidarity: unity (as of a group or class) that produces or is based on community of interests, objectives, and standards

had designed. Alexa thought José might be able to join her in the lab on the weekend, but today was already Friday and they still hadn't successfully obtained the cells from Pecas' mouth.

José had a look of determination on his face as they approached the area where the dolphins were swimming. He looked intently at the frolicking animals, trying to identify Pecas. In the distance, they could see the dolphin facility of Puerto Marino looming ominously[17] on the shore like a huge monstrosity.[18]

"I think I see her!" Alexa exclaimed, pointing the way.

José nodded, slowing the boat and then turning the motor off completely. He threw several fish into the water to get the dolphins' attention. It worked! Pecas came right over, clearly looking for more fish. José lavished[19] praise on the approaching dolphin. The other dolphins stayed behind and eyed the proceedings warily. It was as if they didn't espouse[20] close contact with humans, but nevertheless, they were interested to watch Pecas interact with her human friends.

Alexa made her way back to the end of the boat where José was talking softly to Pecas. He was trying to coax her to take the fish right from his hand instead of tossing the fish to her, which was her customary way of accepting handouts from humans. Alexa tried to keep her balance in the wobbly boat as she walked toward the back, swab and test tube in hand. She steadied herself with a hand on his shoulder and squatted down beside him, trying to get within reach of Pecas.

José talked continually to Pecas in Spanish as he held a fish in his outstretched hand. Alexa wondered what he was saying. Without taking his eyes off of Pecas or relenting in his hypnotic Spanish rhapsody,[21] he

---

[17] Ominously: being or exhibiting an omen, especially foreboding or foreshadowing evil
[18] Monstrosity: an object of great and often frightening size, force, or complexity
[19] Lavish: expending or bestowing profusely
[20] Espouse: to take up and support as a cause; become attached to
[21] Rhapsody: a highly emotional utterance (can also refer to a highly emotional literary work, etc.)

motioned with his free hand for the swab. Alexa knew that he didn't want her to get too close to the dolphin's sharp teeth. She handed the swab over. Pecas took the fish from José's hand and swallowed it rapidly. José quickly readied another fish. As Pecas approached to take the second fish, he quickly swabbed the inside of her cheek with the swab in one hand and then deftly gave her the fish with the other hand.

"I think we've got it!" José exclaimed as he sealed the swab in the sterile test tube.

"It looked good! But we'll see," Alexa replied cautiously. Two days ago they thought they had a sample, but when she returned to the lab, there were no cells on the swab. It probably never even touched the inside of the dolphin's mouth.

José, however, was in no mood for understated[22] optimism. He was assuming that their tenacity[23] had paid off. He stood up on the seat of the boat and held his arms up in victory. "We did it!" he yelled. True to form, he started to lose his balance and soon was flailing comically trying to regain his footing. Down he fell into the water with a resounding splash!

Alexa started laughing at the sight of his exuberance and soon couldn't stop. He had probably fallen on purpose. Nevertheless, his jollity[24] was infectious. Pecas also seemed amused—she squawked animatedly.

"Come swimming with us!" José beckoned.

"OK," Alexa laughed. How could she possibly refrain from indulging?

Pecas, who seemed unfazed by the swabbing, had invented a whimsical[25] new game of fetch that kept them all playing together. The dolphin dove about ten feet down to the bottom and returned with a sponge on her rostrum (the protruding mouth of the dolphin, analogous to the beak

---

[22] Understate: to state or present with restraint, especially for effect
[23] Tenacity: the quality or state of being tenacious (persistent in maintaining or adhering to something)
[24] Jollity: the quality or state of being jolly (full of high spirits)
[25] Whimsical: resulting from or characterized by whim or caprice; lightly fanciful

of a bird) and swam by José, who grabbed it curiously. When he threw the sponge back in the water, Pecas quickly retrieved it and swam by Alexa, as if asking her to do the same. Alexa was delighted to comply.

Inevitably, however, Pecas began her strange behavior of plaintive[26] cries. Swimming again toward Puerto Marino, she would turn back to face her two human friends and desperately beseech them to join her. Alexa and José had begun to notice a pattern with Pecas' actions. She would play with them for a short while, and then, when she had their full attention, she would begin this compulsive[27] behavior.

"It looks like our fun and games are over," José said sadly.

"Yes, I think so too. I really want to get back to the lab anyway," Alexa replied, as she pulled herself into the boat. As the words came out of her mouth, Alexa realized that for the first time, she really meant it— she couldn't wait to get back in the lab.

"I wish I could come with you! I can't wait for tomorrow," José said passionately. José planned to sneak into the lab to join Alexa after he worked his breakfast shift at the Puerto Marino cafeteria. But his enthusiasm for science and his special friendship with Pecas made it hard for him to wait so long. "I want to help you with the experiment! Will you tell me all about it? I want to know *everything*!" he added vehemently.[28]

"Of course," Alexa replied. "But don't worry, you'll be there for the most interesting part—the results, when we find out if Pecas' baby is in there." The two of them climbed into the boat and José took his seat near the outboard engine. He rummaged through his backpack instead of starting the motor, like usual.

---

[26] Plaintive: expressive of suffering or woe; mournful
[27] Compulsive: obsessive, habitual, or irrational behavior
[28] Vehemently: marked by forceful energy

"I have something for you," José said shyly. He handed her a necklace with a large tooth in the center, surrounded by beautiful and delicate pink shells. "It's a shark's tooth, to ward off evil spirits. It's to bring you good luck."

Alexa was stunned into silence. She had never received a gift from a boy before. She was so surprised that she barely could respond. "It's beautiful! Thank you," Alexa managed to say as she accepted the gift and fastened the talisman[29] around her neck.

"I caught the shark myself," José added shyly. He didn't need to embellish[30] this fact with any narratives[31] about his heroic bravery. Alexa was already impressed with his valor and touched by his gesture.

"I love it." Alexa was amazed with José—he could be so courageous as to catch a shark and yet so tender and sweet to make a necklace. And she was filled with unutterable[32] happiness that he had made the necklace for her.

"Alexa," José began in a serious and thoughtful tone of voice, "do you think that you could come to the library tomorrow morning—very early— around six? I want to show you something before I go to work in the morning and before we begin this experiment." José climbed into the boat and looked right into her eyes to underscore[33] the importance of his request.

"Sure," Alexa replied. How could she possibly refuse when she looked into his soft brown eyes? "I think I know where it is—is it right on the main road in town?"

"Yes, with a sign out front saying *biblioteca*."

"But will it be open so early in the morning?" Alexa asked.

"Don't worry, I have a key. Just come. It's important."

"I'll be there," Alexa replied with certainty.

---

[29] Talisman: an object held as a charm to avert evil and bring good fortune
[30] Embellish: to heighten the attractiveness of by adding ornamental details
[31] Narratives: something that is narrated; a story
[32] Unutterable: being beyond the powers of description
[33] Underscore: give emphasis to, highlight

8

Not a Nemesis

Alexa and Janine waited in line at the cafeteria for lunch. Alexa was nervous and excited at the prospect of seeing José again, even though she had just left his company a mere hour and a half ago.

Alexa had returned to the lab, adorned[1] with her new necklace and glowing with joy. She was still in shock, never having received such a tangible form of adulation[2] from a boy. She kept reaching up to touch the sharp tooth, just to check that it was still there. Alexa loved the necklace—she loved the way the rough shark's tooth was couched[3] in the soft pink shells. The combination of the masculine sharp tooth with the feminine pink shells might appear mismatched to some people, but to Alexa, it was strangely harmonious.[4] It was such an original, unique gift—not some hackneyed[5] old heart on a chain or class ring like you might expect from a high school boy.

When Janine first saw Alexa wearing the necklace, she eyed it curiously. It was hardly inconspicuous. But Janine, being ever so discreet, didn't harangue[6] or tease Alexa in the slightest. Janine didn't even mention the

---

[1] Adorned: to enliven or decorate as if with ornaments
[2] Adulation: to flatter or admire excessively or slavishly
[3] Couched: to lay (oneself) down for rest or sleep
[4] Harmonious: having the parts agreeably related; congruous
[5] Hackneyed: lacking in freshness or originality; trite
[6] Harangue: a ranting speech or writing

correlation[7] between the new necklace and Alexa's wet hair. Although Alexa had liked Janine from the beginning, now she really liked her and respected her as a mentor. Janine managed to interweave[8] teaching and her inherent[9] love of science with a great level of caring for Alexa's feelings.

Alexa didn't see José in the kitchen as she and Janine passed through on route to the seating area. Alexa's butterflies calmed as the moment for a brief encounter with José passed by inconsequentially. When they scouted the room for a place to sit, Alexa noticed Charlotte sitting by herself at a corner table like a pariah.[10] It didn't take more than a modicum[11] of perceptiveness[12] to see that Charlotte was lonely.

"Janine, do you mind if I go join my friend for lunch?" Alexa asked.

"Not at all—enjoy yourself. I'll meet you back at the lab at one o'clock."

Charlotte brightened up immediately when she saw Alexa approaching—her morose[13] demeanor was suspended by Alexa's munificence.[14] She gestured at an empty chair for Alexa to sit.

"Hi, why don't you have a seat," Charlotte offered decorously[15] with a trace of Southern drawl.

"Thanks. I also wanted to thank you again for the other night—that was so nice of you to rescue José like that."

---

[7] Correlation: a relationship between two or more things which tend to vary, or occur together in a way not expected on the basis of chance alone

[8] Interweave: to mix or blend together

[9] Inherent: involved in the constitution or essential character of something, belonging by nature or habit

[10] Pariah: outcast

[11] Modicum: a small amount

[12] Perceptiveness: ability to notice and see; discernment, sharpness

[13] Morose: having a sullen or gloomy disposition

[14] Munificence: characterized by great liberality or generosity

[15] Decorous: marked by propriety and good taste

"Oh, it was nothing," Charlotte replied with nonchalance.[16] "It looked like you all were having fun!" Charlotte raised her eyebrows and smiled conspiratorially. "So tell me, is he your boyfriend?"

"Oh, I don't know..." Alexa blushed self-consciously.

"Did he give you that necklace?"

"Yes..." Alexa started to giggle nervously. "He just gave it to me this morning. It's a shark's tooth for good luck. He caught the shark himself!"

"Oh my gosh! He is *definitely* your boyfriend then. No doubt about it."

Alexa laughed. It was fun to have a girlfriend to talk to about these things. And it was especially nice to have a friend who was also a compatriot[17] when they were all so far from home.

"I have a boyfriend back home in Virginia," Charlotte offered. "He didn't refer to me as his girlfriend until we had been dating for four months! They keep us guessing!" Charlotte's hearty laugh permeated[18] the atmosphere.

"Did he give you that bracelet?" Alexa asked with a teasing innuendo[19] in her voice.

"No, actually, my father gave me this—my real father, that is. Colonel Brandt is my stepfather. My real father was also in the Navy...he died when I was ten years old. It was an accident...during training exercises." Charlotte was fingering the silver charm bracelet on her wrist.

"Oh, I'm so sorry," Alexa felt terrible. She had wanted to tease Charlotte about *her* boyfriend, but had mistakenly stumbled onto a very sad and awkward topic of conversation.

---

[16] Nonchalance: having an air of easy unconcern or indifference
[17] Compatriot: fellow countryman
[18] Permeate: to spread or diffuse through
[19] Innuendo: an oblique allusion; hint, insinuation

"It was a long time ago, but it's still difficult to talk about," Charlotte replied, looking down at the table. "Let's talk about something else. I want to hear more about this necklace that you're wearing! My boyfriend never gave me anything like that!"

"Is it hard to be away from him all summer?" Alexa asked.

"Yes! It's killing me! The worst part is that he doesn't return my e-mails very often and I can only talk to him once a week."

"That must be so hard!" Alexa said sympathetically. "I can kind of understand what that must be like—I'm not receiving very many e-mails from my friends at home either. I feel so isolated."

"You *were* feeling isolated, but now you have a *boyfriend*!" Charlotte laughed melodiously.[20]

Alexa couldn't help but laugh as well. All of her earlier misconceptions[21] about Charlotte had been negated.[22] Alexa had thought that Charlotte was narcissistic,[23] pretentious, and narrow-minded. But she wasn't any of these things. Quite the contrary, Charlotte was friendly, fun-loving, and sweet. Alexa realized that it was she, herself, who had been insular[24] in her judgments. She had perceived Charlotte as her nemesis,[25] when in reality, Charlotte wanted to be her friend.

"Do you do any activities or sports back home?" Alexa asked, eager to steer the conversation away from her love life.

"Yes, I play field hockey and I run on the track team, and I also play the piano."

"I run track too! I just started this past year," Alexa replied enthusiastically.

---

[20] Melodiously: having a pleasing sound or melody
[21] Misconception: a mistaken idea or concept
[22] Negate: to cause to be ineffective or invalid
[23] Narcissistic: excessive concern or love of oneself
[24] Insular: characteristic of an isolated people, especially having a narrow or provincial viewpoint
[25] Nemesis: a formidable and usually victorious rival or opponent

"You do? Do you want to go running with me? I'm going running every morning at six. Say you'll go with me! It'll be fun!" Charlotte mandated.[26]

"Well, I don't think I can go tomorrow morning..." Alexa hesitated as she thought about her early-morning rendezvous with José at the library. "But I could join you the day after tomorrow."

"Great! Let's meet in front of this building at 6:00 A.M. the day after tomorrow!"

"I'll be here," Alexa promised.

---

[26] Mandated: to make mandatory, obligatory

9

A Contemptuous Claim

Time: 5:30 A.M.
To: "Laurie"
From: "Alexa"
Subject: early morning rendezvous!

Dear Laurie,

Guess what? It looks like José and I were able to get some cells from Pecas the dolphin! Yesterday we had so much fun swimming together—José and I played in the water with Pecas for a while until it looked like she was trying to tell us something again. When I took the swab back to the lab, there were cells there! We finally did it :-) ! He gave me the most amazing necklace with a shark's tooth. Then he asked me if I would meet him at the library at 6 A.M. Can you believe that I'm up at 5:30? He said he wants to show me something. He looked sooo cute when he asked me! He works part-time at the library in addition to everything else that he does – I'm so impressed. Can't wait to find out what he wants to show me. Gotta run now!

Best friends always,
Alexa

P.S. It turns out that Charlotte is really nice—I think we are going to be friends!

Alexa hit Send and wondered if Laurie would ever respond. It was getting tiring to write all of these things and not receive a reply. But realistically, life is full of inequities,[1] she thought, feeling a bit jaded.[2]

The town was eerily quiet at this early hour as Alexa sped to the library on her motorbike. She parked her bike and took a protracted[3] look at the *biblioteca*, which occupied a prominent[4] position on the main street. Though stylistically[5] grand, the building looked as if it was sorely in need of a major renovation.[6] It had an ornate[7] stucco façade and well-worn wooden steps leading up to a large iron door. The building looked at least 100 years old, Alexa thought as she nervously pulled the ring-shaped door handle. Locked! It didn't look like the door was going to budge.

Alexa peered through the window and knocked gently. José came bounding toward the door, a sheepish grin on his face. He opened the massive door and beckoned to Alexa.

"Come in!" He gestured toward the interior. "I hope you weren't out there too long."

"No, I just got here," Alexa replied, suddenly shy again in the wake of his welcome.

"I want to show you something on the computer." José started walking purposefully[8] toward the desk in the back of the room.

"I was so curious when you told me you wanted to show me something at the library—I thought it would be some sort of book."

"No, it's on the computer, the thing I need to show you. There are some amazing books here—but we don't have time for that now. What I have to show you is very important," he added seriously.

---

[1] Inequities: unequal things or situations
[2] Jaded: world-weary, cynical
[3] Protract: to prolong in time or space
[4] Prominent: widely and popularly known
[5] Stylistic: of or relating especially to literary or artistic style
[6] Renovation: to restore to a former better state (as by cleaning, repairing, or rebuilding)
[7] Ornate: elaborately or excessively decorated
[8] Purposefully: with intent; having a purpose

"Oh my gosh, what kind of computer is that?" Alexa asked with a note of disdain. She had never seen such a worn, antiquated[9] machine. "That looks like a vestige[10] from the 80s!"

"It's the only computer I have access to," José replied defensively. "And it works...at least sometimes it works." After fumbling with the circuitry[11] under the desk, he began madly tapping away on the keyboard, trying to get the screen to respond from its dark repose.[12]

"It looks like you're really good with computers," Alexa complimented. She searched for something soothing and eloquent[13] to say after her earlier faux pas. In truth, Alexa really was impressed with José's abilities. By now he had gotten some bright green words to appear on the black screen and appeared to be programming the computer. Alexa struggled to fathom[14] just what he was coercing the computer to do. He typed quickly, she noticed. His fingers moved knowingly over the well-worn keyboard, the keys' beige veneer[15] effaced[16] by years of use.

"I have to be, to get this thing to work!" José smiled good-naturedly, putting Alexa at ease. He didn't appear to be insulted by her earlier comment. Finally, a familiar sight appeared on the screen as José clicked on the Internet Explorer icon. The familiar sounds of a dial tone followed by electronic dialing filled the silence. "Sometimes it takes awhile to get online. But it should be easy at this hour." They heard the telltale sound of the computer connecting. José quickly typed in an address, and the computer paused for a lengthy moment while it strained to pull up the image.

Finally, the image finished loading and José hopped out of his chair in front of the terminal to let Alexa take his seat.

---

[9] Antiquated: old-fashioned, old or obsolete

[10] Vestige: a trace, mark, or visible sign left by something (as an ancient city or a condition or practice) vanished or lost; relic

[11] Circuitry: the components of an electric circuit

[12] Repose: to lie at rest

[13] Eloquent: vividly or movingly expressive or revealing

[14] Fathom: comprehend

[15] Veneer: a thin sheet of a material; finish, or coating

[16] Efface: to eliminate or make indistinct by or as if by wearing away a surface

"There are lots of things I want to show you, but maybe you can start by reading this," José said solemnly.

Alexa sat in the chair and eagerly looked at the screen. It was an article called "The Dolphins of War" on the Conservation Forum website. Alexa read rapidly. The article described how the military purportedly[17] uses dolphins as guards for naval installments, to locate underwater mines and enemy divers, and to carry out "kamikaze" missions to blow up enemy submarines, among other duties.

"I didn't know dolphins are used in the military. Do you think any of this is true?" Alexa asked incredulously.

"Of course," José answered with emotion coloring his voice. "And I think that the reason you see some military people at Puerto Marino, is that they are here to buy the dolphins. Why else would they be here? Puerto Marino is a business. They capture and train dolphins, and then they sell them. I'll bet some of these dolphins are destined for dolphin shows. But the rest are going to the military."

Alexa felt a growing sense of dread in the face of his logical deduction.[18] She had seen the military personnel, including Colonel Brandt, at Puerto Marino. But she didn't have a clear idea of why they were there. "I thought they were interested in the dolphins' sonar because submarines use sonar...." As soon as the words were out of her mouth, she realized how silly they sounded. Alexa couldn't believe her own oversight. She hadn't even seriously thought about what Puerto Marino was doing with the dolphins. But now it all made sense. José's theory had a ring of truth to it. And her mother was collaborating with these people! It was hard to

---

[17] Purportedly: ostensibly, allegedly

[18] Deduction: a conclusion reached by logic or reasoning

imagine her mother doing anything that could possibly harm the dolphins. But nevertheless, Alexa felt conflicted—her eyes returned to the article searching for a redeeming factor.

"Well, maybe they're studying the dolphins some of the time, but realistically, why would the Navy be interested in dolphins if they weren't going to use them to fight the enemy?" José prodded.

Alexa was silent as she read the words on the screen. "You know, this article is mostly about the old Russian military dolphin unit. It doesn't even exist anymore. It says that the program was abandoned a long time ago," Alexa said hopefully. She didn't want to believe that the dolphins at Puerto Marino were destined to be used for dangerous missions.

"Yes, but the Americans are probably doing similar things," José said contemptuously.[19]

"I don't know that...aren't some of these articles written by animal rights groups? They make such ostentatious[20] claims. I've seen them protesting medical research at the University back home. And in that case, I know some of the things they said were outlandish[21] because my father works in those laboratories. I don't think we can just interpret everything they say literally."[22] Alexa searched for something else to say that would modulate[23] José's growing malice[24] toward Puerto Marino and the American military.

"There are so many articles on the Web—you can read them and decide for yourself. But I have to run to work now. Did you want to stay here?" José asked.

---

[19] Contemptuously: with contempt, disdain
[20] Ostentatious: marked by or fond of conspicuous or vainglorious and sometimes pretentious display
[21] Outlandish: exceeding proper or reasonable limits or standards
[22] Literally: actually, in a literal sense or manner
[23] Modulate: to adjust to or keep in proper measure or proportion; temper
[24] Malice: intent to commit an unlawful act or cause harm without legal justification or excuse

"No, I'm heading to the lab." Alexa's mood had deflated from the height of nervous anticipation to the depths of sober reflection. Her thoughts were a tangled morass[25] of conflicting emotions and alliances.

They decided to ride together on the motorbike, at least until they were in view of the security gate. But not even the thrill of riding the speeding bike with José could lift Alexa's mood and her growing disillusionment[26] with the dolphin facility at Puerto Marino, which had once seemed so captivating.

Time: 10:30 A.M.
To: "Laurie"
From: "Alexa"
Subject: dolphins at war

Dear Laurie,

Well, I found out what José wanted to show me and now I'm really upset. He thinks that the dolphins at Puerto Marino are going to be sold to the Navy. Did you know that dolphins are used in the military? José showed me an article on the Internet. I feel so naive. I thought the military was studying the dolphins, not using them! Apparently they are used to locate underwater mines and enemy divers. I suppose that would be OK, if it were safe for the dolphins. But the article José showed me on the Internet—it didn't look so safe. I wish I could talk to you about this! Please write back soon!

Best friends always,
Alexa

---

[25] Morass: something that traps, confuses, or impedes
[26] Disillusionment: to leave without illusion or naive faith and trust

Alexa clicked Send on the computer in the lab and sighed. It would be so great to talk to Laurie right now, she thought. José seemed so inordinately[27] passionate and rather intemperate[28] whenever the subject of the dolphins came up. Her mother was obviously caught in the middle, as was Charlotte. Alexa longed for an impartial and sympathetic ear to help her work through her complex feelings.

She realized she couldn't even concentrate on the experiment that she and José planned to work on today. Finding out if Pecas' baby was in captivity, a goal that had seemed so compelling before, now paled in comparison to the plight of all of the dolphins.

The first time she saw the dolphin facility, Alexa simply thought that it was amazing. The dolphins *looked* happy and well-cared for...and Alexa didn't have any negative feelings about the dolphins living their life in confinement. It hadn't even occurred to her. But now...now that she had developed such a unique friendship with Pecas, her perspective had changed dramatically. She had to agree with José—dolphins deserved a certain level of respect. It didn't feel right to confine them against their will and to sell them to the highest bidder. It seemed particularly egregious[29] to sell them into a life of military service.

Alexa was thirsty for more information. She sat down at the computer and double-clicked on the Internet Explorer icon. The powerful, modern computer in the lab responded quickly to her commands. Opening up the Google search engine, she typed in "dolphins—military" and clicked Search. The results of the search were displayed in an instant.

---

[27] Inordinately: exceeding reasonable limits; excessively
[28] Intemperate: not temperate (moderate); extreme, immoderate
[29] Egregious: conspicuously bad; flagrant

There were so many links to explore! Alexa scanned the long list, not knowing where to begin. There was one entitled "U.S. Navy Marine Mammal Program." Alexa double-clicked on the link. Jackpot! This brought up the Navy's own website, which included information about the dolphin and sea lion programs. Alexa chuckled at the cartoon of a dolphin and a sea lion in a Navy uniforms.

Alexa clicked on "Frequently Asked Questions" and read eagerly. Here were the answers to all of her questions. She scanned the list. *"Why does the Navy use marine mammals?" "What species of marine mammals are used by the Navy?" "Does the Navy train its dolphins for offensive warfare, including attacks on human swimmers or divers?"* Alexa eagerly read the answer: *"No. The Navy does not now train, nor has it ever trained, its marine mammals to injure humans in any fashion or carry weapons to destroy ships."*

"Does the Navy ask the dolphins and sea lions to do dangerous things? The dolphins locate and mark the location of sea mines that are designed to be set off by large ships, not aquatic animals. Once the marking has been completed, the animals are removed from the area before the mines are disarmed...." In the swimmer detection program, dolphins move so quickly and with such accuracy that human swimmers in dark or murky waters are located and marked before they know what has happened.

Alexa grew more relaxed as she continued reading. It was very reassuring. It looked like the Navy made every effort to keep the dolphins safe and healthy. Alexa couldn't wait to show this to José.

Ding! The computer emitted the telltale bell alerting Alexa to an incoming e-mail. Alexa clicked on her e-mail window. It was from Laurie!

Time: 11:30 A.M.
To: "Alexa"
From: "Laurie"
Subject: Re: dolphins at war

Dear Alexa,

I can't stop thinking about your e-mail. I had no idea dolphins were used in the military either! What a fascinating story. I am going to tell Jeff on Monday—he is my boss at CNN—maybe we can do a story on it! I am his protégé[30]—and I know he would be really impressed if I could bring in a really hot idea for a story. Now I am doing some research on the Web. Did you know that the U.S. military flew dolphins to Iraq to help clear the harbor in the Iraq war? Check out the link to the article below. Don't worry so much about the article that José showed you. If there is one thing I have learned working in the media, it's that you can't believe everything you read. Particularly from lobbyist[31] groups or egotistical political pundits[32] who like to see their name in print at any cost! You have to be really critical about the source. We always have to check our facts over and over again. It's such an onerous[33] task and it's usually the intern who gets the grunt work! Well, anyway, I have to run now! I have so much work to do before Monday!

Love,
Laurie

Finally, a response from Laurie! Alexa breathed a sigh of relief. Laurie hadn't forgotten her! As Alexa reread the e-mail, she couldn't help

---

[30] Protégé: one who is protected or trained or whose career is furthered by a person of experience, prominence, or influence

[31] Lobbyist: a person or group that attempts to influence or sway (as a public official) toward a desired action; activist, campaigner

[32] Pundits: one who gives opinions in an authoritative manner; critic

[33] Onerous: involving, imposing, or constituting a burden

but smile at Laurie's vivacity.[34] She had such a spirited way of jumping into things with both feet. Now she wanted to do a story on dolphins!

Alex clicked on the link in the e-mail to look at the article that Laurie had unearthed[35] on the Internet. It was entitled "Crack sea mammals in training." Alexa scanned the article. It was all about the training of dolphins and sea lions for deployment in Iraq. The article quoted Tom LaPuzza, the man who had run the Navy's Marine Mammal Program since its inception[36] in 1960. Most of the article covered familiar territory, but then Alexa's eyes locked on one quote from Mr. LaPuzza:

"We get them when they're newborns," he said, adding that the mammals lived for around 25 years and never left the service. "They are in the Navy for life."

Alexa paused, her feeling of turmoil and dread returning. The article also mentioned that the Navy obtained its dolphin recruits by purchasing them from other marine mammal facilities. But where were these facilities getting their dolphins? Maybe some of them were born in captivity but ultimately, some of them had to have been captured from the wild. Alexa's emotions were bubbling up inside her. Was this really an ethical thing to do? It was hard to be objective[37] when she couldn't stop thinking about Pecas' baby. Was her baby now destined to be in the Navy for life? Alexa felt that it was now of paramount[38] importance to find out. Where was José? They needed to begin this experiment!

José arrived at 10:45, full of apologies. This morning they had been short-handed in the kitchen at Puerto Marino. Not only did he have to stay late after the breakfast service, he needed to return within a half hour to help with lunch.

---

[34] Vivacity: the quality or state of being vivacious (lively in temper, conduct, or spirit); enthusiasm
[35] Unearthed: brought to light, discovered
[36] Inception: an act, process, or instance of beginning
[37] Objective: expressing or dealing with facts or conditions as perceived without distortion by personal feelings, prejudices, or interpretations; without bias
[38] Paramount: superior to all others; supreme

"Lets take a look at the cells from Pecas. I put them in some media yesterday." Alexa headed toward the tall incubator. A warm draft of air hit her face as she opened the incubator and pulled out a flat, square-shaped bottle that was resting on its side. "This is the dish where I'm growing Pecas' cells."

José could barely contain his excitement as he looked at the dish with amazement. "What is that pink stuff?" he asked incredulously as he pointed to the dish in Alexa's hand. The bottom of the dish was covered with a bright magenta liquid.

"That's media—it's like food and water for the cells that are growing in here—sort of like an organic[39] soup." She carefully brought the dish over to the microscope without disturbing the magenta liquid. She set the dish on the microscope platform and switched on the scope.

"What do you see?" José asked anxiously. "Can I take a look too?" José was very excited at the novelty[40] of being in a sophisticated laboratory. He loved science and its environs.

"Just a second, I'm trying to locate the cells." Alexa concentrated on focusing the microscope.

"Do you see them?"

"Yes! Here they are." Alexa hopped off the chair in front of the microscope and gestured to José. He eagerly took her seat and gazed through the scope.

"Wow! This is *so* awesome!" José reacted as if he was viewing the most opulent[41] jewels in the world.

"Do you see the cells?" Alexa inquired.

---

[39] Organic: of, relating to, or containing carbon compounds
[40] Novelty: something new and fresh
[41] Opulent: exhibiting or characterized by opulence (wealth, affluence); magnificent, lavish

"I think so," José replied as he started to fiddle with the knobs on the side of the scope. "There are so many of them!"

"It's funny you should say that because paradoxically,[42] there aren't enough cells. I don't think we have enough to extract DNA today. I think we need to let these cells grow and divide. I've never extracted DNA from such a small number of cells before. It's just safer if we wait." Alexa spoke carefully, knowing José would be disappointed.

"How long do you think we need to wait?"

"Probably until next weekend," she said tentatively. Alexa was also disappointed to have to wait so long, but she knew from experience that it was prudent[43] to follow the experimental protocol precisely. She knew that if they attempted the experiment too soon, it might not work and then they would have to start all over again. Alexa, being a pragmatist[44] at heart, knew that in all practicality,[45] it was better to wait.

"Oh. That seems like such a long time to wait." José got up from his chair and looked at Alexa.

"I agree." Alexa took the dish out from under the microscope and placed it back in the incubator. "But the cells have already started to proliferate[46] since yesterday, so at least the culture is doing well."

"I'm so impressed that you are such a smart scientist," José said admiringly.

Alexa laughed at the notion that her lowly summer intern status was suddenly exalted[47] to brilliant scientist. Modestly, she refrained from responding to his compliment.

"Do you have time to look at some things on the computer with me? I found some other things about dolphins in the military that I want

---

[42] Paradox: a statement that is seemingly contradictory or opposed to common sense and yet is perhaps true

[43] Prudent: shrewd in the management of practical affairs; sensible

[44] Pragmatist: a person who takes a practical approach to problems and affairs

[45] Practical: of, relating to, or manifested in practice or action; not theoretical or ideal

[46] Proliferate: to grow by rapid production of new parts, cells, buds, or offspring; reproduce, multiply

[47] Exalted: to raise in status (can also mean to praise, glorify, or honor)

you to see." Alexa was eager to show him the information she had found and to talk about the various conflicting stories on the Internet. Some of these articles had to be fallacious,[48] and they needed to talk and resolve[49] their differing perspectives on this issue.

"I would love to, but I have to get back to work." José came over to Alexa and took both of her hands in his. He was gazing admiringly at her. "But maybe I will see you on Monday morning at the shore?" he added softly as his eyes looked directly into hers.

"Yes...sure. I...I'll be there," Alexa managed to reply, even though her heart was racing. She didn't have much experience being kissed by a boy, but intuitively,[50] she felt that this moment was leading up to it.

"Great, see you then. I've got to go now." José gave her hands a squeeze and smiled down at her face. And then he left! The moment felt so anticlimactic.[51]

Alexa tried to catch her breath; her heart was pounding. It seemed like a long time until Monday.

---

[48] Fallacious: untrue; tending to deceive or mislead
[49] Resolve: to deal with successfully, to clear up
[50] Intuitively: known or perceived by intuition (quick and ready insight); instinctively
[51] Anticlimactic: of, relating to, or marked by anticlimax; an event (as at the end of a series) that is strikingly less important than what has preceded it

10

A Conflagration Ignites

Time: 3:30 P.M.
To: "Laurie"
From: "Alexa"
Subject: I think...

Dear Laurie,

I think José might like me too! He held my hands today—just now—for a whole minute! I thought I was going to faint! I thought he was going to kiss me, but it didn't happen! I can't wait for Monday. He didn't ask me to meet him on Sunday—what do you think he's doing?

Did you pitch your story idea to your boss Jeff? I thought I would try to do more investigating about the dolphins here. Maybe my mother will take me to see them. I'm also going running with Charlotte. She's really great—we are eating all our meals together now. I think you would really like her.

Your friend always,
Alexa

Alexa decided to wait in the lab a while longer to see if Laurie replied. If only José wasn't perpetually[1] working, they could have done something fun together today, Alexa pined. Ding! The computer signaled incoming e-mail—it was from Laurie! Alexa perked up, bolstered[2] by Laurie's quick response.

Time: 3:47 P.M.
To: "Alexa"
From: "Laurie"
Subject: I know!

Dear Lexxie,

I know what you should do—you should kiss him!! Of course he likes you! He's only been meeting you at the beach every day! Don't be so ridiculous. I know he likes you. I told Jeff my idea about doing a story on dolphins in the military. He tabled[3] it! He said there are already lots of stories out there so it's not worth doing unless I'm able to find a unique angle. Oh well. Don't forget to write to me tomorrow and tell me about The Big Kiss. Ha ha.

Laurie

Kiss him? Was she crazy? Alexa laughed at the thought of it and immediately discredited[4] the idea. She knew that she would never have the temerity[5] to pull off such a bold action. Well, at least Laurie was writing to her and was making some effort to maintain the rapport they had at home, Alexa thought. That was a huge relief. It was Alexa's greatest fear that in her absence, someone else would supplant[6] her role as Laurie's

---

[1] Perpetually: continuing forever
[2] Bolster: to give a boost to
[3] Tabled: removed from consideration indefinitely
[4] Discredit: to refuse to accept as true or accurate
[5] Temerity: nerve, boldness
[6] Supplant: to supersede (another), especially by force or treachery

best friend. Alexa banished the pessimistic[7] thoughts from her mind. While Laurie had been remiss[8] in her lack of response earlier, her latest e-mails redeemed her in Alexa's eyes. Deep down, she really didn't believe Laurie would be that fickle.[9]

⤮ ⤮

Puerto Marino was quiet early Sunday morning as Alexa jogged slowly to the cafeteria where Charlotte was waiting for her. The only noise came from the birds, who chirped and sang vociferously[10] as they greeting the sunrise. The words of her track coach resonated[11] in her mind as she approached the building. He had admonished the team on their last day of practice to "Keep in shape and run regularly or you'll be sorry!" and added "Consistent training augurs[12] well for success!" True to his prediction, Alexa regretted procrastinating[13] her training. What if Charlotte is really in shape and has an audacious[14] workout planned? Alexa worried. "I hope I can keep up!" she said aloud as she approached Charlotte, who was stretching on the front steps of the building.

"Good morning!" Charlotte greeted her cheerfully.

"Hi. I have a confession to make...I haven't been running in several months—I may not be able to keep up with you," Alexa said with chagrin.[15]

"Don't worry. We'll take it easy. I'm just happy to have the company. If you need to stop, just say so. I'll promise not to chide[16] you for being out of shape!" Charlotte laughed as they started jogging.

"Where are we going?"

---

[7] Pessimistic: negative, gloomy
[8] Remiss: showing neglect or inattention
[9] Fickle: marked by lack of steadfastness, constancy, or stability; given to erratic changeableness
[10] Vociferous: marked by or given to vehement insistent outcry
[11] Resonate: to produce or exhibit resonance (a quality of evoking response)
[12] Augurs: to foretell
[13] Procrastinating: putting off until later
[14] Audacious: intrepidly daring
[15] Chagrin: disquietude or distress of mind caused by humiliation, disappointment, or failure
[16] Chide: reproach in a usually mild and constructive manner; scold

"Oh, I have this route that I usually do—it's about two miles to this beautiful beach down the road. We have to go through this destitute[17] little village—hardly a cosmopolitan[18] town," Charlotte added derisively.[19]

"Yes, I know exactly what you're referring to—José lives in that town!" Alexa replied defensively.

"Oh, I'm sorry! I must have sounded so pompous![20] I didn't mean to insinuate[21] anything derogatory![22] What I meant was it's a quaint little village, not a large, crowded cosmopolitan city." Charlotte artfully restated.[23]

Her penitence[24] sounded genuine, although Alexa was certain her initial comment about the village *was* irreverent.[25] Alexa was in no mood to argue about Charlotte's sweeping generalizations[26] about the local village. Nor was she in any condition to argue—she needed every breath to keep up with Charlotte. "It's OK. I know you didn't mean to insult José. Let's just forget about it."

Charlotte was only too happy to comply. Skillfully, she changed the subject as they ran out onto the main road toward the town.

"Last summer, I was with my stepfather in San Diego for six weeks. He travels so much for his work in the military. He's always going somewhere for a new assignment. I've been to seven schools already and I haven't even graduated yet!"

"Wow, seven schools? I've only been to one!"

"It's so difficult. I hate always being the new person when everybody already has their group of friends. Girls can be so cruel."

"That sounds difficult," Alexa said sympathetically.

---

[17] Destitute: lacking possessions and resources; especially suffering extreme poverty
[18] Cosmopolitan: having wide international sophistication
[19] Derisively: expressing ridicule, scorn, or contempt
[20] Pompous: having or exhibiting self-importance; arrogant
[21] Insinuate: to impart or communicate with artful or oblique reference
[22] Derogatory: expressive of a low opinion: disparaging
[23] Restate: to state again or in another way
[24] Penitence: sorrow for sins or faults
[25] Irreverent: lacking proper respect or seriousness
[26] Generalizations: to make vague or indefinite statements

"It's kind of fun to travel in the summer, though—when school is out. I loved San Diego. And it's really great when I meet a new friend like you!"

"I was really happy to meet you too!" Alexa replied breathlessly. She wanted to tell Charlotte about her parents' divorce, but the rigor[27] of their pace was making it hard for Alexa to converse. She could feel a cramp in her side beginning to get worse, but she was determined to quell[28] her desire to stop and catch her breath.

"Why don't we take a break at the beach up here. We can dangle our feet in the water and catch our breath," Charlotte suggested when she saw that Alexa was struggling.

"Sounds good! I can't believe how out of shape I am!" Alexa was immensely relieved to arrest[29] the strenuous activity. She looked over at Charlotte. It was surprising how her pristine, carefully coiffed appearance belied[30] her adeptness[31] in athletics. On the contrary,[32] Alexa was relieved they had decided to curtail[33] their workout.

"Don't worry, it'll come back to you. Just run with me every day!" Charlotte said cheerfully as they approached the sand.

The beach was serene[34] so early on a Sunday morning. If anything, the peacefulness made the scene even more spectacular. Alexa took a deep breath of the fresh, salty air. She was happy they had deviated[35] from their run to spend a few peaceful moments in this beautiful spot.

"Oh, look! Someone left a bunch of old soda cans over there by the water!" Charlotte was indignant at this impropriety.[36]

---

[27] Rigor: a condition that makes life difficult, challenging, or uncomfortable; severity

[28] Quell: quiet, pacify

[29] Arrest: to bring to a stop

[30] Belie: to give a false impression of

[31] Adeptness: thoroughly proficient; expert

[32] Contrary: a fact or condition incompatible with another; opposite

[33] Curtail: to make less by or as if by cutting off or away some part; shorten

[34] Serene: marked by or suggestive of utter calm and unruffled repose or quietude; peaceful

[35] Deviate: to depart from an established course or norm; stray

[36] Impropriety: an improper or indecorous act or remark; especially an unacceptable use of a word or of language

"That makes me so mad! It is absolutely an insidious[37] offense to desecrate[38] such a beautiful place!"

"Let's pick them up!"

"I agree." The two girls marched over to the litter with the conviction[39] of the righteous.[40]

"It looks like the remains of a boxed lunch from Puerto Marino. Someone from the compound must have come here for lunch and left their trash on the beach," Alexa said.

"I was afraid of that," Charlotte replied with remorse. "There's really no excuse for people to behave like that," she decried.[41] Chatting continuously as they picked up the litter, they realized they had similar outlooks about pollution. Both of them were idealists[42] when it came to issues about the environment. They shared the view that pollution in all forms simply had to stop if the world was going to remain habitable.[43]

"Why don't we stop here at the beach every day on our run and pick up the litter?" Charlotte suggested. "Then at least we can do something to try to counteract[44] this degradation!"[45]

"I agree! That's a great idea." Alexa didn't need any further inducement.[46] This was exactly the type of thing that she liked to do—something

---

[37] Insidious: having a gradual and cumulative effect

[38] Desecrate: to treat disrespectfully, irreverently, or outrageously

[39] Conviction: a strong persuasion or belief

[40] Righteous: arising from an outraged sense of justice or morality

[41] Decry: to express strong disapproval of; condemn

[42] Idealist: one guided by ideals, especially one who places ideals before practical considerations

[43] Habitable: capable of being lived in; suitable for habitation

[44] Counteract: to make ineffective or restrain or neutralize the usually ill effects of by an opposite force

[45] Degradation: the act or process of degrading (to impair in respect to some physical property)

[46] Inducement: a motive or consideration that leads one to action

constructive,[47] yet idealistic. "I'm so glad we became friends, Charlotte. It's great to have a friend like you to do things with. I thought I was going to be so lonely here all summer—but instead..."

"Instead you have me *and* a boyfriend!" Charlotte teased.

Alexa laughed. At least Charlotte was good-natured in her teasing.

"Hey, is that a mirage,[48] or do I see your man on the horizon right now?" Charlotte pointed to a boat in the distance.

"Oh my gosh—it *is* José! Let's go out on the rocks and say hello," Alexa said, her voice filled with excitement.

"Are you sure you want me to come? Did you want to go see him by yourself?" Charlotte inquired, her refined[49] manners always at hand.

"Of course I want you to come! You're my friend and he's my friend! Just come with me, please?"

"OK," Charlotte agreed, making an effort to be pliable,[50] even though she appeared reluctant to go. Alexa started racing down the rocky peninsula, waving madly at José, while Charlotte followed slowly, restrained[51] in her demeanor.

"José!" Alexa yelled as she ran to the end of the rocky outcrop, narrowly avoiding a fall on the abundant detritus.[52]

José waved back and turned the boat in their direction. When he was about 50 yards away, he dropped the anchor and dove into the water, disappearing from sight. Alexa waited anxiously, immobilized[53] with concern. Where did he go? Finally, after what felt like an interminable pause, he surfaced right in front of Alexa.

"Hi!" He grinned infectiously.

---

[47] Constructive: promoting improvement or development

[48] Mirage: an optical effect that is sometimes seen at sea, in the desert, or over a hot pavement, that may have the appearance of a pool of water

[49] Refined: free from what is coarse, vulgar, or uncouth

[50] Pliable: yielding readily to others

[51] Restrained: reserved, controlled; to limit, restrict, or keep under control

[52] Detritus: loose material (such as rock fragments or organic particles) that results directly from disintegration

[53] Immobilized: incapable of moving

"You always find a special way of saying hello!" Alexa laughed. "José, you remember Charlotte..." Alexa introduced.

"Sure. Thanks again for saving me the other night."

"Oh, it was nothing," Charlotte replied.

"Why don't you guys come on in! The water is so nice!" José beckoned.

"I didn't bring my bathing suit—although I guess I could swim like this anyway..." Alexa replied. The water looked so inviting, and she was so hot and sticky from jogging.

"If you don't come in you're going to get wet anyway!" José teased Alexa as he began to splash her playfully.

"I'm getting in, I'm getting in!" Alexa laughed as she climbed down the rocks and jumped into the refreshing, clear blue water. She surfaced near José and turned back to look at Charlotte, who was still on the shore. "Why don't you come in, Charlotte? The water's so nice!"

"I can't. I just got my hair highlighted and the combination of the salt water and the sun would ruin it." Charlotte replied. Her perfect blond hair was tucked neatly under her cap.

Alexa could see José roll his eyes. Knowing him as she did now, she had the insight[54] to know that this was exactly the kind of thing he scorned.[55] Alexa could tell he preferred her naturalness and absence of vanity.[56] He liked the fact that she was unfettered[57] by such superficial[58] beauty concerns and that she didn't color her hair like Charlotte. He also

---

[54] Insight: the power or act of seeing into a situation
[55] Scorn: open dislike and disrespect or derision often mixed with indignation
[56] Vanity: inflated pride in oneself or one's appearance
[57] Unfetter: emancipate, liberate
[58] Superficial: presenting only an appearance without substance or significance

liked her sense of adventure and the way that she just jumped in the water, not minding if her hair got wet or her clothes got sullied.[59] On the one hand, Alexa was admittedly a bit relieved that José hadn't taken a liking to pretty Charlotte. But on the other hand, Charlotte was her friend, and Alexa wanted them to be able to have fun altogether. Thankfully, Charlotte didn't see José's adverse[60] reaction.

"Your hair won't get wet! The water is really shallow here. Why don't you come in?" Alexa pleaded. "There are so many beautiful fish you can see out here and the water feels so good."

"OK," Charlotte agreed unenthusiastically. She made her way down to the water and gingerly stepped in.

"What did you do in San Diego when you were there last summer?" Alexa asked Charlotte, eager to draw her into conversation. José was busy diving to the bottom, retrieving shells and interesting bits of coral.

"I spent most of my time at the beach. My dad was visiting the naval marine mammal facility there," Charlotte replied.

"Charlotte, where does the Navy get the dolphins it uses? And do you know what they use them for?" Alexa seized the opportunity to get more information.

"The marine mammals are an integral[61] part of America's homeland security program and a vital[62] part of our military operations overseas," Charlotte replied assuredly.[63] Evidently, she was a proponent[64] of dolphins

---

[59] Sully: to make soiled or tarnished
[60] Adverse: acting against or in a contrary direction; hostile
[61] Integral: essential to completeness
[62] Vital: concerned with or necessary to the maintenance of life
[63] Assuredly: without a doubt; certainly
[64] Proponent: one who argues in favor of something; advocate

in the military. "The dolphins in particular have great diving abilities and can locate underwater mines and other things that present grave dangers for people. Dolphins have a..."

"Well, then, isn't it dangerous for the dolphins too?" José interjected. He had resurfaced just in time to hear her speech. Alexa cringed when she heard the hostility[65] in José's voice as he impugned[66] her friend. It was like Charlotte had just pushed a hot button and a raging[67] inferno had ignited.

"All military operations have some element of danger to them. That much is obvious. The point is that the civilians of the world, like you and me, are lucky to have a military that protects them! The military deals with the dangerous situations for us. And yes, the dolphins are part of that, and you should be grateful there are people who are willing to risk their lives to protect you!" Charlotte said defiantly, fueling the conflagration.[68]

"Grateful?" José said cynically.[69] He was flabbergasted.[70] "For this?" he added belligerently[71] as he gestured toward the Puerto Marino compound, looming in the distance. "You have to be kidding me! You people come in here like you own our country!" he berated,[72] the hostility in his voice obvious. He was now on the offensive,[73] and his voice wavered with

---

[65] Hostility: deep-seated, usually mutual, ill will

[66] Impugn: to assail by words or arguments; oppose or attack as false or lacking integrity

[67] Raging: violent, wild

[68] Conflagration: fire, especially a large disastrous fire

[69] Cynically: having a sneering disbelief in sincerity or integrity

[70] Flabbergast: to overwhelm with shock, surprise, or wonder

[71] Belligerent: inclined to or exhibiting assertiveness, hostility, or combativeness

[72] Berate: to scold or condemn vehemently and at length

[73] Offensive: making attack

emotion. Alexa could see that he harbored a lot of resentment.[74] In his mind, Puerto Marino and the American military were one and the same. One entity was supplying trained dolphins and the other was buying them and using them for military operations. And Charlotte, who openly condoned[75] the use of dolphins in the military, was a lightning rod for his pent-up anger. And José was not finished yet. "You just move in here, pollute our beaches, steal the dolphins from our waters, and build these monstrous buildings! That cove used to be the most beautiful place in the world, an amazing place where you could catch so many fish just by touching your net to the water. And now look at it!" he said with derision.[76]

"If you think it's so despicable, why do you work there?" Charlotte replied rancorously,[77] close to tears. Alexa knew Charlotte felt passionately about the environment. But touching even deeper, Charlotte felt the loss of her father every day and was profoundly aware of the sacrifices the men and women of the military make. José had hit a nerve. Charlotte was deeply hurt by his comments, but instead of defending herself, she lashed out at him, and the bickering[78] continued.

"Because I have to," José said, his voice breaking. He, too, was close to tears. Charlotte's recrimination[79] touched on an inflammatory[80] subject. José was working for Puerto Marino even though he loathed[81] their presence in his country. He needed the money that his job with Puerto Marino provided, but he obviously didn't condone what they were doing.

---

[74] Resentment: a feeling of indignant displeasure or persistent ill will at something regarded as a wrong, insult, or injury

[75] Condone: to pardon or overlook voluntarily; especially to treat as if trivial, harmless, or of no importance

[76] Derision: the use of ridicule or scorn to show contempt

[77] Rancorously: characterized by bitter, deep-seated ill will

[78] Bickering: to engage in a petulant or petty quarrel

[79] Recrimination: to make a retaliating charge against an accuser

[80] Inflammatory: tending to excite anger, disorder, or tumult

[81] Loathed: to dislike greatly and often with disgust or intolerance

Alexa wanted to burrow[82] into a hole to hide from this calamity.[83] Her allegiances[84] were divided between Charlotte and José. Alexa had the sagacity[85] and empathy[86] to see both sides of their argument. In her eyes, neither one was right nor wrong, they just came from very different perspectives. Both Charlotte and José were so obstinate[87] in their positions that they didn't try to see the issue from the other person's point of view. Alexa searched her mind for something she could do or say to salvage[88] the relationship between her two new friends.

"I'm leaving now!" Charlotte announced as she started swimming toward the shore.

"Wait, Charlotte! I'll go with you!" Alexa called out. Alexa turned to José. "I'll see you later, OK? I'm sorry this turned into such a mess," Alexa whispered to him.

"No, I'm sorry. I didn't mean to hurt her feelings. I took out all of my anger for Puerto Marino and the military on her. It was wrong of me. I will have to find a way to tell her I'm sorry," José said, expressing his repentance.[89]

"That would be good—because you don't even know some things about Charlotte that will make you regret what you've said even more. But right now, I'm going to try to catch up to her."

"OK. See you tomorrow?" José asked hopefully.

"OK. We'll talk then." Alexa swam toward the shore. It would be a good idea for them to talk, Alexa thought. José really needed to talk about

---

[82] Burrow: a hole or excavation in the ground made by an animal (such as a rabbit) for shelter and habitation

[83] Calamity: an extraordinarily grave event marked by great loss and lasting distress

[84] Allegiance: devotion or loyalty to a person, group, or cause

[85] Sagacity: keen in sense of perception and judgment, discerning

[86] Empathy: the action of understanding, being aware of, being sensitive to, and vicariously experiencing the feelings, thoughts, and experience of another of either the past or present without having the feelings, thoughts, and experience fully communicated in an objectively explicit manner

[87] Obstinate: perversely adhering to an opinion, purpose, or course in spite of reason, arguments, or persuasion; stubborn, inflexible

[88] Salvage: to rescue or save especially from wreckage or ruin

[89] Repentance: to feel regret or contrition

some of these issues with someone who could mollify[90] rather than inflame his obstreperous[91] tendencies.

Alexa hopped out of the water and hurriedly put her sneakers on, even though she was soaking wet. Charlotte was already out of sight. Alexa raced to catch up with her. It wasn't difficult; Charlotte had slowed down to a walk. She was sobbing uncontrollably.

"Oh, Charlotte, I'm so sorry that you guys had a fight—I know he didn't mean to be insolent.[92] He doesn't know about what happened to your father—he never would have said anything so flagrantly[93] upsetting if he knew. He's just so emotional when it comes to anything having to do with the dolphins."

"It's not that. Well, maybe it's that too, but I'm really upset because I lost my bracelet!" Charlotte rubbed her bare wrist as the tears streamed down her face.

"The one your father gave you?" Alexa asked with horror.

"Yes!" Charlotte sobbed.

"Let's go look for it!" Alexa said urgently. "It's probably in the water."

"It could be anywhere. It's gone now. I really don't see the point in trying," she replied, shunning[94] Alexa's suggestion.

"But it probably slipped off in the water—and the water is so clear. Maybe we could find it!"

"It's gone. We'll never find it." Charlotte was obdurate[95] in her position.

---

[90] Mollify: to soothe in temper or disposition; placate, calm
[91] Obstreperous: marked by unruly or aggressive noisiness
[92] Insolent: insultingly contemptuous in speech or conduct; overbearing
[93] Flagrant: conspicuously offensive
[94] Shun: to avoid deliberately and especially habitually
[95] Obdurate: resistant to persuasion or softening influences; stubborn

"Well then, I'll go back and look for you. Will you meet me for lunch at the cafeteria at noon?" Alexa was eager to talk things over with Charlotte.

"OK," Charlotte agreed tearfully.

∽   ∾

Alexa turned around and headed back to the beach, careful to keep her eyes on the ground, ever vigilant[96] for any sign of the bracelet. The beach was quiet and she was grateful for the tranquility. This was a good opportunity to ruminate[97] about the shocking argument that seemed to come out of nowhere. The vivid memory of her two friends yelling at each other reverberated[98] through her mind. The surfacing of José's latent[99] anger toward Puerto Marino was surprising, but the sentiment was understandable, given the circumstances.

As she waded through the clear blue water, Alexa thought about the things Charlotte had said. She had to acknowledge that some of Charlotte's points about the military were reasonable and valid. The fact that the men and women of the military put their lives at risk so that others could live in safety was irrefutable.[100] As simple as it sounded, this was actually a new perspective for Alexa to consider. Growing up on a university campus, the pervasive ideology was consistently liberal.[101] There always seemed to be some sort of anti-war protest going on at the university. In this academic microcosm,[102] Alexa rarely encountered conservative political views, and she had never met anyone who could be considered reactionary.[103] But truthfully, Alexa acknowledged to herself,

---

[96] Vigilant: watchful, alert, and attentive

[97] Ruminate: to go over in the mind repeatedly and often casually or slowly

[98] Reverberate: to continue in or as if in a series of echoes; resound

[99] Latent: present and capable of becoming, though not now visible, obvious, or active

[100] Irrefutable: impossible to refute or deny

[101] Liberal: of or constituting a political party advocating or associated with the principles of political liberalism

[102] Microcosm: a little world; especially the human race or human nature seen as an epitome of the world or the universe

[103] Reactionary: ultraconservative in politics

she found it hard to agree with José's complete renunciation[104] of the military. Particularly in light of the cataclysmic[105] and tragic events of 9/11, which underscored the fact that there are some dangerous people out there who want to compromise the safety of Americans. Also, Charlotte's father had died in service to the military, and she must be acutely aware of the risks that he had taken. It wasn't hard for Alexa to see Charlotte's perspective.

But she could also empathize with José's point of view. José wasn't nefarious,[106] he simply resented the entire concept of Puerto Marino. José adamantly repudiated[107] the concept of capturing wild dolphins and selling them into a life of service. It was easy to see why he would have misgivings[108] about such a distasteful business taking root in his own backyard. Alexa knew with all her heart that José was a good person, and that if he knew about Charlotte's father, he never would have been so callous[109] as to malign[110] the military and hurt her feelings. His malediction[111] derived more from his narrow perspective than from a mean spirit on his part.

Alexa could see so clearly both sides of the argument and why it had escalated into a raucous[112] confrontation. If only she had had the

---

[104] Renunciation: the act of refusing to follow, obey, or recognize any further
[105] Cataclysmic: a momentous and violent event marked by overwhelming upheaval and demolition
[106] Nefarious: flagrantly wicked or impious; evil, malicious
[107] Repudiate: to reject or renounce; to refuse to have anything to do with
[108] Misgiving: to suggest doubt or fear to
[109] Callous: feeling no sympathy for others
[110] Malign: to utter injuriously misleading reports about; to speak evil of
[111] Malediction: to speak evil of
[112] Raucous: boisterously, disorderly

clairvoyance[113] to predict and prevent this melodrama[114] from happening in the first place. Now, she thought, it was up to her to mediate[115] the reconciliation[116] of her two friends.

Looking down at the ocean floor through the crystal-clear water, Alexa felt discouraged. Maybe Charlotte was right and the bracelet was lost forever. The refractive[117] property of the water distorted the view of the objects below, although she could clearly see a school of variegated[118] tropical fish swim right by her legs. This was not going to be an easy task, she realized. But she knew that if the antagonism between her friends was ever going to be absolved,[119] the bracelet needed to be found. Alexa decided that she would keep looking tenaciously[120] until she met Charlotte for lunch. And if the bracelet hadn't turned up by then, she would continue looking after lunch and all summer if she had to.

∽ ∾

Walking into the cafeteria to meet Charlotte, Alexa was barely able to suppress[121] her sorrow. As Alexa approached her table, she could see that Charlotte's face was pallid[122] and her eyes were red from a long crying session. Charlotte looked up at her expectantly with a bit of hopefulness in her eyes. But when she saw the look of despair and sympathy on

---

[113] Clairvoyance: the ability to perceive matters beyond the range of ordinary perception
[114] Melodrama: a drama characterized by extravagant theatricality
[115] Mediate: to bring accord out of by action as an intermediary
[116] Reconciliation: a restoration of friendship or harmony
[117] Refractive: distortion of an image by viewing through a medium
[118] Variegated: having discreet markings of different colors
[119] Absolve: to set free from an obligation or the consequences of guilt
[120] Tenacious: persistent in maintaining or adhering to something valued or habitual
[121] Suppress: to keep secret or to stop or prohibit the publication or revelation of
[122] Pallid: abnormally pale or wan

Alexa's face, her optimism was immediately squelched.[123] They didn't need any words to communicate the fact that Alexa had not been able to find the bracelet.

"Charlotte, I'm not giving up! I'm going back to look after lunch."

"I don't think it'll do any good—it's gone," Charlotte replied with a stoic[124] expression.

"Well, I'm not giving up! I know how much it meant to you."

"That's really nice of you," Charlotte replied.

"José feels really bad he said those things to you—I know he's very sorry," Alexa began with a conciliatory[125] gesture in her attempt to restore accord.[126]

"Alexa, I really like having you as a friend. But that doesn't mean I have to like him! The things he said were really appalling!"[127]

Alexa paused. Arbitrating[128] an understanding between José and Charlotte would not be easy. It looked as though their acrimonious[129] dispute had left Charlotte with an aversion[130] for José that would be difficult to overcome. Even more difficult was the thought that Alexa would need to convince Charlotte to see the situation from José's perspective as well. After all, the confrontation had two disputants[131]—it wasn't just José who had berated Charlotte with harsh words; Charlotte had

---

[123] Squelch: to completely suppress
[124] Stoic: not showing passion or feeling
[125] Conciliatory: to make compatible; reconcile
[126] Accord: to bring into agreement
[127] Appalling: inspiring horror, dismay, or disgust
[128] Arbitrating: acting as an arbitrator (one who decides in the case of a dispute)
[129] Acrimonious: caustic, biting, or rancorous, especially in feeling language or manner
[130] Aversion: a feeling of repugnance toward something with a desire to avoid or turn from it
[131] Disputant: one who is engaged in a dispute

drubbed[132] José as well. But for the moment, Alexa had the discretion[133] not to push the divisive[134] issue any further.

"Do you still want to go running with me tomorrow morning and pick up litter at the beach? We could look for your bracelet at the same time," Alexa suggested.

"OK. Maybe we should look on the beach near where we picked up the trash. Maybe it fell off before I even went in the water," Charlotte replied.

"Yes! But let's not defer[135] the search until tomorrow," Alexa pleaded, seizing the opportunity to shake Charlotte out of her impassive[136] state of inactivity. "Let's go now before the tide comes in!"

---

[132] Drub: to abuse with words; berate
[133] Discretion: the quality of being discreet, especially cautious reserve in speech
[134] Divisive: creating disunity or dissension
[135] Defer: postpone, put off
[136] Impassive: giving no sign of feeling or expression

11

A Stealthy Scheme

A contrite[1] and apologetic José steered his boat toward Alexa, who was waiting inanimately[2] on the shore. As he maneuvered the boat closer, she could see that the enmity[3] he displayed so openly in his fight with Charlotte had dissolved. At least José was sorry about the argument, Alexa thought, unlike Charlotte, who was impenitent.[4]

"Alexa, I am so sorry I blew up yesterday with Charlotte," José said sincerely. He plopped the anchor in the water and waded ashore with a sheepish expression on his face. "Is she really angry with me?"

"Well, I don't know if anger is really the right word to characterize it. She is really upset. I know you probably didn't know this, but her real father died in a training exercise for the military when Charlotte was ten. Colonel Brandt is her stepfather. She has every reason in the world to be sensitive about the things you said," Alexa explained. As he absorbed her words, José looked even more discomfited.[5] Alexa felt a rush of sympathy

---

[1] Contrite: grieving and penitent for sin or shortcoming
[2] Inanimate: not endowed with life or spirit
[3] Enmity: deep-seated and typically mutual hatred or ill will
[4] Impenitent: not penitent (feeling or expressing humble or regretful pain or sorrow for sins or offenses)
[5] Discomfited: to put in a state of perplexity and embarrassment

for him. The look of concern on his face was so endearing.[6] José displayed his emotions on his sleeve, Alexa thought. When he was angry, there was no hiding it, and when he was sorry, he was replete with contrition.

"Oh, no!" José was horrified. "The things I said—I still believe they are true...but I never should have said those words to her."

At least he didn't disavow[7] his role in the altercation,[8] Alexa thought. He was definitely intransigent[9] in his views, but at least he was apologetic about the hurt feelings his words precipitated.[10] "Unfortunately, the situation is even worse—yesterday morning Charlotte lost the bracelet her father gave her. I think the real reason she's still upset is probably attributable[11] to the fact we weren't able to find it anywhere."

"No wonder she is upset. But don't worry, Alexa. We will find it," José asserted.

"But how?" Alexa voiced her dissent.[12] "We've already looked everywhere. We looked on the beach, on the road, on the rocks, in the water...Alexa enumerated[13] her list with her fingers.

"It's probably in the water, and if it's there we will find it," José said confidently. The water is shallow and clear, there is not much current, and we've never lost anything in this bay. We've always found whatever we've dropped in these waters. I'm going to come back here with my mask and snorkel at first morning light tomorrow. I'd do it right now, but I have to get to work soon."

"That would be great," Alexa replied, feeling relieved that José was going to emend[14] the situation. "Look over there! Is that Pecas?" Alexa pointed to a group of three dolphins hovering in the distance.

---

[6] Endear: to cause to become beloved or admired
[7] Disavow: deny responsibility for
[8] Altercation: a noisy, heated, angry dispute; also a noisy controversy
[9] Intransigent: refusing to compromise or abandon an extreme position or attitude; uncompromising
[10] Precipitate: to bring about, especially abruptly
[11] Attribute: to explain by indicating a cause
[12] Dissent: to differ in opinion
[13] Enumerated: counted, tallied
[14] Emend: to correct

"It looks like her! Let's hop in the water!" José cried.

They both wasted no time jumping into the shallow water. Pecas swam in closer while the two other dolphins waited in the distance. Pecas swam slowly, encircling Alexa and José as they stood in chest-deep water.

"What's wrong with her?" Alexa asked. They both noticed immediately that something had changed with their dolphin friend. It was as if a light had been extinguished. Whereas Pecas usually seemed animated and full of zealous[15] vigor, she now appeared phlegmatic.[16] The vitality she usually displayed in abundance had diminished[17] significantly. It was as if depression had enervated[18] her. When she finally surfaced to communicate with them, she wasted no time in beginning her plaintive cries and leading them toward Puerto Marino.

"I think we already know what's wrong with her," José said as he looked scornfully in the direction of Puerto Marino.

"I just wish we could do something about it," Alexa said wistfully as she watched Pecas swim away.

"I've been thinking about this for a while. It's time we do something about it!" In José's black-and-white view of the world, this dire[19] situation warranted[20] immediate action.

"What are you talking about? We can't begin our experiment to see if Pecas' baby is captive in there until this weekend," Alexa pointed out logically. "We don't have enough cells to extract the DNA!" she added, substantiating[21] her argument even further.

"We could free all of the baby dolphins at Puerto Marino! Or maybe even all of the dolphins!" José said defiantly.[22]

---

[15] Zealous: filled with or characterized by zeal (eagerness and ardent interest in pursuit of something)
[16] Phlegmatic: having or showing a slow and stolid temperament; apathetic
[17] Diminished: reduced in scope or size
[18] Enervated: lacking physical, mental, or moral vigor; to lessen the vitality or strength of
[19] Dire: arousing terror or causing extreme distress; calling for quick action, urgent
[20] Warranted: sanctioned, authorized
[21] Substantiate: to establish by proof or competent evidence; verify
[22] Defiantly: full of defiance (disposition to resist, willingness to contend or fight)

"What? That's crazy!" Alexa scoffed.[23] Had his idolatry[24] of the dolphins made him lose his senses? At the very least, his perspective was subjective[25] when it came to Puerto Marino, she thought.

"Why is it so crazy? I've been thinking about this for a long time. They took the dolphins from the ocean illegally, and we would just be returning them there. It's not stealing or despoiling."[26] He looked expectantly at Alexa, waiting for her corroboration.[27] "They didn't have a permit to take any dolphins from these waters. It's illegal!" he repeated.

"But we don't even know that Pecas' baby is in there!"

"What if we do the DNA experiment and it turns out her baby is in there? Then we would know for sure that they captured the dolphin illegally. Wouldn't you agree that we should do something about it?"

"Yes," Alexa agreed, complying[28] with his logic. "In that case, if we knew for sure that her baby was confined in Puerto Marino, then I agree—we would need to free her from captivity. But we don't even know that yet!"

"Wouldn't you want to free all of the dolphins anyway? They're all in the same situation. We need to set all of the dolphins free!" José said firmly, as if this notion was the obvious corollary[29] of their decision to free Pecas' baby. In his mind, the emancipation[30] of all of the dolphins at Puerto Marino was not an eccentric[31] wish on his part; it was the dolphins' inviolable[32] right.

---

[23] Scoffed: to treat or address with derision; mocked, ridiculed
[24] Idolatry: immoderate attachment or devotion to something
[25] Subjective: modified or affected by personal views, experience, or background
[26] Despoiling: to strip of belongings and value; pillage
[27] Corroboration: to support with evidence or authority
[28] Complying: to conform or adapt one's actions to another's wishes
[29] Corollary: a deduction or inference
[30] Emancipation: to free from restraint, control, or the power of another
[31] Eccentric: deviating from conventional or accepted usage or conduct, especially in odd or whimsical ways
[32] Inviolable: secure from violation or profanation; unbreakable

"No," Alexa replied firmly. "If we find out for sure that Pecas' baby is in there, I agree we should free her." In Alexa's mind, that piece of irrefutable DNA evidence would consecrate[33] their entitlement[34] to free Pecas' baby. "But I just don't feel right about freeing the dolphins we really don't know anything about. We don't even know what kind of situation we'd be exposing them to out in the open ocean! The baby dolphins might not have a mother waiting for them, and some of the adult dolphins might not even be from this area. They might not even know how to live on their own in the ocean—it can be a treacherous[35] place!"

"I see your point. Maybe we should just start with freeing one dolphin," José compromised.[36] "After we right one wrong in the world we can think carefully about what we can do to help the other dolphins."

"Then I think we have a consensus,"[37] Alexa agreed. But unlike José, Alexa didn't think this would be a facile[38] undertaking. It didn't seem quite real to her—the idea that they would actually carry out this stealthy[39] scheme. Theoretically,[40] reuniting a young dolphin with its mother sounded like the right thing to do. However, Alexa could not trivialize[41] the logistical hurdles the way José could. At times, he resembled a

---

[33] Consecrate: to make inviolable or venerable (can also mean to declare sacred)
[34] Entitlement: the state or condition of being entitled; right
[35] Treacherous: marked by hidden dangers
[36] Compromise: to adjust or settle by mutual concessions
[37] Consensus: general agreement; unanimity
[38] Facile: easily accomplished or attained
[39] Stealthy: intended to escape observation; secret
[40] Theoretically: according to an ideal or assumed set of facts or principles, in theory
[41] Trivialize: to make trivial (of little worth or importance)

doctrinaire[42] idealist. He tended to aspire to lofty principles without thinking too much about the practical difficulties that may be encountered in their implementation.[43] Still, Alexa had to admit she really admired José's idealism. He had high-minded principles and an illimitable[44] sense of purpose. When she was around him, everything they talked about or did together took on a heightened[45] sense of importance. Alexa felt intoxicated, excited, and simply happy to be alive whenever she was around him. So what if José wasn't good at thinking through the practical details—she could help with that. "So how are we possibly going to manage to break into a high-security facility and free this baby dolphin?" she asked.

"Don't worry. We'll figure it out. We are two innovative[46] people—we will find a way," José replied, taking her hand in his as they waded through the water toward the shore.

"José, if we can prove that they captured one of the dolphins in the bay, and it's illegal to do that, why don't we just report it to the police?"

José groaned audibly. "You don't understand what it's like here! Things don't work like that! Puerto Marino has the support of all of the politicians around here. They think that they're doing us a favor by bringing in an industry to stimulate the economy here. I just don't think they would help us if it involved antagonizing Puerto Marino. It would never work. We have to take care of this ourselves!" he pleaded.

"OK. But let's just wait to see the results of the experiment," Alexa replied.

---

[42] Doctrinaire: one who attempts to put into effect an abstract doctrine or theory with little or no regard for practical difficulties

[43] Implementation: to put into practical effect; carry out

[44] Illimitable: incapable of being limited or bounded

[45] Heightened: to increase the amount or degree of

[46] Innovative: characterized by, tending to, or introducing innovations (a new idea, method, or device)

"Sounds like a plan." José took a deep breath as he tried to calm down. When they reached the shallows, he turned to her, looking sincere. "I want to show you something special tomorrow. Have you ever ridden on a kayak?"

"Yes, several times."

"I want to take you kayaking through the estuaries! Will you come?

"What are the estuaries...and where are they?" Alexa asked.

"You'll see! It is so beautiful—so full of life—you have to see it!" he said with his indefatigable[47] passion.

That sounds like fun," Alexa replied, her heart fluttering. José was standing so close to her and holding her hand. Her head was spinning and it was hard to concentrate when she felt this ineffable[48] excitement, but Alexa knew there was no way that she was saying no. She wanted to go kayaking with José.

"Great!" he said, smiling down at her. "I'll look for Charlotte's bracelet in the early morning and then let's meet at the library at the usual time later tomorrow morning. I'll borrow my uncle's pickup truck and we can carry the kayaks in the back. It's just a short drive from here—the place where we launch the kayaks. You're going to love it!" José predicted with his boundless[49] enthusiasm. It was as if the thought of going kayaking had filled him with renewed vigor, and he dropped Alexa's hand and raced though the shallow water to the rocky outcrop. Nimbly, he hopped up ashore, and then turned to Alexa and held his hand out to help her up.

Alexa could barely keep up. She had thought this special moment was destined to culminate[50] in a kiss. But the kiss she had thought was

---

[47] Indefatigable: incapable of being fatigued; untiring
[48] Ineffable: incapable of being expressed in words; indescribable
[49] Boundless: having no boundaries; vast
[50] Culminate: to reach the highest or a climactic or decisive point

inevitable didn't happen. Riding her motorbike back to the lab to check on Pecas' cell culture, she couldn't help but dwell on this shortcoming. Obviously, she couldn't talk about this with Charlotte, given the way Charlotte felt about José. It would have to be Laurie, she thought. She raced back to the lab, filled with a sense of purpose. Not only did she have an important experiment to conduct, she also needed to send a critical e-mail to her friend back home.

Hurrying into the lab, Alexa stowed her backpack and immediately headed over to the incubator to check on Pecas' cells. She always felt intense anticipation when she took her dish of cells out of the incubator and brought it to the microscope. It was particularly exciting to check on the cells first thing in the morning, as the cell culture always changed significantly overnight. Alexa was growing to love the routine of coming to the lab in the morning and checking the status of her various experiments, the most exciting of which concerned Pecas.

Flipping on the microscope light, Alexa placed the dish containing Pecas' cell culture on the stage of the microscope. Eagerly, she peered through the lenses and focused. If there had been any change since she last checked the culture an hour and a half earlier, it was imperceptible.[51] The cells looked like miniature spindles with rounded centers and pinched, pointed ends. They looked healthy and plump, forming a smooth layer that clung to the bottom of the dish. In Alexa's discerning[52]

---

[51] Imperceptible: not perceptible by a sense or by the mind, extremely slight, gradual, or subtle

[52] Discern: to recognize or identify as separate and distinct; discriminate

judgment, the cells were not too crowded. It looked like they had enough room to grow. Probably tomorrow would be the best time to split this culture into two dishes, she surmised.[53] Their experiment seemed to be on schedule. Alexa inferred[54] that they should have 10 million cells by Saturday, and, after an industrious[55] weekend in the laboratory, they should have the factual[56] evidence by Monday.

ᔕ   ᔕ

"Look at that! I think there's an iguana on the road!" José stopped the pickup truck and he and Alexa hopped out to take a closer look.

Alexa looked curiously at the bizarre lizard that somehow appeared ancient. It seemed curiously out of place in the contemporary[57] world—like an anachronistic[58] miniature dinosaur. They watched it amble slowly across the road.

Alexa could hardly contain her excitement as she helped José launch the kayaks into the estuary. Not even the news that José had been unsuccessful in the inexorable[59] search for Charlotte's bracelet could dispel[60] her good mood. They had driven for several miles on an unpaved road through the tropical forest." This is an estuary," José explained, "where the rivers flowing to the sea are bathed by the incoming tides from the ocean. So, the water is a mixture of fresh and salt water."

It's so calm," Alexa noted, "if there's a current at all, it's indiscernible."[61] Paddling through the water was both easy and relaxing. The

---

[53] Surmise: a thought or idea based on scanty evidence

[54] Inferred: derived as a conclusion from facts or premises

[55] Industrious: persistently active; zealous

[56] Factual: restricted to or based on fact

[57] Contemporary: marked by characteristics of the present period; modern

[58] Anachronistic: a person or a thing that is chronologically out of place, especially one from a former age that is incongruously in the present

[59] Inexorable: not to be persuaded or moved by entreaty (pleas); relentless

[60] Dispel: to drive away by or as if by scattering; dissipate

[61] Indiscernible: incapable of being discerned; not recognizable as distinct

abundant foliage[62] formed a canopy over their heads, shading them completely from the unrelenting[63] sun.

"Do you see these trees here? These are mangroves. Look at the roots," José said, pointing to the tangled web of woody roots under the surface of the water. "This is a haven for many small fish—it is where they hide from predatory[64] animals."

"What kinds of animals are in here?" Alexa asked with a bit of trepidation.[65]

"Oh, crocodiles, snakes, deadly parasites[66]...you name it, it's in here!" José laughed, teasing her. "This jungle has a plethora[67] of wildlife. You can see so many species of birds in these trees—you just have to proceed very quietly. Why don't you go first, so I don't scare the birds away before you see them," José urged. He maneuvered his kayak to the side to facilitate[68] her passing in the narrow waterway.

"OK," Alexa agreed, feeling very special to get this private tour of the jungle. She paddled by José, who put his finger to his lips, warning her to avoid startling the wildlife. She could tell by the amused look in his eyes that he was also reminding her of the first time she saw him in the cafeteria, when she had signaled to him to be quiet. She made a motion like she was zipping her lips, just as he had done on that day. They both burst out laughing as they reminisced about that fateful meeting.

Alexa paddled ahead and then let her kayak glide in the calm waters as she absorbed the amazing scene. Now that they had halted their conversation, the sounds of the jungle were readily audible. A delicate and mesmerizing birdsong filled the air, and she looked intently in the trees

---

[62] Foliage: the leaves of one or more plants

[63] Unrelenting: not softening or yielding in determination

[64] Predatory: living by predation (a mode of life in which food is primarily obtained by the killing and consuming of animals)

[65] Trepidation: apprehension, fear

[66] Parasite: an organism living in, with, or on another organism

[67] Plethora: excess, profusion

[68] Facilitate: to make easier, help bring about

for the source of this magical incantation.[69] She looked back at José for guidance, and he pointed silently to the source. Alexa quickly turned her head to catch a glimpse of this melodious creature. But her quick movement must have startled the bird, and her attempt to catch a glimpse of it was foiled.[70]

The waters were easily navigable,[71] and Alexa paddled on. There was so much to see in this amazing place. In the distance, she saw a crocodile slink into the water from its perch on a floating log. She looked back at José with wide eyes. He looked amused and quite satisfied that they had been able to see one of these elusive animals on their foray[72] into the jungle. As Alexa turned back around, she saw a spectacular crimson-colored bird alight[73] by the side of the water.

Up ahead it looked like they had some choices to make. Another estuary joined theirs at an oblique[74] angle, and then the combined waters emptied into a much wider river that was perpendicular to the channel they were on. José pointed to the right, and they paddled out to the large waterway, where José assumed the lead. The current was quite strong here, and they both paddled hard against its force. José pointed to a sandy beach up ahead, which was their apparent goal.

"Let's stop here for a break," José suggested.

"Sounds good," Alexa agreed, relieved to take a respite[75] from the heavy paddling. José helped her out and then pulled the kayaks up onto the beach.

"Let's have a snack here. I brought some things for you to try." José unpacked his backpack under a canopy of palm trees. It was a beautiful

---

[69] Incantation: a use of spells or verbal charms spoken or sung as part of a ritual of magic
[70] Foil: to prevent from attaining an end; thwart
[71] Navigable: deep enough and wide enough to afford passage to ships
[72] Foray: a brief excursion or attempt, especially outside one's accustomed sphere
[73] Alight: to descend from the air and come to rest
[74] Oblique: neither perpendicular nor parallel
[75] Respite: an interval of rest or relief

spot for a picnic. Alexa could see the ocean on one side, the narrow island on the other side, and the verdant jungle across the estuary. She wanted to imprint[76] this memory in her mind so that she could conjure[77] up this scene so full of life and beauty whenever she wanted to.

José poured a pale brown juice into large paper cups and handed one to her. "It's guava juice."

"Thank you." Alexa gingerly took a sip, not quite knowing what to expect. It was delicious. As soon as Alexa started drinking, she realized how thirsty she was. Her cup was empty almost immediately.

José smiled as he refilled her cup. "Here is some fresh pineapple—I cut it myself this morning. And this is a special cake—my mother made it," he added with a smile.

Alexa took a piece of the delicious yellow cake suffused[78] with a milky sweet substance. It was absolutely divine.[79] "This is the best cake I've ever had," she said sincerely.

"Have another piece!" José offered. He looked so pleased that she liked it.

"Oh no, thank you...I think I'll try some of this pineapple now." Alexa summoned all of her willpower to resist the cake. She wasn't exaggerating when she said it was the best cake she'd ever had. She really wanted more, but she didn't want to look like a glutton.[80] The pineapple, sweet and juicy, was equally potent for her palate.[81] Alexa had had pineapple many times before, but somehow it had never tasted like this.

"This is such an amazingly beautiful place," Alexa said, feeling a level of contentment both rare and evanescent.[82] She realized there was

---

[76] Imprint: to fix indelibly or permanently
[77] Conjure: to bring to mind
[78] Suffuse: to spread over or through in the manner of fluid or light
[79] Divine: supremely good
[80] Glutton: one given habitually to greedy and voracious eating and drinking
[81] Palate: the sense of taste
[82] Evanescent: tending to vanish like vapor

nothing in the world, either in the extant[83] world or anything she could possibly conjure up in her imagination, that she would rather be doing than enjoying this moment with José right here and now. It was a moment that was truly ephemeral.[84]

"Yes, this is very beautiful. But I wish I could have shown you the area where Puerto Marino is now. *That* was truly beautiful. Did I tell you that the government expropriated[85] some land from my uncle for the building of Puerto Marino? For an American company! He wasn't even given a choice—he had to give up his land."

"Really?" Alexa asked, as she returned to the present from her reverie. José had managed to curtail her blissful state by bringing up the ponderous[86] issues that vexed[87] them unmercifully. Now, the seizing of his uncle's land was imputed[88] to Puerto Marino on top of the other grievances he had aired previously. She realized that he had layers upon layers of resentment toward Puerto Marino, and, as she got to know him better, he was exposing these layers like an onion being peeled. He resented that an American company was located on his island, he resented the captive state of the dolphins, and he resented the loss of his uncle's beautiful property. Alexa thought he probably resented his servile[89] job there as well. It had to be hard for a person as astute[90] and resourceful as José to work in such a menial position. He had to clean the kitchen while others, such as herself, had an opportunity to work in an interesting and enlightening[91] environment. She knew that he would love to work in a laboratory and learn about DNA, but that opportunity had never been given to him the way it had been given to her. Alexa silently vowed that she would try

---

[83] Extant: currently or actually existing
[84] Ephemeral: lasting a very short time
[85] Expropriate: the action of the state in taking or modifying the property rights of an individual in the exercise of its sovereignty
[86] Ponderous: of very great weight; heavy
[87] Vexed: to bring trouble, stress, or agitation to
[88] Imputed: to lay the responsibility or blame for, often falsely or unjustly; charge, attribute
[89] Servile: of or befitting a slave or a menial person
[90] Astute: having or showing shrewdness and perspicacity
[91] Enlighten: to furnish knowledge to

to invite him to the laboratory as much as possible so that he could also be a beneficiary[92] of her opportunity there. She knew that this gesture couldn't possibly make their situations equitable,[93] but she desperately wanted to do *something*.

"Yes, but I'm sorry I brought that up now," José said as his amiable[94] demeanor returned. He could tell by the look on her face that she did not want to get mired[95] in those loaded issues right now. Tactfully, he steered the conversation to a more benign[96] and pleasant topic. "There are so many beautiful places on this island. I would like to show you all of them!"

"That sounds great. I would love to see them." Alexa warmed at the thought of his gracious[97] offer. It seemed that he liked to make her happy—it was as if he enjoyed her happiness vicariously.[98] "But speaking of time, I should probably be heading back to work. Don't you have to get to work too?"

"Yes, probably," he sighed. "Although my boss is a benevolent[99] dictator—he said that I could come late today. But I don't want to antagonize him by being too late, so we'd better go."

"You have a benevolent dictator for a boss and I have an absent dictator! My boss is hardly ever in the lab. My workplace is more akin to anarchy[100] than dictatorship!" They both broke into laughter over her humorous analogy. Alexa continued on a more serious note. "Did you want to work in the lab with me this weekend? I'm almost sure we will

---

92 Beneficiary: one who benefits from something
93 Equitable: fair
94 Amiable: friendly, sociable, congenial
95 Mire: to cause to get stuck in
96 Benign: having no significant effect; harmless
97 Gracious: marked by kindness and courtesy
98 Vicarious: experienced or realized through imaginative or sympathetic participation in the experience of another
99 Benevolent: marked by or disposed to doing good
100 Anarchy: absence of government

have a profusion[101] of Pecas' cells by then—they have been extremely prolific,"[102] Alexa offered. She knew that he would love this—it was like
offering candy to a child.

"Yes!" he cried, exultant[103] at the thought of it. His eyes were
inflamed[104] with enthusiasm. "But we'll have to remember to keep it
secret—officially, I'm not allowed to go anywhere but the kitchen at
Puerto Marino."

Alexa nodded in sympathy. "Why don't we start in the morning on
Saturday before you have to go to work?" she suggested as they pushed
their kayaks back into the water. It was hard to believe they would
have their answer so soon. Then they would need to figure out what to
do with it.

---

[101] Profusion: great quantity; lavish display or supply
[102] Prolific: abundant growth, generation, or reproduction
[103] Exultant: filled with or expressing great joy or triumph; jubilant
[104] Inflamed: to excite to excessive or uncontrollable action or feeling

The DNA Debacle

Saturday morning dawned sunny and bright, an auspicious[1] beginning to the day that Alexa and José had been anticipating with a mixture of trepidation and excitement. Despite the fact that it was a perfect morning to go to the beach, they were deviating from their usual routine. Today was the day they were going to begin their DNA experiments to find out if Pecas' baby was captive at Puerto Marino.

Alexa waited on the steps of the laboratory with two steaming cups of coffee. José arrived on his ramshackle[2] old bike, wearing a beaming smile that belied the early hour. It was only six o'clock in the morning, but José looked fresh and eager.

"I brought your favorite cake!" José smiled as he waved a brown paper bag in front of her eyes to tease her. It was too early for breakfast at the cafeteria, so the pair had decided to have cake and coffee together before beginning their experiment.

"Sounds good!" Alexa laughed. It was impossible not to feel happy around him, she thought. "I brought you a coffee. Do you mind if we eat out here—we're not supposed to eat in the lab."

---

[1] Auspicious: affording a favorable auspice (a favorable sign)
[2] Ramshackle: appearing ready to collapse

"I like to eat outside," José said as he settled in next to her on the steps of the building. "Then we can hear the howling of the monkeys. Do you hear that?" he asked pointing to the jungle that surrounded the compound. "That's the sound of the howler monkeys. Isn't it fantastic?"

"Those are monkeys that are making that noise?" Alexa inquired as she accepted a piece of cake. "I heard that noise the first night I was here and I had no idea what it was! I was frightened by it!" Alexa laughed.

"They can be very loud. If we have time later, we can go look for them in the treetops. You need to see them—it is quite amazing. I'm so happy they are still around here, that they haven't been eradicated[3] by all of this development." He gestured toward the buildings around them. "Sometimes when the people come, the monkeys must go elsewhere."

"I would love to see them. But we have just enough time to do the DNA extraction from Pecas' cells before you have to go to work. You still want to do that, don't you?"

José laughed. "You know I do! But first, you must have another piece of cake."

"Excellent idea!" Alexa laughed. This time she wasn't so shy about seconds. After they had finished their coffee, they headed into the laboratory to begin.

Alexa led José straight to the incubator to pull out the dishes containing Pecas' cells. "Let's take a look," Alexa said, as she placed the dish on the stage of the microscope. "I think we have enough to enable[4] us to begin right away." She offered José a look.

"Wow...there are so many cells! Do you think there are 10 million?"

"Yes, there should be. In both of these dishes combined."

---

[3] Eradicate: to do away with as if by pulling up from the roots
[4] Enable: to provide with the means or opportunity

"Then let's go! What do we do next?" José asked eagerly.

"We need to collect all of these cells into a test tube. First we'll loosen their attachment to the bottom of the dish and to each other using an enzyme that breaks that bond between them. Then, when the cells are floating freely in the solution, we'll spin them in the centrifuge to make a pellet of cells. Then we break open the cells and pull the DNA out!" Alexa concluded triumphantly.

José was wide-eyed with wonder. "How will we be able to see the DNA—I mean, will we be able to see it?" José asked diffidently.[5]

"Oh, yes, we'll be able to see it!" Alexa answered. She could tell José was a bit embarrassed by his basic questions and lack of knowledge in this area. But Alexa didn't mind that he was a novice.[6] In fact, she relished[7] the thought of being able to show him DNA for the first time. She knew it would be quite a thrill for him, as it had been for her.

Alexa took him through the initial steps of the DNA extraction. José was an exemplary[8] student, absorbing her every word as she showed him how the centrifuge worked and how to handle the samples. He especially liked using the micro pipettes—the specialized hand-held devices used for measuring very small volumes of liquids. Initially, he practiced using them with water, and when he was able to manipulate the instrument smoothly, Alexa had him doing all of the pipetting for the experiment.

Finally, the moment arrived when they added the ethanol to their solution to precipitate[9] the DNA. José deftly pipetted the requisite[10] amount of ethanol into the test tube and closed the cap. Alexa's hand was trembling with excitement as she picked up the tube and inverted it several times to mix the solutions. She held the tube up to the light in

---

[5] Diffident: hesitant in acting or speaking through lack of self-confidence

[6] Novice: beginner

[7] Relish: a strong liking

[8] Exemplary: deserving imitation because of excellence; commendable

[9] Precipitate: to cause to separate from solution or suspension

[10] Requisite: essential, necessary

between them so that they could both see the delicate thread of DNA congeal.[11] Although she had done this before, her previous experience did nothing to diminish the excitement of the moment. Experiencing this moment with José was reminiscent of her own first time seeing DNA.

"Is that it?" José asked with palpable[12] excitement. "The whitish thread there, that is it?"

"Yes it is! We have DNA!" she said triumphantly, handing the tube to José for a closer look.

"Wow! It's just so amazing to me that this white thread in my hand is DNA from a dolphin. From our dolphin friend Pecas! This is awesome!" José's eyes were sparkling with wonder. "What do we do next?"

"Well, we need to centrifuge it again to make a small pellet of that DNA there, and then we resuspend it in a buffer solution. Then we're ready to use it to do the maternity test."

"I'll put it in the centrifuge," José offered. He obviously enjoyed being the one to hold the precious tube and to carry out the manipulations. Alexa didn't mind. It was fun to watch him enjoying himself so much. He carefully placed the tube in the centrifuge and turned it on. After the spin in the centrifuge, he cautiously poured out the ethanol solution, leaving a small pellet about the size of an ant at the bottom of the tube. Then, Alexa instructed José to add the buffer solution to the tube containing the pellet to complete the DNA prep. José held the tube up to the light where they could see the pellet of DNA with a layer of buffer over it.

"It doesn't look like it's dissolving! Isn't the DNA supposed to dissolve in the solution?" José asked worriedly.

---

[11] Congeal: to change from a fluid state to a solid state
[12] Palpable: easily perceptible

"Here, let me try." Alexa reached for the tube. "Sometimes the pellet is really hard and you need to break it up with your pipette tip, like this." Alexa put her pipette tip into the tube and homogenized[13] the solution with the stirring action of her pipette. "There. I think the pellet is dissolved and it's all in solution now. See how viscous[14] the solution is now? It's thick with DNA!" Alexa declared triumphantly. As she held the tube up to the light again for José to see, the tube slipped through her gloved fingers and in an instant, it landed on the floor!

"Oh no!" Alexa cried. "I can't believe that just happened! It just slipped through my fingers." They both could see the small puddle of viscous solution on the floor, the empty plastic tube lying on its side. José looked horrified. His high hopes for the experiment were thwarted[15] by her accident. Alexa knew his heart and mind were consumed with this experiment and she felt terrible for causing such a debacle.[16]

"Don't feel bad. We can always do it over again," José consoled her with his kind words. It didn't take but a moment for him to regain his composure and his limitless empathy. He was most concerned about her. "And maybe there is still some DNA left in here," José added as he picked up the empty tube off the floor, snapped the lid shut, and set it on the counter.

"I feel terrible. It will take us another week to grow the cells again!" Alexa said in despair. "It took us a week just to get the cells from Pecas, then it took us a week to grow them. Now we'll have to wait again!" She felt absolutely disheartened to have put them in such a conundrum[17] when they had been so close to reaching their goal.

---

[13] Homogenize: to blend (diverse elements) into a uniform mixture

[14] Viscous: having or characterized by viscosity (the property of resistance to flow in a fluid or semifluid); a thick liquid

[15] Thwart: to oppose successfully, to defeat the hopes or aspirations of

[16] Debacle: a great disaster; fiasco

[17] Conundrum: an intricate and difficult problem

"Don't feel bad——we'll get there eventually. But speaking of time, I'm five minutes late for work," he said ruefully.[18] He looked hesitant to leave her when she was so upset, but he was already tardy. He pointed to the clock—it was 10:35 A.M. "I need to go. Please don't worry about it. Can you meet me at the beach tomorrow morning?" he asked hopefully on his way out the door.

Alexa nodded and managed to give him a brave smile before he took off. She was thankful that he was not the type to be condescending.[19] By contrast, he was so gracious about her gaffe.[20] Nevertheless, her heart sunk as she returned to her desk. All morning, she had been feeling like a consummate[21] scientist, unraveling a mystery with her partner, who revered her prowess[22] in the laboratory. It had been so much fun up until that horrifying moment when she'd dropped the tube. She felt dejected, embarrassed, and close to tears.

Alexa flung herself into the chair and with her elbows on the desk, rested her head in her hands and felt her eyes fill with tears. She couldn't hold it back any longer. Big tears dropped onto her lab notebook, which lay open on her desk. The words were all blurry through her tears, but Alexa could make out that her tears were falling on the protocol for the DNA maternity test that they had planned to carry out that afternoon. How appropriate, in an ironic sort of way, Alexa thought. It seemed befitting that her tears would stain the instructions for the experiment that was going to elude[23] them for yet another week.

Or would it? she thought as she looked at the protocol. The instructions called for 0.1 micrograms of DNA, she noticed, wiping the tears

---

[18] Rueful: mournful, regretful
[19] Condescending: to assume an air of superiority
[20] Gaffe: a social or diplomatic blunder
[21] Consummate: extremely skilled and accomplished
[22] Prowess: extraordinary ability
[23] Elude: to escape the perception, understanding, or grasp of

from her eyes. Alexa recalled that two weeks ago, when she had made dolphin DNA from Coco, 10 million cells had yielded over a gram of DNA. She hurriedly flipped the pages of her lab notebook back to Coco's DNA extraction. Yes, it had yielded 1.1 grams of DNA. If today's experiment yielded a similar amount, it would have given them 10,000 times more DNA than they needed for the maternity test! So, she calculated excitedly as her spirits rose, even if they spilled 99% of their DNA on the floor and they only had 1% left in the tube, it was still ten times more than they needed!

Alexa ran over to the countertop where José had placed the capped tube. It looked like quite a bit of the viscous solution had stuck to the walls of the test tube. There was probably 20% of the solution still in there, waiting to be analyzed. Alexa was certain now that they had plenty of DNA for the next phase of the experiment. She was elated that her clumsy error wouldn't detract[24] from the progress of their experiment at all.

She brought the precious test tube over to her lab bench to begin the next phase of the experiment. It was a bit embarrassing, she thought as she realized what had happened. Whenever she had made DNA in the past, she had always used a large quantity of cells. By default,[25] she assumed that she had needed to this time as well. But now, she realized they probably could have gotten enough DNA just from the cheek swab itself. How could I have been so obtuse,[26] Alexa chided herself. At least all of their work hadn't been in vain, she thought as she looked at the remaining DNA solution in the test tube.

---

[24] Detract: to diminish the importance, value, or effectiveness of something
[25] Default: a course taken without an active choice
[26] Obtuse: lacking sharpness or quickness of sensibility or intellect

Alexa couldn't wait to tell José their experiment was still on. They could spend all day tomorrow in the lab, she thought with growing jubilation.[27]

But right now was the perfect time to send an e-mail update to Laurie back home, who had been eagerly following the developments in Alexa's life at Puerto Marino. Alexa found that having an online pen pal like Laurie was such a tempting diversion[28] from work. There was so much to talk about—the dolphins, the big experiment, the clandestine plan, and of course, José. Alexa wrote about it all—uncensored,[29] just as if she were talking with Laurie face to face. Lately, Laurie had been writing back almost every day. It was as if their disparate[30] summer experiences gave them so much to talk about that their friendship was growing even when they were thousands of miles apart.

Time: 11:16 A.M.
To: "Laurie"
From: "Alexa"
Subject: the big experiment

Dear Laurie,

I was so happy to get your e-mail this morning! I am glad to hear you like your job at CNN and I concur,[31] you would make an excellent anchorwoman! That would be the perfect career for you. Please tell me more about your new boyfriend! Or better yet, can you send me a picture?

---

[27] Jubilation: an expression of great joy
[28] Diversion: the act or an instance of diverting from a course, activity, or use; deviation
[29] Uncensored: not examined for the purpose of deleting objectionable or sensitive information; unedited
[30] Disparate: containing or made up of fundamentally different and often incongruous elements
[31] Concur: to express agreement

I know you are dying to hear about our experiment. It's working well so far, despite a huge mishap in the lab this morning. But we are all set...and we should know the answer tomorrow! I can hardly wait! I haven't told Charlotte anything about our plan to free Pecas' baby, and, in fact, I don't even mention José when we go running together in the morning. We still haven't found her bracelet and I feel so bad about that. She seems to have accepted the fact that it's gone and it doesn't really seem to get in the way of our friendship like I thought it would. She is a very special friend.

I have to go now—I have a very important experiment to do! I will write to you tomorrow and let you know the answer!

Friends always,
Alexa

Alexa pressed Send, and then immediately set about the task of setting up the next phase of the experiment. In 15 minutes the cafeteria opened for lunch. Hopefully, she would see José so she could give him the good news.

13

A Moral Ambiguity

Alexa waited on the steps of the laboratory early Sunday morning, waiting for José to arrive. It felt like she had never left—even her dreams the night before had been filled with test tubes, cells, and DNA. Today was the day they should have their answer, and it was hard to think about anything else. José looked as if he had a similar single-mindedness as he rode up to the lab on his bike.

"You brought cake!" Alexa cried, delighted when she saw the bag in his hand.

"Yes, and you get one piece for every tube of DNA that you drop!" José teased.

"Very funny," Alexa said, her voice filled with sarcasm. "You are treading perilously[1] on thin ice!" she warned as José handed her a piece of cake.

---

[1] Perilous: full of or involving peril (risk)

"Well, thick ice is kind of hard to find on a tropical island!" he replied, his eyes bright with mischief.

Alexa had to laugh at his perceptive joke. She knew he didn't mean to be malicious[2] in his teasing, nor did he wish to alienate[3] her. He just wanted to make her laugh. So she let it pass good-naturedly. Alexa didn't tell him about how she had miscalculated the amount of DNA that they needed for the maternity test. If he knew about that, she would really be in for a barrage[4] of jokes.

"I can't wait to see the results of this experiment," José tactfully changed the subject. "Do you really think we'll have the answer at the end of the day?"

"Yes—if we start now," Alexa replied, as she finished her cake. "In today's experiment, we're comparing Pecas' DNA to Coco's DNA. So we will definitely get an answer to that. If it turns out Coco is unrelated to Pecas, then we'll need to check the other baby dolphins in separate experiments." They both eagerly headed into the lab.

"I already carried out the PCR of the STRs yesterday, so today, we just need to run the gels to see the answer," Alexa explained.

"Whoa! You've lost me." José looked baffled.[5] "That sounds like an alphabet soup! What's PCR and STR?"

"Well, STR is short for short tandem repeat. It's an area of the chromosome that's highly variable from one individual to the next. But since offspring inherit their chromosomes from their parents, the STRs are usually the same in the parent and the child. So, in other words, if Coco is Pecas' baby, they should have the same STRs. So what we need to

---

[2] Malicious: given to, marked by, or arising from malice (desire to cause pain, injury, or distress to another)

[3] Alienate: to make unfriendly, hostile, or indifferent where attachment formerly existed

[4] Barrage: a vigorous or rapid outpouring or projection of many things at once

[5] Baffle: to defeat or check (as a person) by confusing or puzzling; disconcert

do is to look at a handful of these STRs. If the STRs are completely different, we can say for sure Pecas is not the mother. If they share the same STRs, Pecas is probably the mother. The more STRs we look at, the more certain it becomes. If we look at more than ten and they match, we can be more than 99% certain."

"Wow! That is so awesome," José said. "But how do we look at the STRs?"

"Well, that's where the PCR comes in. PCR is a technique for amplifying segments of DNA. In this case, we are amplifying the STRs. And to look at them, we run a gel." Alexa pointed to the rectangular mold containing the Jell-O-like substance. "We are going to deposit the DNA solution in this slot in the gel and then apply an electric field. Since the DNA has a negative charge, it will migrate toward the positive pole. But the smaller pieces of DNA will move faster and the bigger ones move slower. This will separate the molecules based on their size. It takes about an hour."

José looked at her admiringly as she continued to explain the experiment.

"Then we're going to visualize it on this computer screen here." Alexa pulled up an image of one of her previous experiments. "See—it looks kind of like a bar code. When the bars are at the same position in the gel, you have a matching STR," Alexa pointed out an example on the screen. "And when the bars are at different positions, you have an STR that doesn't match."

"I understand," José nodded. "Let's get started!"

"OK," Alexa replied. It was fun to be the teacher for such an enthusiastic student. "I carried out ten PCRs yesterday, so we'll have data on ten STRs. That should be enough. All we need to do is to get this DNA on the gel and apply the electric field." Alexa gestured toward the ten miniature plastic test tubes that contained less than a drop of liquid each.

The pair worked side by side, conversing constantly while they worked. José was so attuned[6] to the subtleties of lab work that he needed minimal guidance from Alexa. It was fun to spend such a long stretch of time together, Alexa thought. This being Sunday, José didn't have to rush off to work. He loved to talk and he kept her laughing with amusing anecdotes[7] about his family and his fishing adventures.

After carefully setting up the power supply and the wires to apply the electric field to the gel, Alex turned it on. They both watched anxiously, but there was nothing yet to see. "It's going to be at least an hour while this runs." Alexa said. "It's kind of pointless to hover over it now."

"Why don't we go into town and have a quick lunch? That will make the time go faster." José ushered her out the door. "I have a favorite Mexican restaurant—I want to take you there. The authenticity[8] of the tacos there are simply unmatched—you have to try them!" He smiled persuasively.

"But how can they be more authentic than the tacos in Mexico?" Alexa laughed as she hopped on her motorbike behind José.

"Just wait until you try them!" José yelled above the noise of the motor. A short ride later, they parked the bike in front of an unprepossessing[9] establishment. The restaurant looked derelict[10] from the outside.

---

6 Attune: to make aware or responsive

7 Anecdote: a usually short narrative of an interesting, amusing, or biographical incident

8 Authentic: worthy of acceptance or belief as conforming to or based on fact

9 Unprepossessing: not attractive or tending to create a favorable impression

10 Derelict: abandoned, especially by the owner or occupant; run-down

José led them in through the tattered doorway, where they were greeted warmly by the proprietor[11] and ushered into the courtyard. A lovely fountain, a gentle breeze, and beautiful flowers set the scene for their casual repast.[12]

After a delicious lunch of tacos infused[13] with hot sauce and supplemented[14] with extra guacamole, Alexa had to acknowledge that José's claim was substantiated.

José flouted[15] convention by drinking hot tea instead of an ice-cold drink like everyone else at the restaurant. Alexa couldn't resist poking fun at him for a change. "How can you drink something hot when it's hot out, the food is hot, and the hot sauce is even hotter?" Alexa teased as she sipped an ice-cold soda.

"Shhh...it's all part of my secret theory about temperature," José whispered conspiratorially. "You see, if you drink something hot, it precludes[16] the effect of the hot sauce. Now you, for instance, drinking something cold, you will have the polarizing[17] effects of the opposites, which will only make the hot sauce taste hotter!"

"What an innovation!"[18] Alexa laughed, playing along. "You should patent[19] your idea!"

"No, actually I don't drink American sodas because I don't want to," José said seriously. I really loathe the TV advertisements for these things.

---

[11] Proprietor: one who has the legal right or exclusive title to something; owner
[12] Repast: the act or time of taking food
[13] Infused: to cause to be permeated with something
[14] Supplement: something that completes or makes an addition
[15] Flout: to treat with contemptuous disregard
[16] Preclude: to make impossible by necessary consequence, rule out in advance
[17] Polarize: to break up into opposing factions or groupings
[18] Innovation: a new idea, method, or device
[19] Patent: a writing securing to an inventor for a term of years the exclusive right to make, use, or sell an invention

They exemplify[20] everything I detest about American materialism. They pander[21] to people's desires to belong and to be hip. It's just a soda!" he added firmly.

"And I just thought it tasted good," Alexa said, attempting to bring the humor back to their conversation. Alexa had never noticed any lack of integrity[22] in the soda commercials, but she could see that José was staunch[23] in his interpretation.[24] Even though she didn't really agree with his point—in her opinion the commercials were harmless advertising—she admired the fact that José was the type of person to abide by his convictions. "You know, we really need to be heading back. Our gel will be done in ten minutes."

"Let's go! I can't wait to see it!" José enthused. He insisted on paying the bill for their lunch and left some coins on the table for the gratuity.[25] Then the two of them were on their way back to the lab.

There was only one step left in their experiment. They needed to scan the information off of their gels and then look at the picture on the computer screen. The scanning process took only three minutes, but it felt like an eternity. Alexa was tremulous[26] with anticipation as the two of them eagerly waited for the scanner to synthesize[27] the image on the screen.

As their intent gaze was glued to the screen, the image finally appeared, rolling down the screen from top to bottom. The picture on the screen was filled with bands at various positions.

---

[20] Exemplify: to show or illustrate by example
[21] Pander: cater or exploit the weakness of others
[22] Integrity: firm adherence to a code of especially moral or artistic values
[23] Staunch: steadfast in loyalty or principle
[24] Interpretation: the act or the result of interpreting (to conceive in the light of individual belief, judgment, or circumstance)
[25] Gratuity: something given voluntarily or beyond obligation usually for some service; especially a tip
[26] Tremulous: characterized by or affected with trembling or tremors
[27] Synthesize: to combine or produce by synthesis (the composition or combination of parts or elements so as to form a whole)

"What does it say? What does it mean? Did it work? Is Pecas Coco's mother?" José asked urgently. He was beside himself with excitement and pressed Alexa for the answer with his rapid-fire questions.

"Hold on a minute—it's going to take a little bit of time to interpret it," Alexa replied calmly, unruffled[28] by his urgent questions. She continued to scrutinize[29] the image on the screen. "I think it'll be easier if we print out the image and then we can orient ourselves properly," Alexa concluded. "Once we have the picture labeled properly we can interpret it."

"OK," José agreed, but he looked as if she was subjecting[30] him to torture by delaying the answer one more minute. He pulled the paper out of the printer and put it in front of Alexa, who sat at her desk with her lab notebook open. Glancing at her notes, she carefully labeled the picture. José watched intently over her shoulder.

"OK, so right here are the bands from Pecas and here are the bands from Coco," Alexa pointed, feeling like a molecular sleuth.[31] There were several bands in each position, but one band from Pecas was in the exact same position as one of the bands from Coco.

"Look!" José cried. "It matches! Pecas is the mother!" José was wildly excited.

"Hold on a minute! That's a tenuous[32] conclusion at this point. This is only one STR—remember how we need to look at multiple examples to draw a conclusion."

"Yes, of course. But I know it's true! Look here!" José pointed to the next example. "There's another match. And here's another one!"

---

28 Unruffled: poised and serene, especially in the face of setbacks or confusion
29 Scrutinize: to examine closely and minutely
30 Subject: to cause or force to undergo or endure
31 Sleuth: detective
32 Tenuous: having little substance or strength

Alexa nodded excitedly as she too scanned the image quickly. The cumulative[33] data from all of the STRs gave them an undeniable answer. "I think we have a match at all ten STRs!" Alexa turned to look at José. They were both incredulous at their discovery and a bit stunned that they had actually achieved their goal. The profundity[34] of the moment left them momentarily speechless. The conclusion was clear.

"It is so great," José said, pointing to the experiment, "but at the same time it is sad. It means that Pecas' baby is in captivity here." His tone turned serious.

Alexa nodded in response. Pecas' cryptic[35] behavior made so much sense now. They had deciphered what she was trying to tell them.

"We need to free her so that she can go back to her mother where she belongs," José said solemnly.

Alexa suddenly felt jarred out of her complacency.[36] Before they had this answer, she felt justified in postponing any hasty action. But she couldn't sit on the fence any longer. Pecas' baby was in captivity at Puerto Marino, and Alexa needed to decide if she was going to go along with the plan that José had concocted[37] or if she was going to sit on the sidelines. She looked at José's earnest expression and made up her mind.

"Yes. We do need to free her," Alexa said. Finally, she felt that her own conflicting feelings about the dolphins had coalesced. She felt uncomfortable with the way dolphins were treated like commodities.[38] In her view they were more like people—they were sentient,[39] cerebral,[40] social beings that appeared to have a full range of emotions. Although

---

[33] Cumulative: made up of accumulated parts

[34] Profundity: the quality or state of being profound (having intellectual depth or insight)

[35] Cryptic: having or seeming to have a hidden or ambiguous meaning

[36] Complacency: self-satisfaction accompanied by unawareness of actual dangers or deficiencies

[37] Concocted: to prepare by combining raw materials; devise

[38] Commodities: an economic good, as in an article of commerce (something bought or sold), especially when delivered for shipment

[39] Sentient: finely sensitive in perception or feeling; aware

[40] Cerebral: of or relating to the brain or the intellect

Charlotte had brought up some very valid points about dolphins aiding the Navy, Charlotte didn't know Pecas the way Alexa and José did. Allowing her baby to remain in captivity here devalued[41] the very real bond they shared with Pecas. Alexa decided she was going to draw the line here—it was time to take action. "But how are we possibly going to get her out of there? The dolphin facility is so secure."

"Well," José began slowly, "your mother works there, doesn't she?"

"Yes...but how is that going to help us? I can't possibly ask her..."

"If she works there, she has a card key, right? And maybe we could just borrow the card key late at night, set Coco free, and then return the card key while everybody is still sleeping."

Alexa nodded in agreement, but her conscience bothered her. She was uncomfortable at the thought of taking her mother's card key without her knowledge. Alexa pondered this moral dilemma. Does the end result justify the means? In her mind, it would be infinitely better if they could leave her mother out of this subversive[42] plan. The idea of "borrowing" her mother's card key felt a bit unscrupulous.[43] She didn't want her mother to be culpable[44] for her actions. Nevertheless, Alexa could see the logic in José's tactics.[45] Perhaps taking the card key *was* deceitful,[46] but Alexa felt comfortable that their ultimate goal was not. It was the combination of the two actions, one deceitful and one worthy, that presented the moral ambiguity[47] in her mind. Was this furtive[48] plan morally corrupt,[49] or was it a justifiable solution to the wrenching dilemma that they faced? They really had no other way of getting into the dolphin facility. She knew José

---

[41] Devalued: to lessen the value of

[42] Subversive: a cause of overthrow or destruction, especially a systematic attempt to overthrow or undermine a government by persons working secretly within

[43] Unscrupulous: not scrupulous (having moral integrity); unprincipled

[44] Culpable: guilty; meriting condemnation or blame, especially as wrong or harmful

[45] Tactics: a device for accomplishing an end

[46] Deceitful: having a tendency or disposition to deceive; not honest

[47] Ambiguity: the quality or state of being ambiguous (doubtful or uncertain), especially in meaning

[48] Furtive: done by stealth; sly

[49] Corrupt: to change from good to bad in morals, manners, or actions

couldn't get in there without her participation—she was the linchpin[50] of the scheme.

"When do you think we should do this?" Alexa asked nervously.

"The sooner, the better. I think we should do it tonight. All we were waiting for was this experiment to corroborate our suspicions about Coco. Now we know what the situation is beyond the shadow of a doubt." José pointed to the pattern of bands on the computer screen to underscore the validity of his assertion. Then, he turned to look her square in the eyes, his florid[51] complexion revealing the depth of his emotional fervor. "We need to rectify the situation immediately," he concluded.

"Let's think about this for a minute," Alexa said calmly. "I've only been in the dolphin facility three times. I'm pretty sure I would recognize Coco, but I don't know how to work all of those gates and things. Do you know how to do it? Have you ever been in the facility?"

"No, I haven't. But how difficult can it be? Let's just do it. I can stay here in the lab until 3 A.M. We can meet here then. You'll need to bring the card." He looked at her questioningly. "Will you meet me here?" His deep brown eyes beseeched her to collude[52] with him in this daring endeavor.

"Yes," Alexa agreed. "I'll be here."

---

[50] Linchpin: a central cohesive source of support and stability
[51] Florid: flushed with rosy color
[52] Collude: conspire, plot

14

Late-Night Liberation

Alexa had never been so nervous in her entire life. She knew with certainty that sleep would completely elude her. Her mother had finally gone to sleep at 11:30 P.M. Alexa felt a bit disingenuous[1] when she told her mother she wanted to stay up late to write e-mails.

But that uncomfortable feeling she felt when telling a relatively harmless lie paled in comparison to the way she felt now. At this point, her actions made her feel like a dissembler.[2] Here she was rummaging through her mother's wallet, realizing that she was indeed perfidious.[3] Somehow, when she was with José, this plan seemed more credible. His moral certitude[4] was so persuasive. He saw the situation as black and white. Coco held captive in Puerto Marino was a bad thing, and liberating[5] her was a good thing. Alexa, on the other hand, felt mired in shades of gray. However noble their ultimate goal was, Alexa felt terrible about the deviousness[6] of her current actions.

---

[1] Disingenuous: lacking in candor; calculating
[2] Dissembler: one who puts on a false appearance; conceals facts, intentions, or feelings under some pretense
[3] Perfidious: disloyal or faithless
[4] Certitude: the state of being or feeling certain
[5] Liberating: the act of setting free
[6] Deviousness: not straightforward; deceptive

Retrieving the card key from her mother's wallet was easy. There it was, right where it was supposed to be. Alexa took it out and placed it in her back pocket. Looking at the clock, she realized she would need to wait a few more hours before meeting José. It looked like she would have plenty of time to deal with her feelings about deceiving her mother.

It would be so great to talk to Laurie right now, Alexa thought. While her epistolary[7] relationship with Laurie was nice, Alexa really longed to talk to her face to face. But since that was not an option, Alexa sat down to write her friend a long, revelatory[8] e-mail. She explained in painstaking detail the provocative[9] experimental results that proved Pecas' baby was in captivity at Puerto Marino. Then, Alexa explained how she and José were planning on carrying out their radical plan to free the baby dolphin tonight. She punctuated the long letter with confessions of her conflicted feelings. She found that putting all of these feelings into words was cathartic,[10] and ultimately it had a therapeutic[11] effect.

Since the plan to free the baby dolphin was José's conception,[12] Alexa realized that her recurring hesitation about the scheme was in part due to her own aversion to playing a submissive[13] role. She didn't want to go along with the plan just because José wanted her to. She wanted to take part in it of her own volition.[14]

After writing for two hours and vacillating[15] about what was right and what was wrong, Alexa finally felt resolute in her decision to

---

[7] Epistolary: contained in or carried on by letters
[8] Revelatory: serving to reveal something
[9] Provocative: serving or tending to provoke, excite, or stimulate
[10] Cathartic: characterized by a purification or purgation of the emotions that brings about spiritual renewal or release from tension
[11] Therapeutic: providing or assisting in a cure
[12] Conception: the originating of something in the mind; idea
[13] Submissive: to yield oneself to the authority or will of another
[14] Volition: an act of making a choice or decision
[15] Vacillate: to waver in mind, will, or feeling; hesitate in choice of opinions or courses

partake[16] in the scheme. Her actions would not compromise her own beliefs. She honestly felt that carrying out this plan was genuinely altruistic,[17] and it was the right thing to do.

When Alexa looked at the voluminous e-mail, she was tempted to abridge[18] its contents. But instead she augmented[19] the letter further by adding an addendum:[20] "Wish us luck, Laurie, we're going to need it!" Alexa reread the letter and hesitated for a moment. Finally she took a deep breath and pressed Send. She glanced at the clock—it was time to go.

Alexa grabbed the flashlight she had found earlier in the kitchen drawer and went out the door. The quiet atmosphere in the compound only seemed to accentuate[21] the noises emanating[22] from the jungle. She kept her flashlight turned off to avoid attention. She could see her way along the well-worn path easily enough in the moonlight, but she couldn't help but be nervous about the various jungle critters, particularly snakes, that might be lurking in the shadows.

The windows of the laboratory were completely dark. Alexa pulled out her own card key and entered the darkened laboratory. José was nowhere in sight. The ultraviolet light emanating from the tissue culture workspace gave the room an eerie purple hue. She could hear the soft hum of the incubator, but otherwise the room was silent.

Alexa walked slowly toward the back of the room. She felt like every nerve in her body was on high alert. Once she reached the back of the

---

[16] Partake: to take part in or experience something along with others
[17] Altruistic: behavior that is unselfish in its regard for or devotion to the welfare of others
[18] Abridge: to shorten in duration or extent
[19] Augment: to make greater, more numerous, larger, or more intense
[20] Addendum: a thing added; an addition
[21] Accentuate: accent, emphasize
[22] Emanate: to come out from a source

room, she could discern the sound of rhythmic breathing. Alexa smiled. José was asleep under her desk! He was curled up in a ball in the small space.

"José! Wake up!" Alexa whispered.

His eyes opened suddenly. He looked momentarily disconcerted.[23]

"It's me, Alexa."

"*Hola!* Is it time?" José managed a sleepy smile as he climbed out of his space.

"Yes, it's time. Why were you down there? Wouldn't it have been more comfortable stretched out here?" Alexa asked.

"Yes, it definitely would have been more comfortable," he smiled ruefully. "But the guards come around on their watch periodically and look in here. They were here twice already tonight. But they didn't find me!" he declared triumphantly.

"Oh my gosh! That sounds treacherous!" Alexa looked anxious. "Do you think there are guards inside the dolphin facility?"

"No, not inside. There is a guard who makes his rounds once every two hours. I was watching. First he stops at the dolphin facility—he walks in there with his flashlight and checks it out, then he comes to this building and does the same, and so on down this row of buildings. He was just here ten minutes ago, so we should have at least an hour before he comes back. Did you bring the card?" he inquired.

"Yes, I have it right here," Alexa replied. The thought of the guard making rounds instilled[24] a fear in her that made her stomach churn.

---

[23] Disconcert: to throw into confusion
[24] Instill: to impart gradually

"Great. Then let's go!" José started for the door. Predictably, there was no question in his mind about whether or not to carry out the plan. In his mind, all of the problems were tractable,[25] and the obstacles were surmountable.[26] He was not going to be irresolute[27] at this juncture, even with the knowledge that the guard was looming outside in the dark night.

"OK," Alexa said, following José. She was desperately trying to quell her pervasive[28] feelings of fear and anxiety. José didn't appear to have any fear at all—he was intrepid[29] in the face of the challenges before them. He held her hand as they headed out the door. Alexa touched the smooth surface of the shark's tooth that adorned her necklace. If ever there was a moment when she needed to summon her inner reserves and emulate José's bravery, this was it.

They walked the short distance over to the dolphin facility and stood at the door. Alexa pulled her mother's card key out of her back pocket and swiped the card through the scanner. The door clicked audibly.

José, looking gratified, immediately pushed open the door and held it for Alexa. Stepping over the threshold, she felt like she had literally crossed the line. Heretofore,[30] their plan was just that—a plan. Now it was an immutable[31] reality.

The hallway was dimly lit, so the two of them proceeded down it without turning on the flashlight. The imposing[32] double doors at the end of the hallway were closed. These were the doors that opened to the grand dolphin room. Alexa again swiped her mother's card through the scanner. Suddenly, the massive double doors swung open automatically.

---

[25] Tractable: easily handled, managed, or wrought
[26] Surmountable: able to prevail over; able to overcome
[27] Irresolute: indecisive (not resolute or firm)
[28] Pervasive: that pervades (to become diffused throughout every part of) or tends to pervade
[29] Intrepid: characterized by resolute fearlessness, fortitude, and endurance
[30] Heretofore: up to this time; hitherto
[31] Immutable: not capable of or susceptible to change
[32] Imposing: impressive in size, bearing, dignity, or grandeur

José looked at Alexa, his eyes were sparkling with excitement. Exuberantly, he grabbed her hand and the two of them raced through the open doors. On the other side of the threshold, they paused for a moment while their eyes adjusted to the dim light and took in the spectacular scene before them. There was a loud noise as the doors shut audibly behind them.

It felt like they were in another world. The dim lighting was sufficient to see the extent of the capacious[33] facility—there were four pools shimmering in the darkness and the water was teeming with dolphins. Of course, Alexa had been in the facility before, but somehow it was incalculably[34] different at night. It felt otherworldly to be in a place where there were dozens of dolphins and only two people.

Thinking back to the first time she'd walked into this room, Alexa couldn't help but recognize just how much her feelings about it had changed. On that very first tour of Puerto Marino, Alexa was entranced by the dolphin facility—in fact, she had wanted to work there. But her friendship with Pecas changed her perspective profoundly. Now, seeing legions[35] of dolphins in captivity was a bittersweet vision. It was always a pleasure to be around so many of these charismatic creatures, but at this point she viewed their captivity with a critical eye. Now that they had some insight into the lives of Pecas and Coco, Alexa couldn't help but wonder about the other dolphins in the facility. Did they have a heart-rending story to tell as well?

---

[33] Capacious: containing or capable of containing a great deal
[34] Incalculably: not capable of being calculated; not predictable
[35] Legions: a large number; a multitude

José was absolutely stunned by the scene. In the entire time she had known him, Alexa had never seen José at a loss for words. Under normal circumstances, he was not that impressionable.[36] But the panorama before them had rendered him inarticulate.[37]

"We have to try to find Coco," Alexa prompted. In her pragmatic mind, they didn't have any time to waste. She felt so susceptible[38] just standing there. They had a job to complete before the guard came back.

"Yes! Let's start looking. I know I would recognize her. I used to see her every day," José replied, heading toward the nearest pool.

"Whenever I've been in here before, Coco has always been in this pool over here," Alexa pointed to the smaller pool on the right.

"OK, let's check it out," José agreed.

Alexa led the way onto the narrow walkway that separated the pools. José followed more slowly. Dolphins were his passion, and the sheer profusion of them here was mesmerizing. José stopped to talk with several dolphins that followed him curiously. These dolphins were quite well adapted to humans and they communicated without hesitation.

"José, we have to find Coco!" Alexa reminded him.

"Yes, of course, let's go." José stood up on the narrow walkway and teetered precariously, as if he was about to fall in. He had a big grin on his face.

"José—I'm so afraid the guard is going to come back and catch us!" Alexa pleaded. Normally, she would laugh at his frivolity.[39] But this was neither the time nor the place. She knew he was acting silly to make her

---

[36] Impressionable: capable of being easily impressed
[37] Inarticulate: incapable of speech, especially under stress of emotion
[38] Susceptible: open to some stimulus, influence, or agency
[39] Frivolity: playful merriment that lacks substance or purpose

laugh and ease her anxiety, but they really didn't have time for such buf-foonery.[40] Nor did they have time to play with the dolphins indiscrimi-nately.[41] In her mind, the task before them was still a daunting[42] one. They needed to find Coco and figure out a way to liberate her.

"I think I see her already!" José said, pointing to a dolphin in the distant pool. "Can I use the flashlight?"

Alexa handed over the flashlight and José took it with him to the edge of the smallest pool. He knelt down at the edge and started talking softly in Spanish. Interspersed[43] periodically in his soft words he whistled three times, as Alexa had seen him do on many occasions with Pecas. It was his signature call. Alexa ardently[44] hoped that Coco would remember.

A small dolphin surfaced near José, evidently responding to the stimulus.[45] Alexa thought it looked like Coco, but her features were dif-ficult to discern in the dim light. José turned the flashlight on, keeping his hand cupped over the light so he didn't startle the young dolphin.

"That's her! That's Coco!" Alexa exclaimed, trying to keep her voice down to a whisper.

José turned around and nodded in agreement, a big smile on his face. "Now we just have to figure out how to get her out of here," José said, his eyes darted around the large room, probing for an answer to their quest.

"I know that the outer pool over there has a gate that opens directly into the ocean," Alexa pointed.

"Let's go take a look at it," José replied. They quickly scurried down the narrow walkway to the outer pool.

---

[40] Buffoonery: foolish or playful behavior

[41] Indiscriminately: not marked by careful distinction; deficient in discrimination and discernment; haphazard; random

[42] Daunting: something that daunts (lessens one's courage)

[43] Interspersed: to place something at intervals in or among

[44] Ardently: characterized by warmth of feeling, typically expressed in eager zealous support or activity

[45] Stimulus: something that rouses or incites to activity

Alexa had never seen this area configured in such a way before. During the day, the entire back wall of the building lifted up, like a garage door. Apparently at night, the wall was down. The outer pool was now half inside the building and half outside.

"This is going to be easy. There are no dolphins in the outer pool, so all we need to do is to open the gate in between the small pool and the outer pool, and then usher Coco into the outer pool. Then we need to go outside and lift the gate that separates the outer pool from the ocean," José said confidently as he put the final pieces of the puzzle into their scheme. "Let's go take a look at the first gate," he commanded incisively.[46]

Heading back to the narrow walkway that separated the small pool from the outer pool, they focused on the gate mechanism. It looked like it was controlled by a hand crank, which manually lifted the gate. José immediately started to test the gate. As he turned the crank, they could see the gate lifting below the surface. José immediately returned the gate to the closed position.

"Alexa, I think we will need you to operate the gate. I need to lure Coco over to the gate and usher her through, without letting any of the other dolphins through." They counted at least three other dolphins in the pool besides Coco, but their real number was indeterminate[47] in this dark atmosphere. "I'm going to have to get in the water."

"OK—but let's just make sure that I'm strong enough to do it."

"It's actually very easy—here, give it a try," José replied.

Alexa turned the crank and the gate lifted easily. José nodded in approval and then wasted no time hopping in the pool. The dolphins

---

[46] Incisively: impressively direct and decisive (as in manner of presentation)
[47] Indeterminate: not definitely or precisely determined; vague

took immediate notice of José's plunge into their pool, and several her-alded[48] his presence with loud squeaks and high-pitched whistles. José treaded water near the gate and repeated his signature whistle and his soft words in Spanish.

Coco surfaced near José and replied in an animated series of squeaks that encapsulated[49] her delight at seeing him in the water next to her. In an instant, there were three other dolphins surrounding him as well.

"Alexa, could you lift the gate?" he asked. "I'm going to swim through and call to Coco from the other side. As soon as she goes through, you need to try to close the gate before the others follow her."

"OK. Here we go," she replied, cranking the gate up to the open position. José maintained eye contact with Coco and kept talking to her as he inched his way backward through the portal.

Opening the gate had a negligible[50] effect on the dolphins. All of them remained immobile in the small pool. Alexa was so surprised. She had thought that the second they lifted the gate, all of the dolphins would immediately want to get out. Ostensibly,[51] all creatures wanted freedom and the opportunity to live their lives autonomously.[52] But evidently, the situation here was more complicated than that. Not a single one exploited the opportunity to go through the opening.

José moved a little closer to the gate and started repeating his whis-tle. It looked like this strategy was inefficacious,[53] and Alexa was getting increasingly nervous as the minutes ticked away. If only they had thought to bring along some fish to use as a lure. Their scheme for freeing Coco had been based on the premise[54] that the dolphin would eagerly swim

---

[48] Heralded: to greet, especially with enthusiasm; to hail, publicize, or signal
[49] Encapsulated: epitomized
[50] Negligible: so small or unimportant or of so little consequence as to warrant little or no attention
[51] Ostensibly: represented or appearing as such; plausible rather than demonstrably true
[52] Autonomous: existing or capable of existing independently
[53] Inefficacious: lacking the power to produce the desired effect
[54] Premise: a preposition upon which an argument is based or from which a conclusion is drawn

through the gate if it was opened. But that didn't appear to be the case. Alexa barely resisted her impetus[55] to call the whole thing off. It was taking so much longer than they anticipated.

Finally, their persistence paid off. Coco moved closer to the gate as the others lagged behind. Alexa prepared to lower the gate as she saw Coco go through. José lavishly extolled[56] the approaching dolphin while Alexa cranked the gate shut as fast as she could.

"Good job!" Alexa congratulated him for successfully resolving their quandary.[57] The hard part was over. Now all they needed to do was to open the outer gate and watch Coco swim out of the enclosure[58] and into the open ocean.

"I'm going to swim under the wall," José pointed to the barrier that separated them from the outdoor portion of the pool. "Why don't you go through the door and meet me on the other side."

Alexa walked through the doorway leading to the outside. From this vantage point, she couldn't help but notice that it was a spectacular evening. The night sky was clear and illuminated with an abundance of stars. A large crescent moon reflected dreamily on the gentle swells of the ocean.

José and Coco swam right under the wall and José hopped out of the pool. Holding Alexa's hand, they walked down the length of the pool to the outer gate. This was the moment they had been waiting for. José cranked the gate open and kept hold of Alexa's hand so they could experience this extraordinary moment together.

---

[55] Impetus: a driving force; impulse
[56] Extolled: praised highly; glorified
[57] Quandary: a state of perplexity or doubt
[58] Enclosure: something that encloses (to close in)

Coco, however, failed to realize her role in the profound proceedings. She hovered next to the wall, immobile, as if she was pinioned[59] to the spot. Her reluctance to move was a substantial hindrance[60] to the execution[61] of their plan. Alexa was again surprised at this peculiar phenomenon.[62] She had assumed the dolphin would eagerly swim out to the open ocean. Perhaps it had been presumptuous[63] of them to assume they knew what the dolphin wanted, Alexa thought.

"Maybe she doesn't want to go," Alexa said.

"Of course she wants to go." José had no such episodes of self-doubt regarding their venture.[64] "It's just that the dolphins don't like to go through these gates," José countered, debunking[65] her theory. "I think that I have to get in again and coax her out." José hopped into the water without hesitation.

With José in the water, Coco must have felt more reassured. José led her to the gate area and recommenced[66] his tactics. He positioned himself just outside of the gate and beckoned softly. This time the young dolphin followed him readily. José looked up at Alexa and signaled for her to close the gate behind them.

Alexa cranked the gate shut as she watched Coco intently. José climbed out of the water and took her hand in his as they watched Coco. It took the young dolphin a minute to regain her bearings in the open ocean—she was immobile for a protracted moment. But all of a sudden, she realized where she was and swam away into the darkness.

---

[59] Pinioned: to disable or restrain; to bind fast

[60] Hindrance: the state of being hindered (to make slow or difficult the progress of)

[61] Execution: the act or process of executing (to carry out fully, put completely into effect)

[62] Phenomenon: an unusual, significant, or unaccountable fact or occurrence

[63] Presumptuous: overstepping due bounds (as of propriety or courtesy), taking liberties

[64] Venture: an undertaking involving chance, risk, or danger

[65] Debunk: to expose the sham or falseness of

[66] Recommenced: to start again

Alexa felt euphoric[67] at the sight of this momentous[68] event. A tear ran down her face. They had just witnessed a profound moment in time. José turned to her and tenderly wiped the tear from her cheek and spoke softly to her in Spanish. She didn't comprehend what he was saying, but it didn't matter. He held her close and Alexa closed her eyes as his lips touched hers. She didn't even notice that he was soaking wet from his swim.

[67] Euphoric: a feeling of well-being or elation
[68] Momentous: important, consequential

15

Friendship– An Eternal Verity

When the alarm rang, Alexa awoke with a start, feeling immensely disoriented, like she was swimming through a dense fog. It was 6:00 A.M. She had barely gotten an hour of sleep. She had returned to the apartment by 4 A.M., replaced the card key in her mother's wallet, and hopped into bed. It had been impossible to sleep after so much excitement, so she'd gotten up and written another e-mail to Laurie to tell her about their successful mission, replete[1] with details. It had all worked so smoothly, thanks to José's craftiness[2] and his indomitable determination. Alexa had to admit her earlier fears about pulling off this wily[3] stunt had been unfounded.[4]

Unfortunately, now it was time to go running with Charlotte. Alexa wished she had had the foresight to cancel this morning's run. But now Charlotte would be waiting for her, so Alexa dragged her body out of bed and dressed for running.

---

[1] Replete: fully or abundantly provided or filled
[2] Craftiness: skillfulness, cleverness
[3] Wily: full of wiles (a trick or a stratagem intended to ensnare or deceive); crafty
[4] Unfounded: lacking a sound basis; groundless, unsupported

Charlotte was bubbling with excitement when Alexa trotted up to the steps of the cafeteria building.

"You're not going to believe what happened! This place is buzzing with activity!" Charlotte exclaimed.

"What's going on?" Alexa asked. She could feel her stomach react as she began to get more nervous. They started running toward the gate.

"Well, one of the dolphins is missing. Apparently the trainer just noticed it this morning and subsequently,[5] there's been chaos It's really unprecedented[6] here—you know how they are about security. Everybody is running around trying to figure out what happened."

"How do you know about all of this?" Alexa asked.

"Because my stepfather got a call at 5:30 in the morning."

"Do they know what happened to the dolphin? Do they know who did it?" Alexa asked, trying to hide the nervousness in her voice.

"No, not yet. Right now, everybody is busy blaming each other—they're looking for a scapegoat.[7]

Alexa was silent as they ran through the town and approached the beach. But it was hard to keep the dramatic events of the previous night to herself. "Charlotte, can I tell you a secret?" Alexa asked, breathless with exertion.

"Sure," Charlotte replied.

"Would you promise to keep it secret under all circumstances? I really need you to refrain from telling anybody."

"Yes, of course. What is it?" Charlotte's curiosity was piqued after Alexa entreated[8] her so ardently for secrecy.

---

[5] Subsequently: following in time, order, or place

[6] Unprecedented: having no precedent (previous example); novel

[7] Scapegoat: one who bears the blame for others

[8] Entreat: to plead with, especially in order to persuade

"I did it," Alexa confessed. "José and I freed the dolphin last night."

"You did *what?*" Charlotte said incredulously. "That's crazy! Why did you do that?" Charlotte stopped running and faced Alexa. They had arrived at the beach. "José talked you into this, didn't he? He probably had some crazy pretext[9] to justify his actions...but why would *you* want to get involved? Why would you fall for that?"

"I didn't fall for anything! I did what needed to be done! The dolphin was so young—just 12 months old—and her mother lives right out here in the bay." Alexa gestured toward the water. "José has known her for years—her name is Pecas—she is so friendly! If only you could get to know her too, you would understand." Alexa spoke rapidly in her heightened state of emotion. She desperately wanted Charlotte's support and approval. "We proved that it was Pecas' baby—we analyzed their DNA!" Alexa buttressed[10] her argument with her trump[11] card. Alexa looked at Charlotte, gauging[12] her reaction. She could see from the look on her face that Charlotte thought that what they'd done was deplorable.[13]

"I know you and José don't approve of the dolphins being used by the Navy, but have you ever stopped to think about what the alternative is? All of the tasks that dolphins can do so easily are incredibly difficult and risky for people to do. I'm just being practical about it. I think we need to be more protective of the *people* who serve in the military!"

"But Charlotte, if you spent some time with these dolphins, you would see...they are like people! They have feelings and emotions and so much intelligence! Setting a baby dolphin free is not the impious[14] act you make it out to be! It was the right thing to do!"

---

9   Pretext: a purpose or motive alleged or an appearance assumed in order to cloak the real intention or state of affairs

10   Buttress: something that supports or strengthens

11   Trump: a card of a suit any of whose cards will win over a card that is not of this suit

12   Gauge: estimate, judge

13   Deplorable: deserving censure or contempt

14   Impious: not pious, lacking in reverence or proper respect (as for God or one's parents)

"Alexa, I don't want to fight." Charlotte's voice softened. "I don't agree with your point of view, that's all. I'm still your friend—and I'll always be your friend. So don't worry, I'll keep your secret and I'm going to help you get out of this mess. I'll do my best to help you—you're going to need salvation[15] from the firestorm that's sure to ensue[16] when they figure out that you did this. You're going to need all the help you can get!"

"Why do you say that? Maybe no one will find out," Alexa replied.

"Alexa, they are going to figure out who did it. It's just a matter of time. Did you use a card key? If you used a card key to get in, they can easily look at the records to see who entered the building and at what time. Whenever you use a card key, there's an electronic record of it." Charlotte looked at her friend with sympathy.

"Oh no..." Alexa's heart sank as she absorbed the implication[17] of Charlotte's words. She chided herself for being so imperceptive. Last night, when they were carrying out their plan, she had felt so grown-up and in control. But now she felt like a callow[18] young girl who had been caught doing something naughty.

"I'll do everything I can to help you, Alexa," Charlotte said sincerely. "I can talk to my father—he wields[19] a lot of influence with the management here. Maybe we can convince them not to go to the police."

"Thank you. Thank you for being such a good friend." Alexa was fighting back the tears. She was terrified at the thought of the maelstrom[20] that would face her when she returned to Puerto Marino. Inevitably, there would be grave charges levied[21] against her and José. At

---

[15] Salvation: deliverance from danger or difficulty
[16] Ensue: to take place afterward or as a result
[17] Implication: the act of implying, the state of being implied (indicate by inference, association, or necessary consequence rather than by direct statement)
[18] Callow: lacking adult maturity or experience
[19] Wields: to exert one's authority
[20] Maelstrom: a powerful, often violent whirlpool sucking in objects within a given radius
[21] Levy: to impose or collect by legal authority

the same time, she was deeply touched by Charlotte's loyalty and integrity. Charlotte's actions revealed so clearly her honorable priorities—she regarded friendship as an eternal[22] verity.[23]

Alexa looked out at the ocean and pondered[24] her fate. There were going to be some serious repercussions[25] of her actions, and she didn't relish the thought of returning to face the music. As she stared at the ocean pensively,[26] she saw a dolphin jumping in the distance.

"Charlotte, let's go out on the point! Will you come with me? I see a dolphin and I want to see if it's Pecas!" Alexa pleaded.

"OK, let's go," Charlotte readily agreed. She looked as if she would do anything to help Alexa at this moment, she was so consumed with sympathy for her friend. The girls scurried over the rocks to reach the end of the outcrop.

Alexa strained her eyes to see. It looked like two dolphins—one big and one small. Alexa couldn't contain her excitement. Could it be Pecas and her baby, Coco?

"I'm going in the water!" Alexa called back to Charlotte, who lagged behind a few paces. Reaching the end of the outcrop, Alexa hurriedly pulled her sneakers off and jumped in the water. The dolphins continued to swim closer. Alexa could barely contain her excitement.

"It *is* Pecas! And Coco—her baby!" Alexa yelled to Charlotte. "This is the young dolphin we set free and this is her mother, Pecas." Alexa explained to Charlotte, who stood on the rocks with a look of amazement. "You see—they wanted to be together! We could tell, José and I."

---

[22] Eternal: having infinite duration; everlasting
[23] Verity: the quality or state of being true or real, especially a fundamental and inevitably true value
[24] Ponder: to think or consider, especially quietly, soberly, and deeply
[25] Repercussion: a widespread, indirect, or unforeseen effect of an act, action, or event
[26] Pensive: musingly or dreamily thoughtful

As soon as Alexa said his name, she realized that she missed him dearly at this moment. She wished he was here right now to see this—the gratifying result of their endeavor. Pecas and Coco swam closer and Alexa held her arm out to stroke Pecas as she swam by.

"I think I can see why you did it," Charlotte said, as she watched the mother and daughter dolphin swim together. Coco swam on Pecas' right side, just slightly behind her. The two dolphins moved in synchronous[27] harmony as if they were one. Whenever Pecas would dive or surface, Coco would perform the same action in a concomitant[28] fashion. "They really are special animals."

"*Very* special!" Alexa emphasized. She was so elated to see Pecas and her baby together—and free. At least there was one undeniably positive manifestation[29] of their scheme, Alexa thought. It made it much easier to face the inevitable repercussions that she would soon be subjected to.

The two dolphins were in a frolicsome[30] mood as they swam around Alexa playfully. This was the first time Alexa swam alone with the dolphins. Previously, she was always swimming with José. Alexa scanned the horizon, looking for José's fishing boat. It was nowhere in sight. She couldn't help but think about him. She knew that he would love this.

Pecas swam close, allowing Alexa to stroke her as she swam by. Coco mirrored her mother's every move. Pecas surfaced to look directly in Alexa's eyes and then dove under the surface in a way that was so familiar to Alexa. She was diving to retrieve an object, a piece of seaweed or sponge, to play with. Resurfacing, she tossed the object with the tip of her

---

[27] Synchronous: happening, existing, or arising at precisely the same time

[28] Concomitant: occurring or existing at the same time

[29] Manifestation: the act, process, or instance of manifesting (readily perceived by the senses, especially by sight)

[30] Frolicsome: full of gaiety; playful

nose over to Alexa. The shiny object landed in the water right in front of Alexa with a plop, and it sunk to the white, sandy ocean floor at her feet.

Curiously, she looked down through the crystal-clear water at the object below. Alexa went underwater to pick it up and resurfaced with a look of profound amazement. She opened her hand and the sunshine reflected brightly off of the object in her palm. It was Charlotte's bracelet.

16

A Preponderance of Evidence

Alexa returned to the apartment glowing with satisfaction. Pecas had been reunited with Coco, and Charlotte had her beloved bracelet back around her wrist. Alexa felt righteous and invulnerable. She was ready to face the inevitable.

And then she saw her mother's face. Helen was sitting in the kitchenette waiting for Alexa's return. The creases etched on her forehead revealed her strain. She looked puzzled and concerned.

Alexa couldn't bear to meet her gaze. She looked down at the floor.

"Alexa, I got a phone call from Mr. Janowitz—the person who runs the whole operation here. We're supposed to go down to the security building immediately, although I don't know why he would want to talk to us. It sounded urgent. Why are you all wet?"

"I hopped in the water to cool off while Charlotte and I were out for our run," Alexa said softly. The damp, synthetic[1] material of her running outfit felt clammy against her skin.

---

[1] Synthetic: something resulting from synthesis rather than occurring naturally, especially a product (as a drug or plastic) of chemical synthesis

The two of them headed out the door for the short walk to the security building. Alexa thought about explaining everything to her mother, but it seemed like such a daunting task. Before she could even fathom how to begin explaining the whole story, they arrived at their destination.

Alexa felt butterflies in the pit in her stomach as she entered the room. Inside, Mr. Janowitz, Dr. Villeponce, Colonel Brandt, and Myles, the chief security officer, were all sitting around the conference table, waiting for their arrival.

"Please, sit down, Helen and Alexa," Janowitz offered in an overly polite voice. He gestured to the two empty chairs at the conference table.

"Thank you," Helen replied. It took her only a few seconds to assess the grave faces of the men gathered around the table. "I'm anxious to hear why you've asked us here today. Is there some sort of problem?"

"Unfortunately, yes," Janowitz began. "At 5:30 this morning, the dolphin trainers noticed there was one dolphin missing from the facility—dolphin number 36—I think her nickname is Coco."

"Coco is missing? Where did she go?" Helen asked, obviously puzzled.

"We've just figured out where she went. This morning at 3:04, your card key was used to gain access to the dolphin facility."

"But I haven't been in the facility since 6:30 last night when I finished work," Helen said with a puzzled and concerned look on her face.

"We know that," Janowitz replied. "Myles, could you play the tape?"

Myles obediently jumped out of his chair to retrieve the television monitor, which was mounted on a cart with wheels. He positioned the cart at the end of the table and then popped a videotape into the VCR.

"This is a tape from our security cameras," Janowitz said with aplomb.[2] A grainy black-and-white image appeared on the screen.

He might just as well have dropped a bomb in the room for the effect it had on Alexa. Security cameras! Why hadn't she thought of that?

All eyes were on the screen as the image showed Alexa and José in the hallway. It then showed Alexa swiping the card key through the scanner. The room was silent as everybody watched the video intently. The tape was patchy in places, like it was spliced together from different cameras, but the content was unmistakable. The screen now showed an image of Alexa cranking the gate open while José coaxed the dolphin over the threshold and into the outer pool.

The video jumped to an outdoor shot where remarkably, the image quality was much sharper. Everyone in the room watched closely as the screen showed an image of Alexa and José walking hand in hand down the length of the pool. Alexa could feel her face turning crimson with embarrassment. Especially since she knew what was coming next.

The camera angle didn't allow them to see Coco, but the image of José cranking open the gate was clear as a bell. José disappeared from the screen momentarily (Alexa recalled that he had to jump in the water to help Coco get through the last gate) and then he was back and holding Alexa's hand. And then they were kissing. Myles jumped out of his chair and flicked the television off.

Alexa was absolutely mortified.[3] It was bad enough to be censured[4] in front of this roomful of people, but to have her private moment with José aired on the screen for all to view—it was absolutely humiliating. Couldn't they have cut that part out? Perhaps they were trying to

---

[2] Aplomb: complete and confident composure or self-assurance
[3] Mortified: subjected to severe and vexing embarrassment
[4] Censured: to find fault with and criticize as blameworthy

demean[5] her as part of her punishment, Alexa thought. She could feel her cheeks burning.

The room was silent for a moment. There was no question of how the dolphin escaped. The condemning videotape made the situation quite clear. The only question now was, what were they going to do about it? Would they call the police? Alexa looked at the people around the table. Charlotte hadn't had the opportunity to talk to her stepfather yet. It didn't look like there was anyone sympathetic in the room. Alexa looked over at Dr. Villeponce, but he looked down at the table, avoiding eye contact.

"Who is that boy in the video?" Helen asked.

Before Alexa had a chance to answer and begin to tell her side of the story, Myles spoke up. "His name is José Consuales. He's a local who works here in the kitchen. We already reported him to the local authorities and they took him into custody at 6:00 this morning," Myles reported dutifully. "With this preponderance[6] of evidence, I don't think there's any doubt that he'll be convicted of this crime."

"You did what?" Janowitz yelled at Myles. He was livid with anger. "I thought you were under strict instructions to keep all security breaches[7] *internal* unless I say otherwise! We have a strict code of confidentiality here! I can't believe you did that! What were you thinking?"

"This is a disaster!" Colonel Brandt concurred, shaking his head at Janowitz like a disappointed parent would look at a misbehaving child. "You know our contracts have a strict confidentiality clause. If there is a breach, you can forget about renewal."

---

[5] Demean: to lower in character, status, or reputation
[6] Preponderance: a superiority in weight, power, importance, or strength
[7] Breach: infraction or violation of a law, obligation, tie, or standard

"I can go down to the police station and drop the charges. I can tell them it was a big mistake...a misunderstanding," Myles offered meekly.

"Yes! Do it right now. And you had better make it quick, because if the local media gets hold of this..." Janowitz rolled his eyes, looking exasperated.

"I'll run down there right now. It will only take a minute! I'll be right back," Myles replied. He rushed out of the room.

"We'll take care of this. I don't think there's any cause for concern," Janowitz reassured Colonel Brandt.

The Colonel shrugged in response. He was not reassured yet.

"And now for you, young lady. May I ask why? Why did you do this? Did your boyfriend talk you into it?" Janowitz asked pointedly.

"No," Alexa's voice wavered with emotion, but she was determined to fight back the tears. She didn't want to invoke[8] sympathy when she explained the justification for her actions. "I participated based on my own decision." Alexa took a deep breath. "The dolphin that you call Coco, number 36, is only 12 months old. She is the baby of one of the dolphins in the bay that José had known for years. Coco must have been captured here, in this bay, without a permit. Nobody has permission to catch wild dolphins here and put them into captivity. And then sell them. It's illegal according to the local laws," Alexa added, gaining confidence as she spoke. "We merely returned the young dolphin to its rightful home."

"You can't possibly prove that this dolphin was caught around here," Janowitz challenged her.

---

[8]　Invoke: to resort to; use or apply

"Yes, I can," Alexa spoke assuredly now. "We proved by DNA analysis that Coco is the progeny of the dolphin that has lived in this bay for her whole life. The test was 99.999% conclusive. The mother's name is Pecas, and all of the local fishermen know her. Everybody saw Pecas with a baby earlier this year. Then the baby disappeared a month ago, and now her baby is back with her swimming by her side. I saw them this morning out in the bay."

All of the men in the room exchanged looks.

"Look, Janowitz," Colonel Brandt looked at Al like a disappointed parent, "my position is clear. If you guys can't run a clean—I mean immaculate—operation, we will have to sever our relationship with you. Everything has to be squeaky clean—and this doesn't sound good. I was under the impression this whole operation was in accordance with the local laws."

Janowitz tried to maintain his composure in the face of this calamity, but he looked like his world had just come crashing down on his shoulders. His cost-cutting measure was coming back to bite him. The only place where he had a permit that allowed him to capture dolphins was off of the coast of Florida. But it was very expensive to send a team to Florida and then to charter a plane to transport the dolphins back to Central America. He figured nobody would ever know if he occasionally took a dolphin from the local waters. And it certainly increased his profit margin. That was the reason why he convinced the management at the Marino Enterprise (the parent company) to set up Puerto Marino in such a remote location. Even if the local authorities managed to find out he had been taking dolphins from local waters, he thought he could probably handle that situation with a well-placed bribe or two—as long as it was handled secretly. But this situation was getting out of control.

"Helen, why don't you and Alexa step outside for a moment," Janowitz said. We have a few things to discuss here privately. Would you mind waiting in the outer room? We'll call you back in a few moments." Janowitz stood up and opened the door for them. He ushered them out and closed the door behind them.

Alexa and Helen sat on the couch, and Alexa felt the tears start to run down her face. The stress of the past 24 hours had caught up with her. The emotional highs and lows had been precipitous and had taken their toll. She was also extremely worried about José. All of these things, combined with sleep deprivation, had left Alexa in a fragile emotional state. Now she needed to face her mother.

"Mom, I'm sorry I took your card key," Alexa broke down, sobbing. Helen put her arms around her and comforted her.

"Alexa, I wish you had come to me with all of this. There are other ways this problem could have been resolved. I would have helped you. Believe me, I can identify with the concerns that you've raised. But I don't approve of the way you and your friend handled it. I don't agree with taking the law into your own hands."

Alexa nodded. She was too upset to talk coherently. She felt terrible for hurting her mother's feelings and betraying her trust. She rested her head on her mother's shoulder. They sat quietly for a few minutes.

Janowitz popped his head out of the conference room door. "Why don't the two of you come in now." He opened the door and ushered them in. Alexa stood up and courageously walked in to face the inevitable castigation.[9]

---

[9] Castigation: to subject to severe punishment, reproof, or criticism

"I think we have a resolution that will be satisfactory to everyone," Janowitz began. "We would like to keep this incident quiet. We are willing to drop any charges against Alexa, but we would like to have your agreement to confidentiality. As long as this whole incident is kept under wraps, we are willing to absolve Alexa of any charges."

"What about José?" Alexa asked, her voice wavering.

"And may I also ask about my ongoing work here?" Helen asked pointedly. Alexa could see that her mother had little respect for Janowitz and his proposed covenant[10] of silence. Dr. Villeponce, who looked extremely uncomfortable throughout the proceedings, remained silent. It seemed rather self-serving, Alexa thought, the way he preserved his neutrality.[11]

"Helen, I think you would agree that perhaps, given the circumstances, we mutually agree to immediately suspend your consulting contract?" Janowitz raised his eyebrows in a symbolic question mark as he met Helen's direct gaze. "Here at Puerto Marino, we abide by the precepts[12] of honesty and integrity," he added pedantically.[13]

"I see," Helen replied coolly, her eyes narrowing with the anger that was bubbling inside. She didn't appreciate sermonizing[14] in general, and when the source was a hypocrite[15] such as Janowitz—it was too much for her to tolerate. His sanctimonious[16] preaching of ethics was not going to go unchallenged. "And thank you for the lesson in morality—coming from someone who is so eminently[17] qualified to adjudicate,[18] we can all learn from the example you've set," Helen said sarcastically. She was not

---

[10] Covenant: a usually formal, solemn, and binding agreement

[11] Neutrality: the quality or state of being neutral, especially refusal to take part in a war between other powers

[12] Precept: a command or principle intended as a general rule of action

[13] Pedantic: a style of teaching characterized by formality and undue attention to minutiae

[14] Sermonize: to preach to or on at length

[15] Hypocrite: a person who puts on a false appearance of virtue or religion

[16] Sanctimonious: affecting piousness, hypocritically devout

[17] Eminently: to a high degree; very

[18] Adjudicate: to act as judge

the type of person to hurl insults in slang or colloquial[19] expressions. Rather, she preferred veiling[20] her insults in sophisticated language and circumlocutions[21] that were peppered with sarcasm.

Alexa was relieved to see that her mother was on her side and was so supportive. But her mother's staunch devotion only made Alexa feel worse about the ramifications[22] of her own behavior. Now her mother was out of a job, undoubtedly without a good reference from Puerto Marino. And what about José? Alexa felt sick when she thought about the consequences for her friend. If he lost his job, would he ever be able to save enough money to go to college? And what kind of retribution[23] would he face for their actions?

Suddenly, Myles came bursting through the door, gasping for breath. He looked as if he had run all of the way back from the police station in town.

"What's going on, Myles? Did you drop the charges?" Janowitz demanded while Myles struggled to regain his composure. Janowitz was growing increasingly cantankerous.[24]

"I couldn't get into the police station!" Myles said breathlessly. "It was a madhouse of the media there. There were CNN people all over the place! And there's a CNN truck out at the security gate. They are trying to come in to get a statement from you."

"*What?*" Janowitz bellowed. "What's going on?" He was absolutely livid.

---

[19] Colloquial: characteristic of familiar and informal conversation
[20] Veil: to cover, provide, obscure, or conceal with or as if with a veil
[21] Circumlocutions: the use of an unnecessarily large number of words to express an idea
[22] Ramification: consequence, outcome
[23] Retribution: something given or exacted in recompense, especially punishment
[24] Cantankerous: difficult or irritating to deal with

"I think they're doing a story on the dolphin being set free. They said they already got a statement from the boy and from the local police. They've got people talking to the locals..." Myles dutifully delivered the update without skirting[25] the contentious[26] issue, but he looked as reticent as a lamb being sent for a rendezvous with a pack of carnivores.[27]

"This is a disaster!" Janowitz fumed. "How could you have been so stupid!" he yelled with a ferocity[28] that was unparalleled.

"We'd better see what's going on," Colonel Brandt said calmly. He embodied[29] the image of calm under dire circumstances. He rose from his chair, turned on the television, and flipped through the channels to find CNN.

They had a moment to wait while Colonel Brandt found the station, and Alexa was consumed with thought. CNN? Could Laurie have anything to do with this? Alexa had told Laurie via e-mail about the DNA tests and freeing the dolphin. Could her friend be behind this media frenzy?

On the television screen, a well-dressed anchorwoman was reporting on location in front of the ocean. A gentle breeze ruffled her perfectly coiffed hair as she spoke, and her high heels looked incredibly awkward on the rocky terrain. Alexa realized with a start that this was being filmed from the rocky outcrop right here, on the same beach where she went every day!

"This story has all of the heart, all of the compassion of a contemporary *Free Willy* saga. At its heart it is about this dolphin mother and

---

[25] Skirt: to avoid, especially because of difficulty or fear of controversy
[26] Contentious: likely to cause contention (controversy or debate); controversial
[27] Carnivores: any of an order (Carnivora) of typically flesh-eating mammals that includes dogs, foxes, bears, raccoons, and cats
[28] Ferocity: the quality or state of being ferocious (exhibiting or given to extreme fierceness and unrestrained violence and brutality)
[29] Embody: to represent in human or animal form; personify

her baby," the reporter gushed, as if she were an entertainment reporter talking about a movie. The image on the screen switched to a shot of Pecas and Coco, swimming happily next to the boat where the camera was positioned. Her voice turned serious as she continued. "But also at the core of this story is the saga of the dolphins that are captured, trained, and sold into service. Sometimes their lives are filled with frivolity." The image switched to a scene of a dolphin playing with a ball at Marineland. "But for some of these dolphins, their lives are consumed with more serious and dangerous pursuits." The screen shifted to battle scenes from the Vietnam era and then shifted to black-and-white footage of dolphins cavorting.[30]

"Here on a remote island off the east coast of Central America, a private company has set up a dolphin training facility. It is widely purported, although not officially confirmed, that the Navy obtains some of its dolphins from this facility." The screen showed an image of Puerto Marino taken from a vantage point in the bay. "Suffice it to say that the dolphins here are destined to a life in captivity, be it in the military or in one of the numerous dolphin show ventures that can be found in seaside resort communities worldwide. Unless a maverick[31] dissident[32] changes their fate," the reporter intoned dramatically, leading into the next shot, which was José!

Alexa's heart was racing as she saw José's face on the television screen. He looked so composed and intelligent. He calmly stated his position with such an understated eloquence. "My family has lived here and fished in

---

[30] Cavorting: prancing
[31] Maverick: an independent individual who does not go along with a group or party
[32] Dissident: disagreeing with an opinion or group

these waters for generations. If you spend any amount of time here, you will see that the people in this area have a very special relationship with the dolphins that live in this bay. We respect each other and live in harmony. It came to my attention that one of the young dolphins—the daughter of a dolphin that lives right here—was unlawfully captured and held in captivity at Puerto Marino." José took a deep breath and looked squarely into the lens of the camera. He was not squirming or fidgeting under the immense pressure, but faced the issue directly and continued his speech in a self-assured tone. He was a natural orator,[33] Alexa thought.

"Nobody has the right, either legal or ethical, to take a dolphin from these waters. It broke my heart to see this travesty[34] of justice and freedom. I did what any other compassionate person would do." José paused for dramatic effect, like a master elocutionist.[35] "I set the young dolphin free."

A spontaneous cheer arose from the boisterous[36] crowd that was undeniably in support of José and the inspiring ethos[37] he evoked with his words. The camera briefly panned the throng[38] of people and then cut back to the reporter, who explained that José was being held by the local authorities. He was charged with multiple crimes and would face prison time if convicted. Finally, the news piece ended.

Alexa was bursting with emotions. Watching the broadcast was a surreal[39] experience. It was hard to believe that last night she and José had freed a dolphin, and today it was turning into a sensationalized[40] story on international television.

---

[33] Orator: one distinguished for skill and power as a public speaker

[34] Travesty: a debased, distorted, or grossly inferior imitation

[35] Elocutionist: one who is effective in the art of public speaking

[36] Boisterous: noisily turbulent; rowdy

[37] Ethos: the distinguishing character, sentiment, moral nature, or guiding beliefs of a person, group, or institution

[38] Throng: a multitude of assembled persons

[39] Surreal: having the intense irrational reality of a dream

[40] Sensationalize: to present in a manner intended to arouse strong interest, especially by the inclusion of exaggerated or lurid details

Alexa was so proud of José and his ability to stand tall and proud in a situation of great adversity.[41] The way he explained what had taken place, with a combination of emotion and logic, was so compelling that it had a resounding[42] effect. He didn't overtly[43] proselytize,[44] he simply made felicitous[45] comments that argued his position effectively. Taken together with the reporter's provocative editorial,[46] it was almost as if the entire piece was formulated to draw out the emotions of the audience. Just watching it made them want to help those beautiful ocean creatures and the poor young man who had intervened[47] to make the world a better place. It made others feel like it was a grave injustice to imprison this young man who was able to engender[48] such a feeling of idealism with his poignant[49] speech.

Janowitz was fuming at the sight of the images on the television screen. He was living his worst nightmare. Not only was the illegal procurement of Coco exposed, their entire business was shown in a negative light on international television. He preferred to run a quiet operation away from any sort of public exposure. There were so many people who objected to the buying and selling of dolphins as commodities, not to mention all the animal rights groups that didn't like to see any animals in

---

[41] Adversity: a state or condition contrary to one of well-being
[42] Resounding: emphatic, unequivocal
[43] Overtly: in a manner that is open to view
[44] Proselytize: to recruit someone to join one's party, institution, or cause
[45] Felicitous: very well-suited or expressed; apt
[46] Editorial: a newspaper or magazine article that gives the opinions of the editors or publishers; also an expression of opinion that resembles such an article
[47] Intervene: to come in or between by way of hindrance or modification
[48] Engender: to cause to exist or develop
[49] Poignant: deeply affecting; touching

captivity. These factions[50] could cause him grave problems if they organized protests and disseminated[51] negative information. He knew that if he had a tarnished image, the public outcry might cause his government contracts to dry up. Janowitz had purposely picked an extremely remote place to build his business, far away from the prying eyes of the dissenters and the media. Or so he'd thought.

"Myles, did you drop the charges against this young man?" Janowitz fumed, barely able to maintain his composure.

"I tried, but I couldn't get into the police station—it's a madhouse," he replied meekly.

"Then call!" Janowitz yelled.

"I tried...but all of the lines were busy," Myles tried to say something else, but he was gibbering[52] unintelligibly, obviously flustered under the pressure.

"Then send a fax! Now!" Janowitz shouted, his scathing[53] voice filling the room with his fury. His truculent[54] nature was revealing itself. Myles scurried out of the room, and Janowitz turned his attention back to Helen.

"You have my resignation," Helen said coolly. "I'll have a formal letter of resignation on your desk within the hour. And we will leave as soon as I can make the travel arrangements."

"I think that would be best for everyone," Janowitz replied in a much calmer tone. "I will see to it that we arrange for fair and equitable remuneration[55] for you for the time and effort you have put into your work here. In turn, may I ask that you refrain from speaking with the media?"

---

[50] Faction: a party or group (as within a government) that is often contentious or self-seeking
[51] Disseminate: to disperse throughout
[52] Gibbering: to speak rapidly, inarticulately, and often foolishly
[53] Scathing: to assail with withering denunciation
[54] Truculent: feeling or displaying ferocity; cruel, savage
[55] Remuneration: an act or fact of remunerating (to pay an equivalent to someone for a service, loss, or expense); recompense

"We have no intention of speaking to the media," Helen replied in a glacial[56] tone.

"Thank you. I appreciate your cooperation in this area." Janowitz looked relieved. Helen's assurance that she would refrain from talking to the media was like a tonic[57] for Al. He was regaining his composure. "I hope you understand that, given the circumstances, I will need to confiscate[58] your card keys."

Alexa and her mother retrieved their card keys from their respective pockets and laid them on the table. As she surrendered her card key, Alexa realized that now that her freedom to enter the laboratory had been revoked,[59] she couldn't retrieve the DNA evidence that proved Coco was Pecas' baby. Undoubtedly, it would be destroyed by the management here at Puerto Marino.

"If we're all done here, I would like to leave and prepare our travel arrangements," Helen said.

Janowitz nodded in response. Helen and Alexa walked out of the room and a feeling of relief washed over Alexa. This traumatic episode was finally over.

---

[56] Glacial: devoid of warmth and cordiality
[57] Tonic: one that invigorates, restores, refreshes, or stimulates
[58] Confiscate: to seize by or as if by authority
[59] Revoke: to annul by recalling or taking back; rescind

17

A Nebulous Future

When they walked into the apartment, Helen immediately got on the telephone to reschedule their flight home. Alexa plopped down on the couch. It was a huge relief to have the proceedings over, but she was so sad at the thought of leaving this place. Of course she had always known that her stay there was impermanent,[1] but the decision to leave had been made so precipitously, and she didn't have any say in it. It wasn't her choice to come here in the first place, and now, ironically, it wasn't her choice to leave. Her life back home seemed so prosaic[2] in comparison. The thought of reintegrating[3] back into the same old routine at home made her realize that she didn't want to go home just yet.

"Alexa, your father is on the phone." Helen handed the phone to her. She looked weary from stress. "I'm going to take a shower now."

As soon as she heard her father's voice, she broke into tears. She tried to explain to him what had happened. He had already seen the news

---

[1] Impermanent: not permanent; transient
[2] Prosaic: dull, unimaginative
[3] Reintegrating: restoring to a condition of integration or unity

piece on CNN, but was unaware of her involvement. Her father listened calmly while Alexa told him the whole story.

"So that's why you wanted me to send you the papers on how to determine familial relationships through DNA analysis?" her father asked incredulously. "You tested the maternity of a dolphin?"

"Yes," Alexa meekly replied. She was wary of being reprimanded yet again, but on the other hand, she was tired of all the pretense.[4] It was a huge relief to confess this story that she had kept shrouded[5] in secrecy for so long.

"And you carried out the experiment on one dolphin from the wild and one dolphin in captivity?" he inquired, sounding surprised and actually quite proud.

"Yes, we had to get some cells from the dolphin in the wild. José did that part."

"Was that your friend José who I saw on CNN?" he asked.

"Yes, that's him." Alexa started crying as she thought about José and his future. "Dad," Alexa sobbed, "I feel terrible—I don't know what's going to happen to him. At the very least, he's lost his job. That job was the only way he could even conceive of making enough money to go to college. He wants to go to college in the United States—to Cornell, actually. He's so smart and he works so hard. It just doesn't seem fair!" Alexa cried.

"I know, honey." Her father spoke soothingly. "I don't want to lecture you right now about this, but you need to know that I agree with your mother—I don't approve of you taking the law into your own hands. You and your friend are really lucky that you're not headed for incarceration[6]

---

4   Pretense: false show
5   Shroud: something that covers, screens, or guards
6   Incarceration: time spent in prison

or litigation.[7] There are all sorts of grave consequences, as I think you're beginning to see. I'm really sorry to hear about your friend's predicament. It sounds like you really care about him."

"I do care about him...I just wish I'd thought more carefully about what we did and how it might affect his whole future," Alexa said as the tears streamed down her face.

"You really don't need to take that burden upon yourself. I sincerely doubt that you are the bane[8] of his future. People choose their own fates. Did you talk him into this scheme?"

"No," Alexa said, still crying.

"Then it was his own choice. Although I have to say, he did appear quite astute on CNN this morning. His ability to speak in public is quite precocious.[9] If his scholastic aptitude is anywhere near as great as his media acumen,[10] he may be eligible for some type of scholarship. I think some of the charitable[11] donations here at the University are earmarked[12] for foreign student scholarships."

"Really?" Alexa replied.

"Yes. I can look into it if you like. I'll call the financial aid office here and see what types of things he may be eligible for."

"That would be great!" Alexa said, brightening up considerably at the thought of being a benefactor[13] of José's future.

"Yes, but please don't get your hopes up too high—these scholarships are not indiscriminately philanthropic.[14] He would need to be an outstanding student as well. There's always a stringent selection process.

---

[7] Litigate: to contest in law
[8] Bane: a source of harm or ruin; curse
[9] Precocious: exhibiting mature qualities at an unusually early age
[10] Acumen: keenness and depth of perception, discernment, or discrimination, especially in practical matters; shrewdness
[11] Charitable: of or relating to charity (generosity and helpfulness, especially toward the needy)
[12] Earmark: to designate (as funds) for a specific use or owner
[13] Benefactor: one who confers a benefit, especially one who makes a gift or bequest
[14] Philanthropic: of, relating to, or characterized by philanthropy (active effort to promote human welfare)

Do you know if he took the SAT? That would almost certainly be a prerequisite."

"I don't know, but I can find out," Alexa replied.

"Check your e-mail later today—I'll send some information for your friend."

"Thanks, Dad!"

Alexa said goodbye to her father and immediately went to the computer to check her e-mail. She had a sinking feeling about the integrity of her friendship with Laurie. Could Laurie have been behind the story at CNN? Could she have told them everything Alexa had naively revealed to her in great detail?

Alexa opened up her e-mail and sure enough, there was a message waiting from Laurie.

Time: 10:47 A.M.
To: "Alexa"
From: "Laurie"
Subject: the big scoop

Dear Lexxie,

Did you see the story on CNN? It's so incredible, I can't believe it! When I told my boss about how you and José had freed that dolphin, he said that I had ingeniously[15] found a unique angle to position our story! All we needed was some independent confirmation. My boss called the police station in your town to see if anything was going on, and sure enough, they were holding José for setting that dolphin free. And then the story just took

---

[15] Ingenious: marked by originality, resourcefulness, and cleverness in conception or execution

off! And my future career took off with it! I am so excited. José did so well on camera—I can see why you like him. He is really cute! You have to write to me and tell me what's going on now!

Laurie

Alexa reread Laurie's e-mail, her revulsion[16] mounting with each sentence. Friendship is supposed to be synonymous[17] with trust. Didn't Laurie feel the same way? Why couldn't Laurie have honored her most personal revelations as confidential information? Alexa realized that she hadn't explicitly told Laurie her e-mails were secret. But couldn't she have assumed as much? Wasn't it obvious? It was absolutely ludicrous[18] for Laurie to use her secrets as fodder[19] for an international newscast. Alexa couldn't help but think it was patently[20] self-serving for Laurie to betray her this way. She thought for a moment about sending a scathing missive[21] in reply, but then thought better of it. She really needed to see Laurie in person to discuss this.

"Alexa," Helen walked into the room, "we have reservations to leave for home the day after tomorrow. Why don't we leave Puerto Marino now, and go do some sight-seeing before we head home? Or maybe we could go to one of the other islands and spend a day relaxing on the beach."

"Oh, Mom, couldn't we stay one more day? I want to say goodbye to Charlotte and José!" Alexa's heart was in her throat. Everything was happening so fast.

---

[16] Revulsion: a sense of utter distaste or repugnance
[17] Synonymous: having the same connotations, implications, or reference
[18] Ludicrous: amusing or laughable through obvious absurdity, incongruity, exaggeration, or eccentricity
[19] Fodder: inferior or readily available material used to supply a heavy demand
[20] Patently: readily visible or intelligible; obvious
[21] Missive: written communication; letter

"OK," Helen relented. "It does seem a bit abrupt to leave right now. I really need to talk to Dr. Villeponce before we go anyway. I need to try to salvage what I can from this research project."

"Why didn't he say anything at the meeting this morning?" Alexa asked. Under normal circumstances, Dr. Villeponce was always fawning over Helen like a sycophant.[22] But in the proceedings this morning, he never once spoke a word in support of Helen or Alexa.

"Oh, he was probably worried about his own job and his stature in the company. He's in the lofty position of running the dolphin facility and he doesn't want to be deposed.[23] Some people have the fortitude and integrity to stand up for their friends and others don't," Helen said cynically. In her experience, selfish behavior in the context of a friendship was not unprecedented. She was shrugging it off as if it was something she had seen before.

But Alexa couldn't help but dwell on the notion of spurious[24] friendships—relationships that appear to be true friendships, but when they are tested by some sort of external force, buckle under pressure. Was that really the nature of her friendship with Laurie? Alexa wondered. She felt deeply hurt by Laurie's actions. From her perspective, Laurie had been unduly[25] self-serving.

Alexa consciously decided not to think about Laurie right now. She didn't want to squander[26] the precious time she had left at Puerto Marino. While she had always known her stay there was transient,[27] it always seemed like her departure was far off in the nebulous[28] future. Now, it was imminent.

---

[22] Sycophant: a servile self-serving flatterer
[23] Deposed: to remove from a throne or other high position
[24] Spurious: outwardly similar or corresponding to something without having its genuine qualities; false
[25] Unduly: in an undue manner; excessively
[26] Squander: to spend extravagantly or foolishly
[27] Transient: passing through or by a place with only a brief stay or sojourn
[28] Nebulous: indistinct, vague

18

The Proverbial Invitation

The gentle morning sun reflected off the placid water of the bay. Alexa sat on the rocky outcrop as she had done so many mornings before. This time, however, was different. Today was her last day in this beautiful place, and the temperate[1] ocean breeze was suffused with a melancholy[2] aura.

Alexa knew that this was her last opportunity to see José. He didn't even know she was leaving. Yesterday, she had come to the beach hoping to see him, but he wasn't there. The fact that he didn't have a phone was utterly confounding.[3] They had no way of reaching each other. She knew that yesterday must have been a crazy day for him. There were the television cameras, the charges that had been pressed against him and then dropped, and the crowd of supporters to deal with.

---

[1] Temperate: marked by moderation, not extreme or excessive; mild
[2] Melancholy: depression of spirits; dejection
[3] Confounding: baffling, frustrating

Alexa hoped with all of her heart that he wanted to see her, too. If he wanted to see her, she knew he would come here this morning. This was their routine.

Her heart skipped a beat when she saw his boat on the horizon and the familiar wave as he navigated ever closer.

"*Hola!*" José yelled over the noise of the motor. "Let's go to Coconut Bay! The dolphins are there!" Having vanquished[4] the opponents and succeeded at their mission, he looked inestimably[5] content.

They had met like this dozens of times before. The proverbial[6] invitation to seek out the dolphins was the same as always. But Alexa knew this was not the canonical[7] rendezvous it appeared to be. It was their last rendezvous. She felt so encumbered[8] with this heart-rending[9] knowledge that she could barely respond to his invitation.

Even from a distance of 50 feet, José could tell something was wrong. In deference[10] to Alexa's melancholy, he refrained from acting like a jester.[11] Normally, he would perform some silly and humorous antics—something to make her laugh. He was a quintessential[12] comedian. But

---

[4] Vanquish: to defeat in a conflict or contest
[5] Inestimably: incapable of being estimated
[6] Proverbial: that has become a proverb or byword; commonly spoken of
[7] Canonical: conforming to a general rule or acceptable procedure; orthodox
[8] Encumbered: weighed down, burdened
[9] Heart-rending: heartbreaking
[10] Deference: in consideration of
[11] Jester: fool
[12] Quintessential: the most typical example or representative

today's encounter was not a prototype[13] of the many that had preceded it. José turned off the motor, dropped the anchor in the shallow water, and waded toward the outcrop.

"What's wrong?" he asked tenderly when he saw her tears. He put his arms around her. "Tell me, what happened? Was there lots of trouble for you because of what we did?"

"No, it's not that. José...we're leaving tomorrow!"

"Tomorrow! That is so soon!" José replied, stunned. This was an outcome he hadn't anticipated. They sat in silence for a moment, holding each other.

"Well, how am I going to free all the rest of the dolphins at Puerto Marino if my cohort[14] isn't here to help me?" he joked. For José, humor was the universal antidote.[15]

Alexa laughed at the notion of freeing the entire trove[16] of dolphins. Its implausibility[17] made it funny. Now that José was permanently banished[18] from Puerto Marino, it seemed quite dubious[19] he would be able to engineer such a grandiose[20] scheme.

"Well, if I can't be here in person to help you with the sequel, I'll be with you in spirit. And I can follow all of the pertinent[21] developments on CNN!" Alexa added with a wry smile. Now they both burst out laughing.

"Why don't we make the best of our day together? Let's go to Coconut Bay and swim with the dolphins," José urged convincingly.

"I'd like that," Alexa agreed. She took the outstretched hand he offered her and they waded out to the boat.

---

[13] Prototype: a standard or typical example
[14] Cohort: companion, colleague
[15] Antidote: something that relieves, prevents, or counteracts
[16] Trove: a valuable collection; treasure
[17] Implausible: not plausible; provoking disbelief
[18] Banish: to require by authority to leave
[19] Dubious: giving rise to uncertainty
[20] Grandiose: impressive because of uncommon largeness, scope, effect, or grandeur
[21] Pertinent: having a clear decisive relevance to the matter at hand

❦   ❦

The picturesque scenery of Coconut Bay struck Alexa profoundly when they pulled their boat ashore. Its beauty was so uplifting, but it was hard not to dwell on the fact that she might not see this special place again for a long time. Alexa knew she would always feel nostalgic[22] about this spectacular place and the time she spent here.

"I think Pecas and her baby are swimming right over there," José pointed. He took her hand to wade out into deeper water. "Did you see? They are together again! They found each other!" José's voice cracked with emotion.

"I know. I saw them yesterday. Isn't it beautiful?" Alexa remarked.

"It's the way it should be," José replied.

Pecas and Coco swam around them in circles, frolicking playfully. Alexa couldn't believe her good fortune. It seemed unimaginably poetic that on her last day, she would be able to swim together with José, Pecas, and Coco.

"José, what are you going to do now that you can't work at Puerto Marino anymore?" Alexa asked. "Will you be able to find another job to save money for college? You're not going to dive for lobsters, are you?"

"No, don't worry. I promised my father I wouldn't, and I will keep my promise. I don't know where I'll find another job, but I will. I know I won't be able to find something that paid as well as Puerto Marino." He looked serious and pensive for a moment. "It just means that it will take longer for me to get there—to college." He paused again, as if he were

---

[22] Nostalgic: a wistful or excessively sentimental, sometimes abnormal yearning for return to or of some past period or irrecoverable condition

choosing his words carefully. "But I have no regrets about what we did. Some things are worth the consequences, whatever they may be."

"My father e-mailed me some information on scholarships at Cornell. There are a few you would be qualified for," Alexa said hopefully.

"Really?" José replied, brightening up considerably. "There are scholarships for foreigners?"

"Yes," Alexa nodded. "If you want, maybe we could spend this afternoon at the library. If we can use the computer there, I can pull up his e-mail and we can start to fill out some of the applications."

"That sounds great!" José said. He looked so touched that she had looked into this for him. "Thank you so much. That's the nicest thing anyone has ever done for me...aside from my mother, of course!" José laughed.

"Oh, it was nothing, really," Alexa brushed off his compliment. "Oh—my dad said you would need to take the SAT to be considered for the scholarships."

"I already did."

"You did?" Alexa was a bit surprised. Evidently, José was quite serious about going to an American university. Although he scorned American soda, he lauded[23] American institutions of higher learning. He must have at least considered emigrating[24] to the United States for college if he took the SAT.

"How did you do?" Alexa asked hesitantly. She didn't want to put him on the spot, but it *was* pertinent to their discussion.

---

[23] Lauded: praise, extol
[24] Emigrate: to leave one's place of residence or country to live elsewhere

"I got a 1590," he answered simply, without a trace of self-aggrandizement.[25] He was not a braggart.[26] She had asked him, and he had merely complied with a straightforward answer.

"Oh my gosh! That's amazing! You'll have an excellent chance of getting a scholarship! How did you do it? I don't know anyone who scored that well! That's nearly perfect!" Alexa was astounded.

"Well, actually...I did score perfectly on the math section, but the verbal section was my nemesis. I think I missed one or two questions because of the vocabulary—it always boils down to whether or not you know the words!"

---

[25] Self-aggrandizement: to make oneself appear greater; to praise oneself
[26] Braggart: a loud, arrogant boaster

Vocabulary Exercises

Chapter 1

A Futile Request

1. hierarchy
2. incessantly
3. speculate
4. emulate
5. conventional
6. exacerbate
7. exclusive
8. pretentious
9. haughty
10. disdainful
11. miff
12. perpetuate
13. incline
14. contemporaries
15. incongruous
16. transformation
17. modest
18. demeanor
19. detached
20. venerate
21. rudiment
22. machination
23. emergent
24. interlude
25. embroil
26. unswerving
27. vocation
28. burgeoning
29. chasm
30. inept
31. lurid
32. indifferent
33. aesthetics
34. adept
35. abhor
36. mundane
37. archetypal
38. cloying
39. bereft
40. enduring

41. gregarious
42. camaraderie
43. endorsement
44. cherished
45. elation
46. ardor
47. imminent
48. persevere
49. brooding
50. cognizant
51. perception
52. cajole
53. clientele
54. esteem
55. reverence
56. preamble
57. gingerly
58. volubly
59. disparaging
60. invariably
61. rhetoric
62. discourse
63. ambivalent
64. tacit
65. flippancy
66. futile
67. resolute

1. The **mundane rhetoric** and passive **demeanor** of the mayoral candidate left the assembled crowd feeling _____ about his candidacy.
   A. **evoked**
   B. **embroiled**
   C. **ambivalent**
   D. **cherished**
   E. **ardor**

2. After years of enduring the **incessant** scrutiny of the media, the governor had learned to become _____ of how his actions were perceived by others.
   A. **haughty**
   B. **cajoling**
   C. **bereft**
   D. **disparaging**
   E. **cognizant**

3. The **esteemed** teacher was **cherished** by her students for her _____ style of teaching. She managed to convey the _____ of history in an **unconventional** manner that kept her students chuckling while they learned the essentials.

    A. invariable...preamble

    B. gregarious...rudiments

    C. inept...chasm

    D. resolute...contemporaries

    E. exacerbated...perception

4. The genuine _____ among the members of the baseball team was an integral part of their **enduring** team spirit.

    A. camaraderie

    B. interlude

    C. speculation

    D. disdain

    E. transformation

5. Suzanne was a(n) _____ salesperson who always tried to **cajole** her **clients** into spending more money than they initially intended.

    A. futile

    B. disparaging

    C. detached

    D. archetypal

    E. inept

6. Sam, a **burgeoning** political activist, **abhorred** the _____ that many of his **contemporaries** showed for political debates.

    A. rapport

    B. indifference

    C. machinations

    D. elation

    E. perseverance

7. Once she picked her intended **vocation**, Clairissa was _____ in her choice, despite the plethora of career options available to her.

   A. **flippant**

   B. **lurid**

   C. **miffed**

   D. **detached**

   E. **unswerving**

8. The **cloyingly** sweet final scene was a(n) _____ ending to a play that began with such a dark, **brooding** tone.

   A. **incongruous**

   B. **ambivalent**

   C. **innate**

   D. **perpetual**

   E. **disparaging**

9. Since he knew that lucrative commercial **endorsements** were _____, the **venerated** quarterback was inclined to stay with his hometown team, despite the **modest** salary.

   A. **cognizant**

   B. **reverent**

   C. **tacit**

   D. **imminent**

   E. **emulated**

10. The **pretentious** _____ of the **exclusive** resort contrasted sharply with the **modest** dwellings around it.

   A. **hierarchy**

   B. **discourse**

   C. **chasm**

   D. **ascetic**

   E. **aesthetics**

Answers Chapter 1

1. C ambivalent
2. E cognizant
3. B gregarious...rudiments
4. A camaraderie
5. D archetypal
6. B indifference
7. E unswerving
8. A incongruous
9. D imminent
10. E aesthetics

Chapter 2

Captivating Creatures

68. genial
69. affable
70. harbor
71. pique
72. punctuate
73. extenuating
74. evoke
75. innate
76. rapport
77. procure
78. arid
79. utopia
80. garish
81. crass
82. voluminous
83. oblivious
84. embittered
85. emissary
86. vivid
87. cartographer
88. foreboding
89. encompasses
90. perplexed
91. oration
92. unyielding
93. undermine
94. strife
95. interlocutor
96. portentously
97. interminable
98. enveloped
99. remote
100. verdant
101. prompt
102. peruse
103. legitimacy
104. perfunctory
105. profoundly
106. sarcastically
107. admonish
108. nondescript
109. colossal
110. austere
111. collaborator
112. portal
113. vast
114. torpid
115. charismatic
116. potentate
117. supple
118. captivate
119. precarious
120. contiguous
121. periphery
122. periodically
123. presiding
124. rambled
125. rousing
126. preempted
127. comparatively

128. compelling
129. arduous
130. formidable
131. assiduous
132. fortitude
133. awestruck
134. cordial
135. articulate
136. yearning

137. compassionately
138. coerce
139. exasperated
140. empathetic
141. forlorn
142. foster
143. redeeming
144. grievance

1. Despite her **grievances** about the **voluminous** length of the text-book, Kara attacked the **colossal** assignment _____.
   A. **assiduously**
   B. **remotely**
   C. **contiguously**
   D. **comparatively**
   E. **precariously**

2. The audience was **awestruck** by the **rousing oration** of the candidate who managed to **articulate** his ideas in such a(n) _____ fashion.
   A. **torpid**
   B. **compelling**
   C. **supple**
   D. **unyielding**
   E. **periodic**

3. The **remote** island _____ thousands of species of birds in its _____ jungle.
   A. **enveloped...portal**
   B. **evoked...punctuated**
   C. **admonished...arid**
   D. **harbored...verdant**
   E. **captivated...crass**

4. **Exasperated** by her _____ collaborator, Gigi was **prompted** to seek the advice of her supervisor.

   A. **vivid**

   B. **redeeming**

   C. **affable**

   D. **genial**

   E. **unyielding**

5. The poignant plea for peace from the **forlorn** orphan managed to _____ **compassion** among the warring tribes, while the more **coercive** tactics of the government failed to alleviate the continual **strife** in the region.

   A. **foster**

   B. **embitter**

   C. **austere**

   D. **innate**

   E. **extenuate**

6. **Embittered** by the **indifference** of his supervisor, John decided to seek a new mentor who would not be so _____ to his **formidable** efforts.

   A. **procured**

   B. **oblivious**

   C. **crass**

   D. **cordial**

   E. **supple**

7. The jury looked _____ while the prosecutor **rambled** on _____ in a **portentous** opening argument.

   A. **foreboding...succinctly**

   B. **charismatic...profoundly**

   C. **utopian...remotely**

   D. **perplexed...interminably**

   E. **arduous...comparatively**

8. The teacher **admonished** Jared for his **sarcastic** remark about the Watergate scandal, even though his comment had a rather insightful nuance that _____ her interest.

   A. yearned

   B. exasperated

   C. presided

   D. undermined

   E. piqued

9. The discerning judge **presiding** over the case _____ the documents provided by the prosecution in order to verify their legitimacy.

   A. perused

   B. coerced

   C. compelled

   D. enveloped

   E. punctuated

10. The corporation's designated **interlocutor** made a **perfunctory** statement that failed to _____ the growing aura of scandal that **enveloped** the embattled CEO.

   A. procure

   B. embitter

   C. preempt

   D. admonish

   E. yearn

11. Although the crime itself was **garish**, the **extenuating** circumstances of the perpetrator's upbringing garnered _____ from the jury.

   A. fortitude

   B. orations

   C. strife

   D. utopia

   E. empathy

Answers Chapter 2

1. A assiduously
2. B compelling
3. D harbored...verdant
4. E unyielding
5. A foster
6. B oblivious
7. D perplexed...interminably
8. E piqued
9. A perused
10. C preempt
11. E empathy

Chapter 3

A Serendipitous Find

145. animated
146. domestic
147. limitation
148. covet
149. deliberate
150. cultivating
151. desolate
152. wary
153. usurp
154. consign
155. debatable
156. comrade
157. flourish
158. denounce
159. disgruntled
160. emphatically
161. affirming
162. asserted
163. upstart
164. hospitable
165. elaborate
166. protocol
167. empowering
168. impulsively
169. omnipresent
170. authoritatively
171. impetuous
172. parched
173. ubiquitous
174. franchise

175. encampment
176. perspective
177. deprived
178. mendicant
179. beseech
180. subsist
181. penurious
182. patrons
183. ethnicity
184. ostracized
185. scurried
186. translucent
187. serendipitously
188. decadent
189. archaic
190. dingy
191. unintelligible
192. deflect
193. lithe
194. exorbitantly
195. extricate
196. evade
197. perspicacity
198. proximity
199. divulge
200. indiscretion
201. discretionary
202. feigned
203. efficaciously
204. inundate

205. foraged
206. corrosive
207. soluble
208. dénouement
209. lull
210. coalesce

211. enigmatic
212. propensity
213. debilitating
214. bequeathing
215. invigorating

1. In order to keep her **lithe** frame toned and trim for the upcoming track season, Sandy _____ herself to a summer filled with **invigorating** exercise.
   A. **consigned**
   B. **feigned**
   C. **foraged**
   D. **parched**
   E. **animated**

2. Although the directions were **unintelligible**, Harry _____ found his way to the **desolate** location.
   A. **beseechingly**
   B. **hospitably**
   C. **translucently**
   D. **serendipitously**
   E. **elaborately**

3. During a **lull** in the debate, Jill's **elaborate** strategy _____ in her mind.
   A. **bequeathed**
   B. **coalesced**
   C. **coveted**
   D. **parched**
   E. **deprived**

4. Even though his security guards were **omnipresent**, the Army captain was increasingly _____ of the rebels in the neighboring **encampment**.

    A. **dingy**
    B. **archaic**
    C. **flourished**
    D. **wary**
    E. **scurried**

5. The _____ expensive purchase of **decadent** chocolate was an **impulsive** decision that exceeded the spending _____ David and Sue had set for themselves.

    A. **animatedly...franchise**
    B. **corrosively...denouement**
    C. **exorbitantly...limitations**
    D. **domestically...comrade**
    E. **enigmatically...mendicant**

6. After setting strict _____ on her budget, Rory was able to save for college quite **efficaciously**, although at times, she felt _____ of luxurious treats.

    A. **limitations...deprived**
    B. **indiscretions...asserted**
    C. **upstarts...empowered**
    D. **lulls...deflected**
    E. **encampments...evaded**

7. The _____ employee emphatically **denounced** the deplorable working conditions at the fast-food **franchise** before handing in his resignation.

    A. **flourished**
    B. **serendipitous**
    C. **protocol**
    D. **affirming**
    E. **disgruntled**

8. At times, Sheila was **ostracized** from her group of friends because of her _____ to **divulge** secrets.

   A. **perspicacity**
   B. **propensity**
   C. **proximity**
   D. **discretionary**
   E. **protocol**

9. Even though the prosecution's witness had received numerous death threats and his safety was **debatable**, none of the authorities had the _____ to enroll him in a witness protection program.

   A. **perspicacity**
   B. **cultivation**
   C. **indiscretion**
   D. **lithe**
   E. **limitation**

10. After **deliberating** over the restaurant's décor, Angie decided that she would attempt to **cultivate** an international aura that would complement the _____ cuisine.

    A. **parched**
    B. **ethnic**
    C. **discretionary**
    D. **soluble**
    E. **wary**

Answers Chapter 3

1. A consigned
2. D serendipitously
3. B coalesced
4. D wary
5. C exorbitantly...limitations
6. A limitations...deprived
7. E disgruntled
8. B propensity
9. A perspicacity
10. B ethnic

Chapter 4

An Old Maxim

216. stifling
217. uplifting
218. sensibilities
219. explicitly
220. prophetic
221. surreptitiously
222. fervently
223. universal
224. anemic
225. gourmand
226. affront
227. envision
228. affectation
229. frugal
230. ensemble
231. vitiate
232. bourgeois
233. parsimony
234. eclectic
235. fantasize
236. maxim
237. pigeonhole
238. dimension
239. querulous
240. confrontation
241. mechanisms
242. coherently
243. livid
244. indecorous
245. dissipated
246. digress
247. toady
248. untenable
249. unalterable

1. The **uplifting** quality of the concerto was _____ by the abhorrent acoustics of the auditorium.

   A. **livid**
   B. **vitiated**
   C. **gourmand**
   D. **pigeonholed**
   E. **envisioned**

2. After halting a violent **confrontation** between two students, the teacher made it clear that such _____ behavior was simply **untenable** in the classroom.

    A. gourmand
    B. frugal
    C. ensemble
    D. parsimonious
    E. indecorous

3. **Digressing** into an **eclectic** variety of topics, Randy's essay failed to focus on a(n) _____ theme.

    A. coherent
    B. maxim
    C. toady
    D. stifling
    E. ensemble

4. The _____ debate in the student council meeting was an **affront** to their advisor, who always taught them to resolve their differences in a well-mannered fashion.

    A. mechanism
    B. dimension
    C. dissipated
    D. querulous
    E. unalterable

5. Gillian's desire to buy a designer handbag **dissipated** when she decided that the highly visible designer labels on the exterior were a(n) _____ symbol that she did not aspire to own.

    A. parsimonious
    B. bourgeois
    C. envisioned
    D. dissipated
    E. querulous

6. The **stifling** heat in the auditorium gave Adam a(n) _____ desire to slip out of the back door **surreptitiously**.

   A. fervent
   B. frugal
   C. livid
   D. anemic
   E. toady

Answers Chapter 4

1. B vitiated
2. E indecorous
3. A coherent
4. D querulous
5. B bourgeois
6. A fervent

Chapter 5

A Surprising Revelation

250. unambiguously
251. arbitrarily
252. apathetic
253. alleviate
254. anticipating
255. resplendent
256. wavered
257. immerse
258. transparent
259. iridescent
260. idealistic
261. languidly
262. restorative
263. stagnating
264. cacophony
265. kinship
266. legitimating
267. circumscribe
268. linguistic
269. visceral
270. lummox
271. penchant
272. jovial
273. propelled

274. sentiment
275. indomitable
276. juxtaposition
277. introspective
278. intelligentsia
279. elusive
280. predetermined
281. subsidize
282. disparity
283. elitist
284. egalitarian
285. malinger
286. reiterate
287. tentatively
288. ignite
289. exploit
290. illicit
291. tranquility
292. deftly
293. apparatus
294. revelation
295. fritter
296. inauspicious
297. surfeit

*

1. After **frittering** away the first 30 minutes of her allotted time, Alicia finally _____ herself in the task of writing an essay.

   A. reiterated
   B. immersed
   C. circumscribed
   D. predetermined
   E. idealized

2. The **juxtaposition** of the **resplendent** hotel next to the **subsidized** housing unit underscored the _____ between the tourists and the local population.

   A. arbitrary
   B. tranquility
   C. apparatus
   D. iridescence
   E. disparity

3. The dictator's intent to **exploit** his country's resources of natural gas was **unambiguously** demonstrated by his _____ statements at the environmental summit meeting.

   A. elusive
   B. frittering
   C. kinship
   D. transparent
   E. stagnating

4. David's _____ attitude toward his homework **legitimated** his mother's growing concern about his education.

   A. apathetic
   B. deft
   C. reiterated
   D. surfeit
   E. linguistic

5. The _____ of the mountain retreat was conducive to
languid afternoons spent in **introspective** thought.

A. **cacophony**

B. **disparity**

C. **revelation**

D. **transparency**

E. **tranquility**

6. Far from being an **elitist** politician, the councilman _____ his
egalitarian policies several times during his speech.

A. **frittered**

B. **reiterated**

C. **alleviated**

D. **maligned**

E. **circumscribed**

7. Bill's _____ for old cars **propelled** him to visit even the
most **inauspicious** places to look for **elusive** car parts.

A. **apparatus**

B. **egalitarian**

C. **tentative**

D. **penchant**

E. **utopian**

8. Suzanne's **deft** maneuvers on the **apparatus ignited** the crowd
of gymnastics enthusiasts into a(n) _____ of applause
and cheers.

A. **cacophony**

B. **exploitations**

C. **stagnation**

D. **languid**

E. **intelligentsia**

9. The startling _____ about a new planet in the solar system was eagerly **anticipated** by the press, many of whom had heard rumors about the exciting discovery.

   A. **exploitation**
   B. **juxtaposition**
   C. **revelation**
   D. **disparity**
   E. **lummox**

Answers Chapter 5

1. B immersed
2. E disparity
3. D transparent
4. A apathetic
5. E tranquility
6. B reiterated
7. D penchant
8. A cacophony
9. C revelation

Chapter 6

Pecas' Plea

298. ascetic
299. utilitarian
300. sparsely
301. virtuoso
302. pronouncement
303. preoccupied
304. discourteous
305. encroaching
306. wrath
307. indefensible
308. combativeness
309. placating
310. rectify
311. advocate
312. adversary
313. vindictive
314. exculpate
315. preconceptions
316. unmitigated
317. solicitous
318. botched
319. amorphous
320. assurance
321. analogous
322. cynicism
323. satire
324. meticulously
325. methodically
326. refurbish
327. circuitous
328. delineated
329. feral
330. reticent
331. folly
332. ethical
333. heinous
334. inconsequential
335. indignant
336. illogical
337. antagonistic
338. entangled
339. friction
340. impassion
341. erratic
342. goading
343. alacrity
344. quest
345. uncanny
346. symptomatic
347. theorized
348. specter
349. condemn
350. reprehensible
351. promulgate
352. statute
353. razed
354. incumbent
355. formulate
356. rational

1. After an unsuccessful attempt to unseat the incumbent, Bill was _____ to run for office again when the **specter** of defeat **preoccupied** his mind.

    A. **reticent**
    B. **promulgated**
    C. **feral**
    D. **unmitigated**
    E. **formulated**

2. The defendant was **indignant** that the _____ evidence was omitted from the trial due to the **botched** police investigation.

    A. **ascetic**
    B. **preoccupied**
    C. **virtuoso**
    D. **exculpatory**
    E. **encroaching**

3. The **heinous** act of aggression was _____ by the international community.

    A. **refurbished**
    B. **condemned**
    C. **encroached**
    D. **razed**
    E. **reticent**

4. Ruth ignored the _____ comments by her **adversary** in the debate because she didn't want to become **entangled** in a _____ exchange of insults.

    A. **rational...folly**
    B. **illogical...placating**
    C. **sparse...uncanny**
    D. **statute...satire**
    E. **antagonistic...vindictive**

5. In an attempt to **formulate** a **rational** hypothesis, Doug reviewed the evidence _____.
   A. **methodically**
   B. **illogically**
   C. **indefensibly**
   D. **inconsequentially**
   E. **discourteously**

6. After **encroaching** on the **feral** bear's territory, John attempted to _____ the **combative** animal.
   A. **placate**
   B. **refurbish**
   C. **formulate**
   D. **quest**
   E. **delineate**

7. The _____ concerns raised by the board of directors were vindicated when they discovered that the company's bookkeeping had not been carried out in a **meticulous** fashion.
   A. **feral**
   B. **analogous**
   C. **virtuoso**
   D. **utilitarian**
   E. **ethical**

8. Gina _____ taking a **circuitous** route back to the trailhead, even though her exhausted fellow hikers thought that her idea was **illogical**.
   A. **exculpated**
   B. **advocated**
   C. **botched**
   D. **encroached**
   E. **refurbished**

9. The spate of **impassioned** anti-war rallies in the 1960s was **symptomatic** of the growing _____ the citizens felt about their involvement in the Vietnam War.

   A. cynicism
   B. goading
   C. alacrity
   D. quest
   E. assurance

10. Chris typically didn't require any **goading** from his parents about doing his homework, but this particular assignment was so _____ and poorly **delineated**, he didn't know where to begin.

   A. methodical
   B. incumbent
   C. rational
   D. amorphous
   E. preoccupied

Answers Chapter 6

1. A reticent
2. D exculpatory
3. B condemned
4. E antagonistic...vindictive
5. A methodically
6. A placate
7. E ethical
8. B advocated
9. A cynicism
10. D amorphous

Chapter 7

The Clandestine Mission

357. agile
358. clandestine
359. endeavor
360. crystallize
361. cunning
362. ecstatic
363. hypothesis
364. preconceived
365. notions
366. scrupulous
367. radical
368. vengeance
369. scheme
370. conjecture
371. verifiable
372. solidarity
373. ominously
374. monstrosity
375. lavish
376. espouse
377. rhapsody
378. understate
379. tenacity
380. jollity
381. whimsical
382. plaintive
383. compulsive
384. vehemently
385. talisman
386. embellish
387. narratives
388. unutterable
389. underscore

1. Jerry **vehemently** refused to _____ Terry's **hypothesis** because he thought that Terry did not **scrupulously** analyze the data.

    A. **espouse**
    B. **agile**
    C. **conjecture**
    D. **understate**
    E. **talisman**

2. After working **tenaciously** for a whole year on a big project, Velma was **ecstatic** to complete the _____ endeavor.

   A. vengeance
   B. notion
   C. plaintive
   D. monstrous
   E. underscored

3. Throughout the **narrative**, the _____ cry of the wolf symbolized the anguish of the animals in the burning forest and **underscored** the prevailing theme of man's destruction of nature.

   A. whimsical
   B. jolly
   C. verifiable
   D. clandestine
   E. plaintive

4. The _____ style of the hotel lobby lacked the extravagant furniture and **lavish embellishments** that are prevalent in contemporary decorating **schemes**.

   A. unutterable
   B. understated
   C. rhapsodic
   D. solidarity
   E. preconceived

5. Once the soldier came to grips with the _____ reality of his capture, a **cunning** plan of escape **crystallized** in his mind.

   A. whimsical
   B. agile
   C. ominous
   D. lavish
   E. compulsive

Answers Chapter 7

1. A espouse
2. D monstrous
3. E plaintive
4. B understated
5. C ominous

Chapter 8

Not a Nemesis

390. adorned
391. adulation
392. couched
393. harmonious
394. hackneyed
395. harangue
396. correlation
397. interweave
398. inherent
399. pariah
400. modicum
401. perceptiveness
402. morose

403. munificence
404. decorous
405. nonchalance
406. compatriot
407. permeate
408. innuendo
409. melodiously
410. misconception
411. negate
412. narcissistic
413. insular
414. nemesis
415. mandated

1. After being **harangued** and outcast by his teammates, Sean tried to act **nonchalant**, but in reality, he felt deeply saddened to be treated like a(n) _____ .

   A. **innuendo**
   B. **morose**
   C. **hackneyed**
   D. **pariah**
   E. **compatriot**

2. Having grown up in a(n) _____ environment with little exposure to world politics, Gary's outlook was **permeated** with **misconceptions** about the United Nations.

   A. **insular**
   B. **adorned**
   C. **negated**
   D. **permeated**
   E. **inherent**

3. It only took a **modicum** of _____ to understand the thinly veiled **innuendo** of the political cartoon.

   A. **decorum**

   B. **adulation**

   C. **nonchalance**

   D. **mandate**

   E. **perceptiveness**

4. **Interweaving** words of _____ for the military with sharp criticism for the president, the political candidate hoped that his **compatriots** would see him as a compassionate leader who cared deeply for the fate of the young men and women in the armed forces.

   A. **harangue**

   B. **adulation**

   C. **misconception**

   D. **narcissism**

   E. **negation**

5. Harry enjoyed handing out lavish gifts at the orphanage because the kids showered him with **adulation** and genuinely seemed to appreciate his _____.

   A. **nemesis**

   B. **misconception**

   C. **decorum**

   D. **munificence**

   E. **nonchalance**

Answers Chapter 8

1. D pariah
2. A insular
3. E perceptiveness
4. B adulation
5. D munificence

Chapter 9

A Contemptuous Claim

416. inequities
417. jaded
418. protract
419. prominent
420. stylistic
421. renovation
422. ornate
423. purposefully
424. antiquated
425. vestige
426. circuitry
427. repose
428. eloquent
429. fathom
430. veneer
431. efface
432. purportedly
433. deduction
434. contemptuously
435. ostentatious
436. outlandish
437. literally
438. modulate
439. malice
440. morass
441. disillusionment
442. inordinately
443. intemperate
444. egregious
445. protégé
446. lobbyist
447. pundits
448. onerous
449. vivacity
450. unearthed
451. inception
452. objective
453. paramount
454. organic
455. novelty
456. opulent
457. paradox
458. prudent
459. pragmatist
460. practical
461. proliferate
462. exalted
463. fallacious
464. resolve
465. intuitively
466. anticlimactic

1. John **intuitively** knew that it was of **paramount** importance to rectify the _____ in the report before anyone read the **outlandish** lies.

   A. **novelties**

   B. **fallacies**

   C. **inceptions**

   D. **practicalities**

   E. **protégés**

2. The compelling speech **eloquently** expressed the political **objectives** of the **lobby** group without getting mired down in a(n) _____ discussion of the complicated issue.

   A. **protracted**

   B. **prudent**

   C. **pragmatic**

   D. **practical**

   E. **unearthed**

3. When the **novelty** of staying at the **opulent** hotel wore off, Kara _____ thought about her strained budget.

   A. **stylistically**

   B. **ostentatiously**

   C. **prudently**

   D. **exaltedly**

   E. **fallaciously**

4. Although his **objective** was **purposefully malicious**, _____ , his actions resulted in a vastly improved working environment.

   A. **vivaciously**

   B. **opulently**

   C. **organically**

   D. **prominently**

   E. **paradoxically**

5. Since its **inception**, the **ostentatious** restaurant _____ to serve the best French food in all of Chicago.

   A. purported
   B. jaded
   C. fathomed
   D. effaced
   E. unearthed

6. The _____ of the **organic** cuisine wore off rather quickly for the _____ clientele.

   A. practicality...anticlimactic
   B. novelty...jaded
   C. repose...prominent
   D. proliferation...exalted
   E. malice...pundit

7. Although the palace had undergone extensive **renovations** in recent years, it retained some **vestiges** of its _____ past.

   A. lobbyist
   B. pundit
   C. protégé
   D. organic
   E. opulent

8. Even though Alice had **resolved** to tackle _____ assignments with a good attitude, she resented being coerced into the _____ boring task of filing a mountain of papers.

   A. onerous...inordinately
   B. prudent...vivaciously
   C. egregious...vivaciously
   D. deduced...paradoxically
   E. fathomed...eloquently

Answers Chapter 9

1. B fallacies
2. A protracted
3. C prudently
4. E paradoxically
5. A purported
6. B novelty...jaded
7. E opulent
8. A onerous...inordinately

Chapter 10

A Conflagration Ignites

467. perpetually
468. bolster
469. tabled
470. discredit
471. temerity
472. supplant
473. pessimistic
474. remiss
475. fickle
476. vociferous
477. resonate
478. augurs
479. procrastinating
480. audacious
481. chagrin
482. chide
483. destitute
484. cosmopolitan
485. derisively
486. pompous
487. insinuate
488. derogatory
489. restate
490. penitence
491. irreverent
492. generalizations
493. rigor
494. quell
495. arrest
496. belie

497. adeptness
498. contrary
499. curtail
500. serene
501. deviate
502. impropriety
503. insidious
504. desecrate
505. conviction
506. righteous
507. decry
508. idealist
509. habitable
510. counteract
511. degradation
512. inducement
513. constructive
514. mirage
515. refined
516. pliable
517. restrained
518. detritus
519. immobilized
520. insight
521. scorn
522. vanity
523. unfetter
524. superficial
525. sully
526. adverse

527. integral
528. vital
529. assuredly
530. proponent
531. hostility
532. impugn
533. raging
534. conflagration
535. cynically
536. flabbergast
537. belligerent
538. berate
539. offensive
540. resentment
541. condone
542. derision
543. rancorously
544. bickering
545. recrimination
546. inflammatory
547. loathed
548. burrow
549. calamity
550. allegiance
551. sagacity
552. empathy
553. obstinate
554. salvage
555. repentance
556. mollify
557. obstreperous
558. insolent
559. flagrant
560. shun
561. obdurate
562. vigilant
563. ruminate
564. reverberate
565. latent
566. irrefutable
567. liberal
568. microcosm
569. reactionary
570. renunciation
571. cataclysmic
572. nefarious
573. repudiate
574. misgiving
575. callous
576. malign
577. malediction
578. raucous
579. clairvoyant
580. melodrama
581. mediate
582. reconciliation
583. refractive
584. variegated
585. absolve
586. tenacious
587. suppress
588. pallid
589. squelch
590. stoic
591. conciliatory
592. accord
593. appalling
594. arbitrating

595. acrimonious	599. discretion
596. aversion	600. divisive
597. disputant	601. defer
598. drub	602. impassive

1. The _____ dispute over the **divisive** issue of taxes was an **appalling** display of _____ **bickering**.
   - A. **acrimonious...rancorous**
   - B. **pallid...burrow**
   - C. **conviction...derogatory**
   - D. **desecrated...tabled**
   - E. **destitute...cosmopolitan**

2. The **disputants** _____ each other **tenaciously** before the **mediator** intervened to _____ the **raucous** fight.
   - A. **ruminated...reverberate**
   - B. **scorned...pompous**
   - C. **drubbed...mollify**
   - D. **resonated...augur**
   - E. **curtailed...mirage**

3. Jim's **flagrantly callous** behavior lacked _____.
   - A. **reverberation**
   - B. **scorn**
   - C. **microcosm**
   - D. **assuredness**
   - E. **discretion**

4. Hal's **conciliatory** gesture was ignored by Jill, as she was still feeling **resentful** about the _____ comments he made earlier.
   - A. **bolstered**
   - B. **salvaged**
   - C. **vigilant**
   - D. **derisive**
   - E. **integral**

5. After a lengthy period of **arbitration**, a peace **accord** was signed that attempted to_____ the persistent _____ between the **belligerent** countries.

A. **restate...rigor**

B. **absolve...hostility**

C. **sully...sagacity**

D. **shun...empathy**

E. **immobilize...condoning**

6. Fred's _____ judgment in stock purchases allowed him to **perpetually** overcome **adverse** market conditions.

A. **insolent**

B. **scorned**

C. **penitent**

D. **inflammatory**

E. **sagacious**

7. Although the truth of the matter was **irrefutable**, Gina **loathed** being wrong and she continued to argue _____.

A. **vociferously**

B. **procrastinating**

C. **calamity**

D. **immobilized**

E. **clairvoyantly**

8. Feeling _____ about his **idealistic** viewpoint, Nolan was an **obstinate** _____ of the environmental conservation movement.

A. **remiss...detritus**

B. **vanity...obdurate**

C. **nefarious...clairvoyant**

D. **righteous...proponent**

E. **latent...reactionary**

9. The audience watching the debate was **flabbergasted** when the conservative candidate _____ his **liberal** opponent with **inflammatory** remarks about his personal life.

   A. **impugned**
   B. **salvaged**
   C. condoned
   D. loathed
   E. reverberated

10. The endless _____ continued as the **scorned** candidate **decried** his opponent's shady business dealings.

    A. **mollifying**
    B. **restraint**
    C. **vitality**
    D. **proponent**
    E. recrimination

11. Although the prince never formally _____ his rights to the throne, his **misgivings** about the **superficial** duties of the reigning monarchy were evident in his comments to the press.

    A. **variegated**
    B. **bolstered**
    C. renounced
    D. refined
    E. ruminated

12. Tom **squelched** his desire to verbalize a vindictive retort to the **offensive** insult and instead maintained a _____ silence.

    A. **stoic**
    B. raucous
    C. salvaged
    D. **habitable**
    E. **fickle**

13. The _____ act of **hostility** was so **inflammatory** that it derailed the fragile peace in the war-torn region.
    A. serene
    B. pallid
    C. shunned
    D. insightful
    E. nefarious

14. The _____ pressures of working on Wall Street eventually caused Frank to become **cynical** about material desires.
    A. restrained
    B. insidious
    C. clairvoyant
    D. vigilant
    E. habitable

15. Claire's _____ ranting **belied** the **serene** disposition that she normally displayed at the office.
    A. integral
    B. sullied
    C. counteracted
    D. obstreperous
    E. tabled

Answers Chapter 10

1. A acrimonious...rancorous
2. C drubbed...mollify
3. E discretion
4. D derisive
5. B absolve...hostility
6. E sagacious
7. A vociferously
8. D righteous...proponent
9. A impugned
10. E recrimination
11. C renounced
12. A stoic
13. E nefarious
14. B insidious
15. D obstreperous

Chapter 11

A Stealthy Scheme

603. contrite
604. inanimate
605. enmity
606. impenitent
607. discomfited
608. endear
609. disavow
610. altercation
611. intransigent
612. precipitate
613. attribute
614. dissent
615. enumerated
616. emend
617. zealous
618. phlegmatic
619. diminished
620. enervated
621. dire
622. warranted
623. substantiate
624. defiantly
625. scoffed
626. idolatry
627. subjective
628. despoiling
629. corroboration
630. complying
631. corollary

632. emancipation
633. eccentric
634. inviolable
635. consecrate
636. entitlement
637. treacherous
638. compromise
639. consensus
640. facile
641. stealthy
642. theoretically
643. trivialize
644. doctrinaire
645. implementation
646. illimitable
647. heightened
648. innovative
649. indefatigable
650. ineffable
651. boundless
652. culminate
653. imperceptible
654. discern
655. surmise
656. inferred
657. industrious
658. factual
659. contemporary
660. anachronistic

661. inexorable
662. dispel
663. indiscernible
664. foliage
665. unrelenting
666. predatory
667. trepidation
668. parasite
669. plethora
670. facilitate
671. incantation
672. foil
673. navigable
674. foray
675. alight
676. oblique
677. respite
678. imprint
679. conjure
680. suffuse
681. divine
682. glutton
683. palate

684. evanescent
685. extant
686. ephemeral
687. expropriate
688. ponderous
689. vexed
690. imputed
691. servile
692. astute
693. enlighten
694. beneficiary
695. equitable
696. amiable
697. mire
698. benign
699. gracious
700. vicarious
701. benevolent
702. anarchy
703. profusion
704. prolific
705. exultant
706. inflamed

1. Mike's **astute** insight about the potential of embryonic stem cells _____ an enormous amount of **innovation** in the field.

   A. **precipitated**
   B. **foiled**
   C. **expropriated**
   D. **antagonized**
   E. **taunted**

2. **Theoretically**, the task before them was **facile**; however, Joe worried about getting _____ in the myriad of details.
   A. emancipated
   B. expropriated
   C. mired
   D. endeared
   E. imprinted

3. With **boundless** enthusiasm, George worked _____ to **implement** legislation that reflected his viewpoint on the issue of abortion.
   A. obliquely
   B. contritely
   C. ephemerally
   D. benignly
   E. zealously

4. The growing _____ between the two neighboring countries began with a **trivial altercation** between two diplomats, but it ultimately **culminated** in a **treacherous** battle.
   A. idolatry
   B. enmity
   C. beneficiary
   D. palate
   E. evanescence

5. Sam's **prolific** reading about European monarchies allowed him to experience _____ the life of a royal.
   A. stealthily
   B. endearingly
   C. intransigently
   D. vicariously
   E. imperceptibly

6. Giving the data a **discerning** review, Velma **enumerated** the inconsistencies with the evidence and _____ that no conclusions could be drawn.

    A. inferred

    B. antagonized

    C. facilitated

    D. entitled

    E. diminished

7. The teacher looked **scornfully** at the **dire** situation in the unruly classroom and decided that the circumstance _____ immediate action on her part.

    A. enumerated

    B. vexed

    C. compromised

    D. warranted

    E. suffused

8. Looking with _____ at the **profusion** of poisonous ants on the trail, Fred shuddered with fear and decided to abort his **foray** into the jungle.

    A. graciousness

    B. benevolence

    C. respite

    D. idolatry

    E. trepidation

9. The tell-all book was _____ with details about the **eccentric** rock star that **corroborated** earlier articles in the tabloid press.

    A. replete

    B. alight

    C. indiscernible

    D. dispelled

    E. disavowed

10. Her face flushed with embarrassment, Suzanne looked
    _____ when the **unrelenting** taunting became increas-
    ingly personal.

    A. **exultant**

    B. **navigable**

    C. **zealous**

    D. **discomfited**

    E. **equitable**

11. The _____ figure skating of champion Michelle Kwan is
    attributable to her **indefatigable** competitive attitude and her
    divine talent.

    A. **foiled**

    B. **illimitable**

    C. **palate**

    D. **imperceptible**

    E. **consensus**

12. Taking a brief _____ from his **servile** duties as a janitor,
    Gerry sat down and **pondered** how he might find a job that was
    more challenging for his active mind.

    A. **respite**

    B. **foliage**

    C. **imprint**

    D. **beneficiary**

    E. **implementation**

13. The _____ opinion put forth by the victim's family
    inflamed the feud over the death penalty.

    A. **subjective**

    B. **objective**

    C. **benign**

    D. **navigable**

    E. **alighted**

Answers Chapter 11

1. A precipitated
2. C mired
3. E zealously
4. B enmity
5. D vicariously
6. A inferred
7. D warranted
8. E trepidation
9. A replete
10. D discomfited
11. B illimitable
12. A respite
13. A subjective

Chapter 12

The DNA Debacle

707. auspicious
708. ramshackle
709. eradicate
710. enable
711. diffidently
712. novice
713. relish
714. exemplary
715. precipitate
716. requisite
717. congeal
718. palpable
719. homogenize
720. viscous
721. thwart
722. debacle

723. conundrum
724. rueful
725. condescending
726. gaffe
727. consummate
728. prowess
729. elude
730. detract
731. default
732. obtuse
733. jubilation
734. diversion
735. uncensored
736. disparate
737. concur

1. Although the debate began **auspiciously** for Brenda, the judges **concurred** that her **gaffe** in the second half _____ from her overall performance.

A. **homogenized**
B. **detracted**
C. **congealed**
D. **relished**
E. **uncensored**

2. Sara's _____ behavior off of the tennis court belied the **prowess** she displayed when playing on the Grand Slam circuit.
   A. **diffident**
   B. **ramshackle**
   C. **relished**
   D. **enabled**
   E. **homogenized**

3. The **debacle** about his shady real estate deal besmirched the candidate's otherwise **exemplary** record and ultimately _____ his efforts to get elected.
   A. **condescended**
   B. **jubilated**
   C. **enabled**
   D. **congealed**
   E. **thwarted**

4. The couple's _____ views on the **eradication** of the death penalty provided the source for many heated debates.
   A. **viscous**
   B. **disparate**
   C. **rueful**
   D. **auspicious**
   E. **ramshackle**

5. Ruth was a(n) _____ chef who **relished** fussing over the nuances of each dish she prepared.
   A. **eluded**
   B. **obtuse**
   C. **diverted**
   D. **consummate**
   E. **gaffe**

Answers Chapter 12

1. B detracted
2. A diffident
3. E thwarted
4. B disparate
5. D consummate

Chapter 13

A Moral Ambiguity

738. perilous
739. malicious
740. alienate
741. barrage
742. baffle
743. attune
744. anecdote
745. authentic
746. unprepossessing
747. derelict
748. proprietor
749. repast
750. infused
751. supplement
752. flout
753. preclude
754. polarize
755. innovation
756. patent
757. exemplify
758. pander
759. integrity
760. staunch
761. interpretation
762. gratuity
763. tremulous

764. synthesize
765. unruffled
766. scrutinize
767. subject
768. sleuth
769. tenuous
770. cumulative
771. profundity
772. cryptic
773. complacency
774. concocted
775. commodities
776. sentient
777. cerebral
778. devalued
779. subversive
780. unscrupulous
781. culpable
782. tactics
783. deceitful
784. ambiguity
785. furtive
786. corrupt
787. linchpin
788. florid
789. collude

1. The boy's **cryptic** behavior _____ his parents.
   A. repast
   B. baffled
   C. infused
   D. corrupted
   E. synthesized

2. Because of the _____ actions of a few criminals, all air-line passengers are now **subjected** to increased **scrutiny** at the airport security checkpoints.
   A. unscrupulous
   B. complacent
   C. cerebral
   D. patent
   E. sleuth

3. After Greg _____ the rules of play and came close to injuring a teammate, his position on the football team was **tenuous**.
   A. cumulated
   B. polarized
   C. supplemented
   D. florid
   E. flouted

4. Brenda came **perilously** close to _____ her friend when she accosted her with a **barrage** of criticism.
   A. colluding
   B. alienating
   C. supplementing
   D. unprepossessing
   E. authenticating

5. Although everyone **interpreted** her absence at the fundraiser as a(n) _____ of her duties as campaign manager, Fiona was **unruffled** in the face of the harsh criticism.

   A. innovation

   B. commodity

   C. exemplification

   D. gratuity

   E. dereliction

6. _____ the **subversive tactics** of career criminals, Captain Hines was a perceptive detective.

   A. **Attuned to**

   B. **Deceitful of**

   C. **Culpable for**

   D. **Baffled by**

   E. **Precluded of**

7. Karen was **staunch** in her opinion that the search for _____ life forms in outer space was a quest of unparalleled **profundity**.

   A. devalued

   B. concocted

   C. anecdotal

   D. sentient

   E. proprietary

8. The marketing team **concocted** a reprehensible ad campaign that _____ to the consumer's basest emotions.

   A. repast

   B. pandered

   C. unruffled

   D. cumulated

   E. flouted

Answers Chapter 13

1. B baffled
2. A unscrupulous
3. E flouted
4. B alienating
5. E dereliction
6. A Attuned to
7. D sentient
8. B pandered

Chapter 14

Late-Night Liberation

790. disingenuous
791. dissembler
792. perfidious
793. certitude
794. liberating
795. deviousness
796. epistolary
797. revelatory
798. provocative
799. cathartic
800. therapeutic
801. conception
802. submissive
803. volition
804. vacillate
805. partake
806. altruistic
807. abridge
808. augment
809. addendum
810. accentuate
811. emanate
812. disconcert
813. instill
814. tractable
815. surmountable
816. irresolute
817. pervasive
818. intrepid
819. heretofore

820. immutable
821. imposing
822. capacious
823. incalculably
824. legions
825. impressionable
826. inarticulate
827. susceptible
828. frivolity
829. buffoonery
830. indiscriminately
831. daunting
832. interspersed
833. ardently
834. stimulus
835. incisively
836. indeterminate
837. heralded
838. encapsulated
839. negligible
840. ostensibly
841. autonomous
842. inefficacious
843. premise
844. impetus
845. extolled
846. quandary
847. enclosure
848. pinioned
849. hindrance

850. execution
851. phenomenon
852. presumptuous
853. venture

854. debunk
855. recommenced
856. euphoric
857. momentous

1. Although it was rather **presumptuous** of Gina to _____ on Sara's hospitality for so long, Sara appeared to enjoy the company.

   A. **inarticulate**
   B. **impose**
   C. **liberate**
   D. **disconcert**
   E. **instill**

2. Before **recommencing** the **daunting** task of reading *War and Peace*, Jane decided to **partake** of some more _____ works of fiction that were filled with **buffoonery** rather than serious social issues.

   A. **irresolute**
   B. **intrepid**
   C. **immutable**
   D. **frivolous**
   E. **instilled**

3. Although the lucrative consulting contract with the pharmaceutical company would have significantly **augmented** his own salary, Dr. Reed decided not to accept because he did not want to compromise his _____ goal of making life-saving **therapies** affordable for the poor.

   A. **interspersed**
   B. **disingenuous**
   C. **devious**
   D. **epistolary**
   E. **altruistic**

4. The **revelatory** article about the candidate was _____ in nature, although **ostensibly** it outlined the main issues of the election.

   A. provocative
   B. pinioned
   C. enclosed
   D. emanating
   E. instilled

5. The general's own disloyal behavior inspired many _____ acts among the enlisted men, who succumbed to the **pervasive** sentiment in that battalion.

   A. capacious
   B. perfidious
   C. heralded
   D. indeterminate
   E. extolled

6. The _____ version of *Frankenstein* managed to **encapsulate** the major elements of the plot in a **tractable** fashion; however, the shortened version wasn't nearly as **provocative** as the original.

   A. vacillating
   B. quandary
   C. therapeutic
   D. susceptible
   E. abridged

7. At a **momentous** meeting of the National Academy of Sciences, the prize-winning scientist _____ the widely **heralded** theory of how life began and then **incisively** outlined his own new theory.

   A. debunked
   B. recommenced
   C. enclosed
   D. emanated
   E. stimulated

8. Since his parents were not there to **impose** their strict rules on his behavior, Fred was tempted to exploit his _____ at college by staying out late every night.

    A. **phenomenon**
    B. **addendum**
    C. **hindrance**
    D. **autonomy**
    E. **epistolary**

9. With convincing **certitude**, the Scout leader proclaimed that the challenges they faced were indeed _____ and that their **venture** would be successful.

    A. **interspersed**
    B. **surmountable**
    C. **executed**
    D. **impetus**
    E. **inarticulate**

10. Trying to **accentuate** the positive aspects of their performance, the conductor of the orchestra _____ the musicians and **instilled** a sense of pride in the group of novices.

    A. **pinioned**
    B. **dissembled**
    C. **interspersed**
    D. **extolled**
    E. **recommenced**

Answers Chapter 14

1. B impose
2. D frivolous
3. E altruistic
4. A provocative
5. B perfidious
6. E abridged
7. A debunked
8. D autonomy
9. B surmountable
10. D extolled

Chapter 15

Friendship—An Eternal Verity

858. replete
859. craftiness
860. wily
861. unfounded
862. subsequently
863. unprecedented
864. scapegoat
865. entreat
866. pretext
867. buttress
868. trump
869. gauge
870. deplorable
871. impious
872. salvation

873. ensue
874. implication
875. callow
876. wields
877. maelstrom
878. levy
879. eternal
880. verity
881. ponder
882. repercussion
883. pensive
884. synchronous
885. concomitant
886. manifestation
887. frolicsome

1. Staring **pensively** out the window, David _____ the inevitable **repercussions** of his **deplorable** act of disloyalty.
   A. **pondered**
   B. **unfounded**
   C. **buttressed**
   D. **trumped**
   E. **frolicked**

2. Helga _____ state and local officials to **levy** an additional tax to pay for the new social programs.
   A. **unprecedented**
   B. **buttressed**
   C. **pondered**
   D. **entreated**
   E. **deplored**

3. The **callow** young man gave a statement to the press that ignited a _____ of controversy.

   A. frolic

   B. verity

   C. wily

   D. replete

   E. maelstrom

4. The wide-ranging _____ of the scientific discovery **manifest** themselves in a variety of different disciplines.

   A. synchronous

   B. implications

   C. gauging

   D. wiles

   E. frolics

5. Michael's _____ remark at the church service shocked his fellow parishioners and inspired the congregation to pray for his **salvation**.

   A. impious

   B. frolicsome

   C. synchronous

   D. pensive

   E. subsequent

Answers Chapter 15

1. A pondered
2. D entreated
3. E maelstrom
4. B implications
5. A impious

Chapter 16

A Preponderance of Evidence

888. synthetic
889. aplomb
890. mortified
891. censured
892. demean
893. preponderance
894. breach
895. invoke
896. castigation
897. covenant
898. neutrality
899 precept
900. epedantic
901. sermonize
902. hypocrite
903. sanctimonious
904. eminently
905. adjudicate
906. colloquial
907. veil
908. circumlocutions
909. ramification
910. retribution
911. cantankerous
912. skirt
913. contentious
914. carnivores
915. ferocity
916. embody
917. cavorting

918. maverick
919. dissident
920. orator
921. travesty
922. elocutionist
923. boisterous
924. ethos
925. throng
926. surreal
927. sensationalize
928. adversity
929. resounding
930. overtly
931. proselytize
932. felicitous
933. editorial
934. intervene
935. engender
936. poignant
937. faction
938. disseminate
939. gibbering
940. scathing
941. truculent
942. remuneration
943. glacial
944. tonic
945. confiscate
946. revoke

1. After feeding the lions regularly for three years, the zookeeper knew that ample portions of meat acted as a(n) _____ for the **ferocious carnivores**.

   A. **surreal**
   B. **tonic**
   C. **aplomb**
   D. **condemnation**
   E. **ramification**

2. The **throng** of people **castigated** the _____ for his **resounding** criticism of the government.

   A. **truculent**
   B. **engendered**
   C. **ethos**
   D. **intervened**
   E. **dissident**

3. His first public speech managed to _____ the contentious issue with **sanctimonious** preaching and poetic **circumlocutions**.

   A. **skirt**
   B. **confiscate**
   C. **intervene**
   D. **revoke**
   E. **aplomb**

4. After **cavorting** with the enemy, Bob faced the _____ of his cohorts, many of whom viewed him as a **hypocrite**.

   A. **engendering**
   B. **retribution**
   C. **synthetic**
   D. **covenant**
   E. **neutrality**

5. After the supervisor **disseminated scathing** criticism to all of his employees, the atmosphere in the meeting became _____.
   A. colloquial
   B. invoked
   C. sensationalized
   D. glacial
   E. confiscated

6. Relentlessly **proselytizing** and **sermonizing**, John worked tirelessly to communicate the _____ of his beloved faith.
   A. factions
   B. throngs
   C. veiling
   D. truculence
   E. precepts

7. Penelope's driver's license was _____ when she **overtly** ran a red light and then acted **cantankerous** when the police officer confronted her.
   A. demeaned
   B. adjudicated
   C. revoked
   D. skirted
   E. resounded

8. The _____ ending of the movie **invoked** the sentiments of the audience.
   A. intervened
   B. gibbering
   C. synthetic
   D. breached
   E. poignant

9. The guard was _____ by his angry employer after a
   major **breach** in security happened during his watch.

   A. **engendered**

   B. **disseminated**

   C. **confiscated**

   D. **censured**

   E. **maverick**

Answers Chapter 16

1. B tonic
2. E dissident
3. A skirt
4. B confiscate
5. D glacial
6. E precepts
7. C revoked
8. E poignant
9. D censured

Chapter 17

A Nebulous Future

947. impermanent	961. ingenious
948. prosaic	962. revulsion
949. reintegrating	963. synonymous
950. pretense	964. ludicrous
951. shroud	965. fodder
952. incarceration	966. patently
953. litigate	967. missive
954. bane	968. sycophant
955. precocious	969. deposed
956. acumen	970. spurious
957. charitable	971. unduly
958. earmark	972. squander
959. benefactor	973. transient
960. philanthropic	974. nebulous

1. Sam, a generous _____ of several **charitable** organizations, always **earmarked** his donations for specific **philanthropic** endeavors.

   A. **bane**
   B. **prosaic**
   C. **benefactor**
   D. **sycophant**
   E. **missive**

2. The **nebulous** apparition, seen only in the dim light of the moon, was **shrouded** in mystery and served as _____ for many ghost stories.

   A. **squander**
   B. **impermanent**
   C. **incarceration**
   D. **revulsion**
   E. **fodder**

3. Although the accusation was **patently** false, the attorney knew that it was going to take all of his **litigation** skills to acquit the accused of the _____ charge.

   A. **spurious**
   B. **synonymous**
   C. **precocious**
   D. **prosaic**
   E. **transient**

4. Although the published review described the book as **ingeniously** poetic and imaginative, Rory disagreed when she described the book as _____.

   A. **earmarked**
   B. **deposed**
   C. **prosaic**
   D. **philanthropic**
   E. **synonymous**

Answers Chapter 17

1. C benefactor
2. E fodder
3 A spurious
4. C prosaic

Chapter 18

The Proverbial Invitation

975. temperate	988. cohort
976. melancholy	989. antidote
977. confounding	990. trove
978. vanquish	991. implausible
979. inestimably	992. banish
980. proverbial	993. dubious
981. canonical	994. grandiose
982. encumbered	995. pertinent
983. heart-rending	996. nostalgic
984. deference	997. lauded
985. jester	998. emigrate
986. quintessential	999. self-aggrandizement
987. prototype	1000. braggart

1. The **temperate** climate of the South provides the perfect
_____ for those who are tired of the frigid, snow-laden
winters of the North.
   A. **melancholy**
   B. **proverb**
   C. **antidote**
   D. **jester**
   E. **deference**

2. Although his **cohort** insisted that he had completed the task,
Jerry was _____ because it seemed rather **implausible** that
he could have finished the work so quickly.
   A. **nostalgic**
   B. **banished**
   C. **temperate**
   D. **lauded**
   E. **dubious**

3. Although he was not typically such a **braggart**, Josh indulged in a bit of _____ when he launched into **nostalgic** tales of his own heroic bravery during the war.
   A. self-aggrandizement
   B. pertinence
   C. vanquish
   D. dubiousness
   E. emigration

4. Although the couple did not want to be **encumbered** with the bills incurred by such a **grandiose** wedding, they had a large reception in _____ to their parents.
   A. implausibility
   B. deference
   C. melancholy
   D. vanquish
   E. self-aggrandizement

5. The **jester** was _____ from the king's court when he told a heart-rending, **melancholy** tale rather than the humorous stories that the king preferred.
   A. encumbered
   B. trove
   C. lauded
   D. confounded
   E. banished

Answers Chapter 18

1. C antidote
2. E dubious
3. A self-aggrandizement
4. B deference
5. E banished

Vocabulary List

Abhor   to regard with extreme repugnance; loathe

Abridge   to shorten in duration or extent

Absolve   to set free from an obligation or the consequences of guilt

Accentuate   accent, emphasize

Accord   to bring into agreement

Acrimonious   caustic, biting, or rancorous, especially in feeling language or manner

Acumen   keenness and depth of perception, discernment, or discrimination, esp. in practical matters; shrewdness

Addendum   a thing added; an addition

Adept   thoroughly proficient; skillful

Adeptness   thoroughly proficient; expert

Adjudicate   to act as judge

Admonish   to express warning or disapproval especially in a gentle, earnest, or solicitous manner

Adorned   to enliven or decorate as if with ornaments

Adulation   to flatter or admire excessively or slavishly

Adversary   one who contends with, opposes, or resists; opponent, rival

Adverse   acting against or in a contrary direction; hostile

Adversity   a state or condition contrary to one of well-being

Advocate   one who pleads the cause of another; specifically one who pleads the cause of another before a tribunal or judicial court

Aesthetics   a pleasing appearance or effect; beauty

Affable   being pleasant and at ease talking to others

Affectation   mannerisms, especially pretentious ones

Affirming   expressing dedication

Affront   to insult especially to the face by behavior or language

Agile   marked by a ready ability to move with a quick, easy grace

Alacrity   promptness in response; cheerful readiness

Alienate   to make unfriendly, hostile, or indifferent where attachment formerly existed

Alight   to descend from the air and come to rest

Allegiance   devotion or loyalty to a person, group, or cause

Alleviate   to make (as suffering) more bearable her sympathy *alleviated* his distress; ease, lessen,

Altercation   a noisy, heated, angry dispute; also a noisy controversy

Altruistic   behavior that is unselfish in its regard for or devotion to the welfare of others

Ambiguity   the quality or state of being ambiguous (doubtful or uncertain), especially in meaning

Ambivalent   simultaneous and contradictory feelings (as attraction and repulsion) toward an object, person, or action

Amiable   friendly, sociable, congenial

Amorphous   without shape or form

Anachronistic   a person or a thing that is chronologically out of place, especially one from a former age that is incongruously in the present

Analogous   showing an analogy or a likeness that permits one to draw an analogy

Anarchy   absence of government

Anecdote   a usually short narrative of an interesting, amusing, or biographical incident

Anemic   lackluster, insipid

Animated   full of movement and activity

Antagonistic   marked by or resulting from antagonism (actively expressed opposition or hostility)

Anticipating   to look forward to as certain; expect

Anticlimactic   of, relating to, or marked by anticlimax; an event (as at the end of a series) that is strikingly less important than what has preceded it

Antidote   something that relieves, prevents, or counteracts

Antiquated   old-fashioned, old or obsolete

Apathetic   having little or no interest or concern; indifferent

Aplomb   complete and confident composure or self-assurance

Appalling   inspiring horror, dismay, or disgust

Apparatus   an instrument or appliance designed for a specific operation

Arbitrarily   based on or determined by individual preference or convenience rather than by necessity or the intrinsic nature of something

Arbitrating   acting as an arbitrator (one who decides in the case of a dispute)

Archaic   characteristic of an earlier or more primitive time

Archetypal   classic example, model example

Ardently   characterized by warmth of feeling, typically expressed in eager zealous support or activity

Ardor   extreme vigor or energy; intensity

Arduous   hard to accomplish or achieve

Arid   excessively dry

Arrest   to bring to a stop

Articulate   expressing oneself readily, clearly, or effectively

Ascetic   plain, stark, simple; austere in appearance, manner, or attitude (not to be confused with aesthetic, which means pleasing in appearance or effect; beauty)

Asserted   to declare forcefully

Assiduous   marked by careful unremitting attention or persistent application

Assurance   something that inspires or tends to inspire confidence

Assuredly   without a doubt; certainly

Astute   having or showing shrewdness and perspicacity

Attribute   to explain by indicating a cause

Attune   to make aware or responsive

Audacious   intrepidly daring

Augment   to make greater, more numerous, larger, or more intense

Augurs   to foretell

Auspicious   affording a favorable auspice (a favorable sign)

Austere   stern and cold in appearance or manner

Authentic   worthy of acceptance or belief as conforming to or based on fact

Authoritatively   with authority, commandingly, convincingly

Autonomous   existing or capable of existing independently

Aversion   a feeling of repugnance toward something with a desire to avoid or turn from it

Awestruck   filled with awe (emotion in which dread, veneration, and wonder are variously mingled)

Baffle   to defeat or check (as a person) by confusing or puzzling; disconcert

Bane   a source of harm or ruin; curse

Banish   to require by authority to leave

Barrage   a vigorous or rapid outpouring or projection of many things at once

Belie   to give a false impression of

Belligerent   inclined to or exhibiting assertiveness, hostility, or combativeness

Benefactor   one who confers a benefit, esp. one who makes a gift or bequest

Beneficiary   one who benefits from something

Benevolent   marked by or disposed to doing good

Benign   having no significant effect; harmless

Bequeathing   handing down, transmitting

Berate   to scold or condemn vehemently and at length

Bereft   deprived or robbed of possession of something

Beseech   to beg for urgently or anxiously

Bickering   to engage in a petulant or petty quarrel

Boisterous   noisily turbulent; rowdy

Bolster   to give a boost to

Botched   to foul up hopelessly; failed, spoiled

Boundless   having no boundaries; vast

Bourgeois   marked by a concern for material interests and respectability and a tendency toward mediocrity, usually used disparagingly

Braggart   a loud, arrogant boaster

Breach   infraction or violation of a law, obligation, tie, or standard

Brooding   to dwell gloomily on a subject, worrying

Buffoonery   foolish or playful behavior

Burgeoning   growing and expanding rapidly

Burrow   a hole or excavation in the ground made by an animal (such as a rabbit) for shelter and habitation

Buttress   something that supports or strengthens

Cacophony   harsh or discordant sound; dissonance

Cajole   to persuade with flattery or gentle urging, especially in the face of reluctance

Calamity   an extraordinarily grave event marked by great loss and lasting distress

Callous   feeling no sympathy for others

Camaraderie   a spirit of friendly good fellowship

Canonical   conforming to a general rule or acceptable procedure; orthodox

Cantankerous   difficult or irritating to deal with

Capacious   containing or capable of containing a great deal

Captivate   to influence and dominate by some special charm, art, or trait and with an irresistible appeal

Carnivores   any of an order (Carnivora) of typically flesh-eating mammals that includes dogs, foxes, bears, raccoons, and cats

Cartographer   one who makes maps

Castigation   to subject to severe punishment, reproof, or criticism

Cataclysmic   a momentous and violent event marked by overwhelming upheaval and demolition

Cathartic   characterized by a purification or purgation of the emotions that brings about spiritual renewal or release from tension

Cavorting   prancing

Censured   to find fault with and criticize as blameworthy (note that the word censure is similar in appearance to the word censor (footnote 733), but different in meaning)

Cerebral   of or relating to the brain or the intellect

Certitude   the state of being or feeling certain

Chagrin   disquietude or distress of mind caused by humiliation, disappointment, or failure

Charismatic   having, exhibiting, or based on charisma (a special magnetic charm or appeal)

Charitable   of or relating to charity (generosity and helpfulness especially toward the needy)

Chasm   a marked division, separation, or difference

Cherished   to hold dear; feel or show affection for

Chide   reproach in a usually mild and constructive manner; scold

Circuitous   having a circular or winding course; roundabout, indirect

Circuitry   the components of an electric circuit

Circumlocutions   the use of an unnecessarily large number of words to express an idea

Circumscribe   to surround by or as if by a boundary

Clairvoyant   the ability to perceive matters beyond the range of ordinary perception

Clandestine   marked by, held in, or conducted with secrecy

Clientele   customers, patrons

Cloying   excessively sweet or sentimental

Coalesce   to arise from the combination of distinct elements; to unite into a whole

Coerce   to compel to an act or choice

Cognizant   knowledgeable about something, especially through personal experience; mindful

Coherently   logically or aesthetically ordered or integrated

Cohort   companion, colleague

Collaborator   co-worker, colleague; a person working jointly with others, especially in an intellectual endeavor

Colloquial   characteristic of familiar and informal conversation

Collude   conspire, plot

Colossal   of a bulk, extent, power, or effect approaching the stupendous or incredible

Combativeness   marked by eagerness to fight or contend

Commodities   an economic good as in an article of commerce (something bought or sold), especially when delivered for shipment

Comparatively   considered as if in comparison to something else; relatively

Compassionately   having or showing compassion (sympathetic consciousness of others' distress, together with a desire to alleviate it)

Compatriot   fellow countryman

Compelling   demanding attention

Complacency   self-satisfaction accompanied by unawareness of actual dangers or deficiencies

Complying   to conform or adapt one's actions to another's wishes, to a rule, or to a necessity

Compromise   to adjust or settle by mutual concessions (see also footnote 802 for a different usage)

Compulsive   obsessive, habitual, or irrational behavior

Comrade   an intimate friend or associate; companion

Conception   the originating of something in the mind; idea

Conciliatory   to make compatible; reconcile

Concocted   to prepare by combining raw materials; devise

Concur   to express agreement

Condemn   to declare to be bad, wrong, or evil

Condescending   to assume an air of superiority

Condone   to pardon or overlook voluntarily; *especially* to treat as if trivial, harmless, or of no importance

Confiscate   to seize by or as if by authority

Conflagration   fire, especially a large disastrous fire

Confounding   baffling, frustrating

Confrontation   the clashing of forces or ideas; conflict

Congeal   to change from a fluid state to a solid state by or as if by cold

Conjecture   a conclusion deduced by surmise or guesswork

Conjure   to bring to mind

Consciousness   the quality or state of being aware especially of something within oneself

Consecrate   to make inviolable or venerable (can also mean to declare sacred)

Consensus   general agreement; unanimity

Consign   commit, especially to a final destination or fate

Constructive   promoting improvement or development

Consummate   extremely skilled and accomplished

Contemporaries   one of the same age or nearly the same age as another

Contemporary   marked by characteristics of the present period; modern

Contemptuously   with contempt, disdain

Contentious   likely to cause contention (rivalry, competition)

Contiguous   touching or connected throughout in an unbroken sequence

Contrary   a fact or condition incompatible with another; opposite

Contrite   grieving and penitent for sin or shortcoming

Conundrum   an intricate and difficult problem

Conventional   according with, sanctioned by, or based on convention (a principle or procedure accepted as true or correct); ordinary, conformist, predictable

Conviction   a strong persuasion or belief

Cordial   warmly and genially affable

Correlation   a relation existing between phenomena or things or between mathematical or statistical variables which tend to vary, be associated, or occur together in a way not expected on the basis of chance alone

Corroboration   to support with evidence or authority

Corrosive   having the power to break down or eat away at something (can also mean very sarcastic)

Corrupt   to change from good to bad in morals, manners, or actions

Cosmopolitan   having wide international sophistication

Couched   to lay (oneself) down for rest or sleep

Counteract   to make ineffective or restrain or neutralize the usually ill effects of by an opposite force

Covenant   a usually formal, solemn, and binding agreement

Covet   to wish for enviously

Craftiness   skillfulness, cleverness

Crass   having or indicating such grossness of mind as precludes delicacy and discrimination

Cryptic   having or seeming to have a hidden or ambiguous meaning

Crystallize   to cause to take a definite form

Culminate   to reach the highest or a climactic or decisive point

Culpable   guilty; meriting condemnation or blame, especially as wrong or harmful

Cultivating   fostering, furthering, encouraging

Cumulative   made up of accumulated parts

Cunning   displaying keen insight

Curtail   to make less by or as if by cutting off or away some part; shorten

Cynically   having a sneering disbelief in sincerity or integrity

Cynicism   having or showing the attitude or temper of a cynic (a fault-finding captious critic)

Daunting   something that daunts (lessens one's courage)

Debacle   a great disaster; fiasco

Debatable   arguable, worthy of debate or consideration

Debilitating   impairing the strength of

Debunk   to expose the sham or falseness of

Decadent   self-indulgent

Deceitful   having a tendency or disposition to deceive; not honest

Decorous   marked by propriety and good taste

Decry   to express strong disapproval of; condemn

Deduction   a conclusion reached by logic or reasoning

Default   a selection automatically used by a computer program in the absence of a choice made by the user; a course taken without an active choice

Defer   postpone, put off

Deference   in consideration of

Defiantly   full of defiance (disposition to resist, willingness to contend or fight)

Deflect   to turn from a straight course or fixed direction; bend

Deftly   characterized by facility and skill

Degradation   the act or process of degrading (to impair in respect to some physical property)

Deliberate   characterized by or resulting from careful and thorough consideration

Delineated   to mark the outline of; demarcated

Demean   to lower in character, status, or reputation

Demeanor   behavior toward others, outward manner; conduct

Dénouement   finale, conclusion

Denounced   to pronounce, especially publicly, to be bad, blameworthy, or evil

Deplorable   deserving censure or contempt

Deprived   marked by deprivation, especially a lack of the necessities of life or of healthful environmental influences

Derelict   abandoned, esp. by the owner or occupant; run-down

Derision   the use of ridicule or scorn to show contempt

Derisively   expressing ridicule, scorn, or contempt

Derogatory   expressive of a low opinion, disparaging

Desecrate   to treat disrespectfully, irreverently, or outrageously

Desolate   deserted, isolated

Despoiling   to strip of belongings and value; pillage

Destitute   lacking possessions and resources; especially suffering extreme poverty

Detached   exhibiting an aloof objectivity; disconnected, removed

Detract   to diminish the importance, value, or effectiveness of something

Detritus   loose material (such as rock fragments or organic particles) that results directly from disintegration

Devalued   to lessen the value of

Deviate   to depart from an established course or norm; stray

Deviousness   not straightforward; deceptive

Diffidently   hesitant in acting or speaking through lack of self-confidence

Digress   to turn aside especially from the main subject of attention or course of argument

Dimension   one of the elements or factors making up a complete personality or entity

Diminished   reduced in scope or size

Dingy   dirty, discolored

Dire   warning of disaster

Disavow   deny responsibility for

Discern   to recognize or identify as separate and distinct; discriminate

Discomfited   to put in a state of perplexity and embarrassment

Disconcert   to throw into confusion

Discourse   talk, converse

Discourteous   lacking courtesy; rude, impolite

Discredit   to refuse to accept as true or accurate

Discretion   the quality of being discreet, especially cautious reserve in speech

Discretionary   left to discretion, exercised at one's own discretion (the quality of being discreet; cautious reserve in speech)

Disdainful   full of a feeling of contempt for what is beneath one; scornful

Disgruntled   discontent, unhappy

Disillusionment   to leave without illusion or naive faith and trust

Disingenuous   lacking in candor; calculating

Disparaging   to speak slightingly about; decry

Disparate   containing or made up of fundamentally different and often incongruous elements

Disparity   containing or made up of fundamentally different and often incongruous elements

Dispel   to drive away by or as if by scattering; dissipate

Disputant   one who is engaged in a dispute

Dissembler   one who puts on a false appearance; conceals facts, intentions or feelings under some pretense

Disseminate   to disperse throughout

Dissent   to differ in opinion

Dissident   disagreeing with an opinion or group

Dissipated   to cause to spread thin or scatter and gradually vanish (one's sympathy is eventually *dissipated*)

Diversion   the act or an instance of diverting from a course, activity, or use; deviation

Divine   supremely good

Divisive   creating disunity or dissension

Divulge   reveal, tell

Doctrinaire   one who attempts to put into effect an abstract doctrine or theory with little or no regard for practical difficulties

Domestic   devoted to home duties and pleasures

Drub   to abuse with words; berate

Dubious   giving rise to uncertainty

Earmark   to designate (as funds) for a specific use or owner

Eccentric   deviating from conventional or accepted usage or conduct, especially in odd or whimsical ways

Eclectic   composed of elements drawn from different sources

Ecstatic   of, relating to, or marked by ecstasy (a state of overwhelming emotion, especially rapturous delight)

Editorial   a newspaper or magazine article that gives the opinions of the editors or publishers; also an expression of opinion that resembles such an article (a television *editorial*)

Efface   to eliminate or make indistinct by or as if by wearing away a surface

Efficaciously   effective; having the power to achieve the desired effect

Egalitarian   one who believes in human equality, especially with respect to social, economic, and political rights

Egregious   conspicuously bad; flagrant

Elaborate   give details, expand upon a subject

Elation   marked by high spirits; exultant

Elitist   consciousness of being or belonging to an elite (a socially superior group)

Elocutionist   one who is effective in the art of public speaking

Eloquent   vividly or movingly expressive or revealing

Elude   to escape the perception, understanding, or grasp of

Elusive   tending to elude, as in tending to evade grasp or pursuit

Emanate   to come out from a source

Emancipation   to free from restraint, control, or the power of another

Embellish   to heighten the attractiveness of by adding ornamental details

Embittered   having bitter feelings

Embody   to represent in human or animal form; personify

Embroil   to involve in conflict or difficulties

Emend   to correct

Emergent   newly formed or prominent

Emigrate   to leave one's place of residence or country to live elsewhere

Eminently   to a high degree; very

Emissary   one designated as the agent of another

Empathetic   being understanding of, aware of, and sensitive to the feelings, thoughts, and experiences of another

Empathy   the action of understanding, being aware of, being sensitive to, and vicariously experiencing the feelings, thoughts, and experience of another of either the past or present without having the feelings, thoughts, and experience fully communicated in an objectively explicit manner

Emphatically   with emphasis, forcefully

Empowering   yielding power or authority

Emulate   try to be like, imitate

Enable   to provide with the means or opportunity

Encampment   the state of being encamped (to place or establish in a camp)

Encapsulated   epitomized

Enclosure   something that encloses (to close in)

Encompasses   to form a circle about, enclose

Encroaching   to enter by gradual steps or by stealth into the possessions or rights of another

Encumbered   weighed down, burdened

Endear   to cause to become beloved or admired

Endeavor   to attempt (as the fulfillment of an obligation) by exertion of effort

Endorsement   backing, sanction, approval

Enduring   lasting

Enervated   lacking physical, mental, or moral vigor; to lessen the vitality or strength of

Engender   to cause to exist or develop

Enigmatic   something hard to understand or explain; mysterious

Enlighten   to furnish knowledge to

Enmity   positive, active, and typically mutual hatred or ill will

Ensemble   a complete costume of harmonizing or complementary clothing and accessories

Ensue   to take place afterward or as a result

Entangled   to involve in a perplexing or troublesome situation

Entitlement   the state or condition of being entitled; right

Entreated   to plead with, esp. in order to persuade

Enumerated   counted, tallied

Enveloped   to enclose or enfold completely with or as if with a covering

Envision   to picture to oneself

Ephemeral   lasting a very short time

Epistolary   contained in or carried on by letters

Equitable   fair

Eradicate   to do away with as if by pulling up from the roots

Erratic   characterized by lack of consistency, regularity, or uniformity; deviating from what is ordinary or standard

Espouse   to take up and support as a cause; become attached to

Esteem   to regard highly

Eternal   having infinite duration; everlasting

Ethical   involving or expressing moral approval or disapproval

Ethnicity   ethnic quality or affiliation

Ethos   the distinguishing character, sentiment, moral nature, or guiding beliefs of a person group or institution

Euphoric   a feeling of well-being or elation

Evade   avoid, dodge

Evanescent   tending to vanish like vapor

Evoke   to call forth or up; conjure

Exacerbate   to make more violent, bitter, or severe

Exalted   to raise in status (can also mean to praise, glorify, or honor)

Exasperated   irritated or annoyed

Exclusive   restricted in distribution, use, or appeal because of expense

Exculpate   to clear from alleged fault or guilt

Execution   the act or process of executing (to carry out fully; put completely into effect)

Exemplary   deserving imitation because of excellence; commendable

Exemplify   to show or illustrate by example

Exorbitantly   excessively; exceedingly

Explicitly   clearly, unambiguously

Exploit   a deed or an act

Expropriated   the action of the state in taking or modifying the property rights of an individual in the exercise of its sovereignty

Extant   currently or actually existing

Extenuating   to mitigate; to lessen or try to lessen the serious or extent of by making partial excuses

Extolled   praised highly; glorified

Extricate   get out, remove oneself

Exultant   filled with or expressing great joy or triumph; jubilant

Facile   easily accomplished or attained

Facilitate   to make easier, help bring about

Faction   a party or group (as within a government) that is often contentious or self-seeking

Factual   restricted to or based on fact

Fallacious   untrue; tending to deceive or mislead

Fantasize   to indulge in fantasy or reverie; daydream

Fathom   comprehend

Feigned   fictitious, faked; artificial

Felicitous   very well suited or expressed; apt

Feral   not domesticated or cultivated; wild

Ferocity   the quality or state of being ferocious (exhibiting or given to extreme fierceness and unrestrained violence and brutality)

Fervently   exhibited or marked by great intensity of feeling; zealously

Fickle   marked by lack of steadfastness, constancy, or stability; given to erratic changeableness

Flabbergast   to overwhelm with shock, surprise, or wonder

Flagrant   conspicuously offensive

Flippancy   unbecoming levity or pertness, especially in respect to grave or sacred matters

Florid   tinged with red

Flourish   grand gesture, display (also has another meaning, to thrive)

Flout   to treat with contemptuous disregard

Fodder   inferior or readily available material used to supply a heavy demand

Foil   to prevent from attaining an end; thwart

Foliage   the leaves of one or more plants

Folly   lack of good sense or normal prudence and foresight; foolishness

Foraged   searched; rummaged

Foray   a brief excursion or attempt especially outside one's accustomed sphere

Foreboding   to have an inward conviction of (as coming ill or misfortune)

Forlorn   being in poor condition; miserable

Formidable   causing fear, dread, or apprehension

Formulate   to reduce to or express in a formula

Fortitude   strength of mind that enables a person to encounter danger or adversity with courage

Foster   to promote the growth or development of

Franchise   the license granted to an individual or group to market a company's goods or services in a particular territory

Friction   the clashing between two persons or parties of opposed views

Fritter   to spend or waste bit by bit on trifles, or without commensurate return

Frivolity   playful merriment that lacks substance or purpose

Frolicsome   full of gaiety; playful

Frugal   characterized by economy in the expenditure of resources

Futile   serving no useful purpose; completely ineffective

Gaffe   a social or diplomatic blunder

Garish   offensively or distressingly bright; glaring

Gauge   estimate, judge

Generalizations   to make vague or indefinite statements

Genial   marked by sympathy or friendliness; kindly

Gibbering   to speak rapidly, inarticulately and often foolishly

Gingerly   very cautiously or carefully

Glacial   devoid of warmth and cordiality

Glutton   one given habitually to greedy and voracious eating and drinking

Goading   to incite or rouse as if with a goad; provoking, prodding

Gourmand   one who is heartily interested in good food and drink

Gracious   marked by kindness and courtesy

Grandiose   impressive because of uncommon largeness, scope, effect, or grandeur

Gratuity   something given voluntarily or beyond obligation usually for some service, esp. a tip

Gregarious   marked by or indicating a liking for companionship; sociable

Grievance   a cause of distress (as an unsatisfactory working condition) felt to afford reason for complaint

Habitable   capable of being lived in; suitable for habitation

Hackneyed   lacking in freshness or originality; trite

Harangue   a ranting speech or writing

Harbor   to hold a thought or feeling of

Harmonious   having the parts agreeably related; congruous

Haughty   blatantly and disdainfully proud; snooty, conceited

Heart-rending   heartbreaking

Heightened   to increase the amount or degree of

Heinous   hatefully or shockingly evil

Heralded   to greet, especially with enthusiasm; to hail, publicize, or signal

Heretofore   up to this time; hitherto

Hierarchy   the classification of a group of people according to ability or to economic, social, or professional standing; pecking order, chain of command

Hindrance   the state of being hindered (to make slow or difficult the progress of)

Homogenize   to blend (diverse elements) into a uniform mixture

Hospitable   promising or suggesting generous and cordial welcome

Hostility   deep-seated, usually mutual, ill will

Hypocrite   a person who puts on a false appearance of virtue or religion

Hypothesis   a tentative assumption made in order to draw out and test its logical or empirical consequences; theory

Idealism   the practice of forming ideals or living under their influence

Idealist   one guided by ideals, especially one who places ideals before practical considerations

Idealistic   characteristic of idealism (the practice of forming ideals or living under their influence)

Idolatry immoderate attachment or devotion to something

Ignite to heat up; excite

Illicit not permitted; against the rules or law

Illimitable incapable of being limited or bounded

Illogical not observing the principles of logic; not reasonable or sound

Immerse to plunge into something that surrounds or covers; especially to plunge or dip into a fluid

Imminent ready to take place; looming, about to happen

Immobilized incapable of moving

Immutable not capable of or susceptible to change

Impassion to arouse the feelings or passions of

Impassive giving no sign of feeling or expression

Impenitent not penitent (feeling or expressing humble or regretful pain or sorrow for sins or offenses)

Imperceptible not perceptible by a sense or by the mind, extremely slight, gradual, or subtle

Impermanent not permanent; transient

Impetuous marked by impulsive vehemence or passion

Impetus a driving force; impulse

Impious not pious; lacking in reverence or proper respect (as for God or one's parents)

Implausible not plausible; provoking disbelief

Implementation to carry out; to give practical effect to and ensure of actual fulfillment by concrete measures

Implication the act of implying, the state of being implied (indicate by inference, association, or necessary consequence rather than by direct statement)

Imposing impressive in size, bearing, dignity, or grandeur

Impressionable capable of being easily impressed

Imprint to fix indelibly or permanently

Impropriety   an improper or indecorous act or remark; especially an unacceptable use of a word or of language

Impugn   to assail by words or arguments; oppose or attack as false or lacking integrity

Impulsively   spontaneously, on a whim

Imputed   to lay the responsibility or blame for, often falsely or unjustly; charge, attribute

Inanimate   not endowed with life or spirit

Inarticulate   incapable of speech, esp. under stress of emotion

Inauspicious   not auspicious or favorable; ominous

Incalculably   not capable of being calculated as in not predictable

Incantation   a use of spells or verbal charms spoken or sung as part of a ritual of magic

Incarceration   to put in prison

Inception   an act, process, or instance of beginning

Incessantly   non-stop, never ending

Incisively   impressively direct and decisive (as in manner of presentation)

Incline   to lean, tend, or become drawn toward an opinion or course of conduct

Incongruous   lacking congruity, not harmonious, incompatible

Inconsequential   of no significance or importance

Incumbent   obligatory, imposed as a duty (is also commonly used to refer to a politician who is currently in office)

Indecorous   not decorous; conflicting with accepted standards of good conduct or good taste

Indefatigable   incapable of being fatigued; untiring

Indefensible   incapable of being justified or excused; inexcusable

Indeterminate   not definitely or precisely determined; vague

Indifferent   apathetic, unconcerned

Indignant   filled with or marked by indignation (anger aroused by something unjust, unworthy, or mean)

Indiscernible   incapable of being discerned; not recognizable as distinct

Indiscretion   something (an act or a remark) marked by a lack of discretion

Indiscriminately   not marked by careful distinction; deficient in discrimination and discernment; haphazard; random

Indomitable   incapable of being subdued; unconquerable

Inducement   a motive or consideration that leads one to action

Industrious   persistently active; zealous

Ineffable   incapable of being expressed in words; indescribable

Inefficacious   lacking the power to produce the desired effect

Inept   generally incompetent; bungling

Inequities   unequal things or situations

Inestimably   incapable of being estimated

Inexorable   not to be persuaded or moved by entreaty (pleas); relentless

Inferred   derived as a conclusion from facts or premises

Inflamed   to excite to excessive or uncontrollable action or feeling

Inflammatory   tending to excite anger, disorder, or tumult

Infused   to cause to be permeated with something

Ingenious   marked by originality, resourcefulness, and cleverness in conception or execution

Inherent   involved in the constitution or essential character of something, belonging by nature or habit

Innate   existing in, belonging to, or determined by factors present in an individual from birth

Innovation   a new idea, method, or device

Innovative   characterized by, tending to, or introducing innovations (a new idea, method, or device)

Innuendo   an oblique allusion; hint, insinuation

Inordinately   exceeding reasonable limits; excessively

Insidious   having a gradual and cumulative effect

Insight   the power or act of seeing into a situation

Insinuate   to impart or communicate with artful or oblique reference

Insolent   insultingly contemptuous in speech or conduct; overbearing

Instill   to impart gradually

Insular   characteristic of an isolated people, especially having a narrow provincial viewpoint

Integral   essential to completeness

Integrity   firm adherence to a code of especially moral or artistic values

Intelligentsia   intellectuals who form an artistic, social, or political vanguard or elite

Intemperate   not temperate (moderate); extreme, immoderate

Interlocutor   those who take part in a dialogue or conversation

Interlude   an intervening or interruptive period, space or event; interval

Interminable   having or seeming to have no end

Interpretation   the act or the result of interpreting (to conceive in the light of individual belief, judgment, or circumstance)

Interspersed   to place something at intervals in or among

Intervene   to come in or between by way of hindrance or modification

Interweave   to mix or blend together

Intransigent   refusing to compromise or abandon an extreme position or attitude; uncompromising

Intrepid   characterized by resolute fearlessness, fortitude, and endurance

Introspective   a reflective looking inward; an examination of one's own thoughts and feelings

Intuitively   known or perceived by intuition (quick and ready insight); instinctively

Inundate   to overwhelm; to cover with a flood

Invariably   not changing or capable of change; constant

Invigorating   stimulating, energizing

Inviolable   secure from violation or profanation; unbreakable

Invoke   bring about; cause

Iridescent   a lustrous rainbowlike play of color caused by differential refraction of light waves (as from an oil slick, soap bubble, or fish scales) that tends to change as the angle of view changes

Irrefutable   impossible to refute or deny

Irresolute   indecisive (not resolute or firm)

Irreverent   lacking proper respect or seriousness

Jaded   world-weary, cynical

Jester   fool

Joie de vivre   (French) joy of living; keen or buoyant enjoyment of life

Jollity   the quality or state of being jolly (full of high spirits)

Jovial   markedly good-humored, especially as evidenced by jollity and conviviality

Jubilation   an expression of great joy

Juxtaposition   the act or an instance of placing two or more things side by side

Kinship   the quality or state of being kin; relationship

Languidly   lacking force or quickness of movement; slow

Latent   present and capable of becoming, though not now visible, obvious, or active

Lauded   praise, extol

Lavish   expending or bestowing profusely

Legitimacy   the quality or state of being legitimate (being exactly as purposed, neither spurious nor false)

Legitimating   to show or affirm to be justified

Levy   to impose or collect by legal authority

Liberal   of or constituting a political party advocating or associated with the principles of political liberalism

Liberate   to set free

Limitation   something that limits; restraint

Linchpin   one that serves to hold together the elements of a complex

Literally   actually, in a literal sense or manner

Lithe   characterized by easy flexibility and grace

Litigate   to contest in law

Livid   very angry; enraged

Loathed   to dislike greatly and often with disgust or intolerance

Lobbyist   one who attempts to influence or sway (as a public official) toward a desired action; activist, campaigner

Ludicrous   amusing or laughable through obvious absurdity, incongruity, exaggeration, or eccentricity

Lull   quiet period

Lummox   clumsy person

Lurid   causing horror or revulsion; ghastly

Machination   a scheming or crafty action or artful design intended to accomplish some usually evil end

Maelstrom   a powerful often violent whirlpool sucking in objects within a given radius

Malediction   to speak evil of

Malice   intent to commit an unlawful act or cause harm without legal justification or excuse

Malicious   given to, marked by, or arising from malice (desire to cause pain, injury, or distress to another)

Malign   to utter injuriously misleading reports about; to speak evil of

Malinger   to pretend incapacity (as illness) so as to avoid duty or work; shirk

Mandated   to make mandatory, obligatory

Manifestation   the act, process, or instance of manifesting (readily perceived by the senses, esp. by sight)

Maverick   an independent individual who does not go along with a group or party

Maxim   a saying of a proverbial nature; adage

Mechanisms   a process or technique for achieving a result

Mediate   to bring accord out of by action as an intermediary

Melancholy   depression of spirits; dejection

Melodiously   having a pleasing sound or melody

Melodrama   a drama characterized by extravagant theatricality

Mendicant   beggar

Methodically   habitually proceeding according to method; systematically

Meticulously   extremely carefully, painstakingly

Microcosm   a little world; especially the human race or human nature seen as an epitome of the world or the universe

Miff   to put into ill humor; offend

Mirage   an optical effect that is sometimes seen at sea, in the desert, or over a hot pavement, that may have the appearance of a pool of water

Mire   a troublesome or intractable situation

Misconception   a mistaken idea or concept

Misgiving   to suggest doubt or fear to

Missive   written communication; letter

Modest   unassuming, unpretentious; limited in size, amount, or scope

Modicum   a small amount

Modulate   to adjust to or keep in proper measure or proportion; temper

Mollify   to soothe in temper or disposition; placate, calm

Momentous   important, consequential

Monstrosity   an object of great and often frightening size, force, or complexity

Morass   something that traps, confuses, or impedes

Morose   having a sullen or gloomy disposition

Mortified   subjected to severe and vexing embarrassment

Mundane   characterized by the practical, transitory, and ordinary; commonplace

Munificence   characterized by great liberality or generosity

Naïve   deficient in worldly wisdom or informed judgment

Narcissistic   excessive concern or love of oneself

Narratives   something that is narrated; a story

Navigable   deep enough and wide enough to afford passage to ships

Nebulous   indistinct, vague

Nefarious   flagrantly wicked or impious; evil, malicious

Negate   to cause to be ineffective or invalid

Negligible   so small or unimportant or of so little consequence as to warrant little or no attention

Nemesis   a formidable and usually victorious rival or opponent

Neutrality   the quality or state of being neutral, esp. refusal to take part in a war between other powers

Nonchalance   having an air of easy unconcern or indifference

Nondescript   lacking distinctive or interesting qualities; dull

Nostalgic   a wistful or excessively sentimental, sometimes abnormal, yearning for return to or of some past period or irrecoverable condition

Notions   a theory or belief held by a person or group

Novelty   something new and fresh

Novice   beginner

Obdurate   resistant to persuasion or softening influences; stubborn

Objective   expressing or dealing with facts or conditions as perceived without distortion by personal feelings, prejudices, or interpretations; without bias

Oblique   neither perpendicular nor parallel

Oblivious   lacking active conscious knowledge or awareness

Obstinate   perversely adhering to an opinion, purpose, or course in spite of reason, arguments, or persuasion; stubborn, inflexible

Obstreperous   marked by unruly or aggressive noisiness

Obtuse   lacking sharpness or quickness of sensibility or intellect

Offensive   making attack

Ominously   being or exhibiting an omen, especially foreboding or foreshadowing evil

Omnipresent   present in all places at all times

Onerous   involving, imposing, or constituting a burden

Opulent   exhibiting or characterized by opulence (wealth, affluence); magnificent, lavish

Oration   speech; an elaborate discourse delivered in a formal and dignified manner

Orator   one distinguished for skill and power as a public speaker

Organic   of, relating to, or containing carbon compounds

Ornate   elaborately or excessively decorated

Ostensibly   being such in appearance; plausible rather than demonstrably true

Ostentatious   marked by or fond of conspicuous or vainglorious and sometimes pretentious display

Ostracized   to exclude from a group by common consent

Outlandish   exceeding proper or reasonable limits or standards

Overtly   in a manner that is open to view

Palate   the sense of taste

Pallid   deficient in color; wan

Palpable   easily perceptible

Pander   cater or exploit the weakness of others

Paradox   a statement that is seemingly contradictory or opposed to common sense and yet is perhaps true

Paramount   superior to all others; supreme

Parasite   an organism living in, with, or on another organism

Parched   dehydrated

Pariah   outcast

Parsimony   the quality of being careful with money or resources; thrift

Partake   to take part in or experience something along with others

Patent   a writing securing to an inventor for a term of years the exclusive right to make, use, or sell an invention

Patently   readily visible or intelligible; obvious

Patrons   customers

Pedantic   a style of teaching characterized by formality and undue attention to minutiae

Penchant   a strong and continued inclination; liking

Penitence   sorrow for sins or faults

Pensive   musingly or dreamily thoughtful

Penurious   marked by a cramping and oppressive lack of resources (as in money)

Perception   capable of or exhibiting keen perception; observant

Perceptiveness   ability to notice and see; discernment, sharpness

Perfidious   disloyal or faithless

Perfunctory   characterized by routine or superficiality

Perilous   full of or involving peril (risk)

Periodically   occurring or recurring at regular intervals

Periphery   the external boundary or surface of a body

Permeate   to spread or diffuse through

Perpetually   continuing forever

Perpetuate   to make perpetual or to cause to last indefinitely

Perplexed   filled with uncertainty; puzzled

Persevere   to persist in a state, enterprise, or undertaking in spite of counter influences, opposition, or influences

Perspective   point of view

Perspicacity   acute mental vision or discernment; keen

Pertinent   having a clear decisive relevance to the matter in hand

Peruse   to examine or consider with attention and in detail; study

Pervasive   something that pervades (to become diffused throughout every part of) or tends to pervade

Pessimistic   negative, gloomy

Phenomenon   an observable fact or event

Philanthropic   of, relating to, or characterized by philanthropy (active effort to promote human welfare)

Phlegmatic   having or showing a slow and stolid temperament; apathetic

Pigeonhole   a neat category which usually fails to reflect actual complexities

Pinioned   to disable or restrain; to bind fast

Pique   to excite or arouse by a provocation, challenge, or rebuff

Placating   to soothe or mollify, especially by concessions; appease

Plaintive   expressive of suffering or woe; mournful

Pliable   yielding readily to others

Poignant   deeply affecting; touching

Polarize   to break up into opposing factions or groupings

Pompous   having or exhibiting self-importance; arrogant

Ponder   to think or consider especially quietly, soberly, and deeply

Ponderous   of very great weight; heavy

Portal   a door or entrance, especially a grand or imposing one

Portentously   something that foreshadows a coming event

Practical   of, relating to, or manifested in practice or action; not theoretical or ideal

Pragmatist   a person who takes a practical approach to problems and affairs

Preamble   an introductory statement

Precarious   characterized by a lack or security or stability that threatens with danger

Precepts   a command or principle intended as a general rule of action

Precipitate   to bring about, especially abruptly; to cause to separate from solution or suspension

Precipitous   very steep, perpendicular, or overhanging in rise or fall (a *precipitous* slope)

Preclude   to make impossible by necessary consequence, rule out in advance

Precocious   exhibiting mature qualities at an unusually early age

Preconceived   to form (as an opinion) prior to actual knowledge or experience

Preconceptions   opinions that are formed prior to actual knowledge or experience

Predatory   living by predation (a mode of life in which food is primarily obtained by the killing and consuming of animals)

Predetermined   to determine beforehand

Preempted   to take the place of

Preoccupied   engrossed, busy, or occupied with thought

Preponderance   a superiority in weight, power, importance, or strength

Presiding   occupying a place of authority; acting as president, chairman, or moderator

Presumptuous   overstepping due bounds (as of propriety or courtesy); taking liberties

Pretense   false show

Pretentious   making usually unjustified or excessive claims (as of value or standing); showy, ostentatious

Pretext   a purpose or motive alleged or an appearance assumed in order to cloak the real intention or state of affairs

Procrastinating   putting off until later

Procure   to get possession of; obtain by particular care and effort

Profoundly   characterized by intensity of feeling or quality

Profundity   the quality or state of being profound (having intellectual depth or insight)

Profusion   great quantity; lavish display or supply

Proliferate   to grow by rapid production of new parts, cells, buds, or offspring; reproduce, multiply

Prolific   abundant growth, generation, or reproduction

Prominent   widely and popularly known

Prompt   to move to action; incite

Promulgate   to put (a law) into action or force

Pronouncement   a usually formal declaration of opinion

Propelled   to drive forward or onward by or as if by means of a force that imparts motion; pushed

Propensity   an often intense natural inclination or preference

Prophetic   foretelling events; predictive

Proponent   one who argues in favor of something; advocate

Proprietor   one who has the legal right or exclusive title to something

Prosaic   dull, unimaginative

Proselytize   to recruit someone to join one's party, institution, or cause

Protégé   one who is protected or trained or whose career is furthered by a person of experience, prominence, or influence

Protocol   the plan of a scientific experiment

Prototype   a standard or typical example

Protract   to prolong in time or space

Proverbial   something that has become a proverb or byword; commonly spoken of

Provocative   serving or tending to provoke, excite, or stimulate

Prowess   extraordinary ability

Proximity   nearness, closeness

Prudent   shrewd in the management of practical affairs; sensible

Punctuate   to break into or interrupt at intervals

Pundits   one who gives opinions in an authoritative manner; critic

Purportedly   ostensibly, allegedly

Purposefully   with intent; having a purpose

Quandary   a state of perplexity or doubt

Quell   quiet, pacify

Querulous   argumentative

Quest   a person or group of persons who search or make inquiry; mission, expedition

Quintessential   the most typical example or representative

Radical   tending or disposed to make extreme changes in existing views, habits, conditions, or institutions

Raging   violent, wild

Rambled   to talk or write in a long-winded, wandering fashion

Ramification   consequence, outcome

Ramshackle   appearing ready to collapse

Rancorously   characterized by bitter, deep-seated ill will

Rapport   relation marked by harmony, conformity, accord, or affinity

Rational   relating to, based on, or agreeable to reason; lucid

Raucous   boisterously, disorderly

Reactionary   ultraconservative in politics

Recommenced   to start again

Reconciliation   a restoration of friendship or harmony

Recrimination   to make a retaliating charge against an accuser

Rectify   to set right; remedy, correct

Redeeming   to release from blame or debt

Refined   free from what is coarse, vulgar, or uncouth

Refractive   distortion of an image by viewing through a medium

Refurbish   to brighten or freshen up; renovate

Reiterate   to state or do over again or repeatedly, sometimes with wearying effect

Relish   a strong liking

Remiss   showing neglect or inattention

Remote   isolated, secluded, far from activity

Remuneration   an act or fact of remunerating (to pay an equivalent to for a service, loss, or expense); recompense

Renovation   to restore to a former better state (as by cleaning, repairing, or rebuilding)

Renunciation   the act of refusing to follow, obey, or recognize any further

Repast   the act or time of taking food

Repentance   to feel regret or contrition

Repercussion   a widespread, indirect, or unforeseen effect of an act, action, or event

Replete   fully or abundantly provided or filled

Repose   to lie at rest

Reprehensible   deserving criticism

Repudiate   to reject or renounce; to refuse to have anything to do with

Requisite   essential, necessary

Resentment   a feeling of indignant displeasure or persistent ill will at something regarded as a wrong, insult, or injury

Resolute   marked by firm determination; resolved

Resolve   to deal with successfully, to clear up

Resonate   to produce or exhibit resonance (a quality of evoking response)

Resounding   emphatic, unequivocal

Respite   an interval of rest or relief

Resplendent   shining brilliantly; characterized by a glowing splendor

Restate   to state again or in another way

Restorative   something that serves to restore to consciousness, vigor, or health

Restrained   reserved, controlled; to limit, restrict, or keep under control

Reticent   restrained in expression, presentation, or appearance

Retribution   something given or exacted in recompense, esp. punishment

Revelation   the act of revealing an enlightening or divine truth

Revelatory   serving to reveal something

Reverberate   to continue in or as if in a series of echoes; resound

Reverence   honor or respect felt or shown; deference; especially profound or adoring awed respect

Revoke   to annul by recalling or taking back; rescind

Revulsion   a sense of utter distaste or repugnance

Rhapsody   a highly emotional utterance (can also refer to a highly emotional literary work, etc.)

Rhetoric   a type or mode of language or speech; also insincere or lofty language

Righteous   arising from an outraged sense of justice or morality

Rigor   a condition that makes life difficult, challenging, or uncomfortable; severity

Rousing   giving rise to excitement; stirring

Rudiment   a basic principle, element, or fundamental skill

Rueful   mournful, regretful

Ruminate   to go over in the mind repeatedly and often casually or slowly

Sagacity   keen in sense of perception and judgment, discerning

Salvage   the act of saving or rescuing property in danger (as from fire)

Salvation   deliverance from danger or difficulty

Sanctimonious   affecting piousness, hypocritically devout

Sarcastically   having the character of sarcasm (a mode of satirical wit depending for its effect on bitter, caustic, and often ironic language that is usually directed against an individual)

Satire   wit, irony, or sarcasm used to expose and discredit vice or folly

Scapegoat   one that bears the blame for others

Scathing   to assail with withering denunciation

Scheme   a plan or program of action, especially a crafty or secret one

Scoffed   to treat or address with derision; mocked, ridiculed

Scorn   open dislike and disrespect or derision often mixed with indignation

Scrupulous   punctiliously exact; painstaking

Scrutinize   to examine closely and minutely

Scurried   scampered; to move in or as if in a brisk rapidly alternating step

Self-aggrandizement   to make oneself appear greater; to praise oneself

Sensationalize   to present in a sensational (arousing or tending to arouse [as by lurid details] a quick, intense, and usually superficial interest, curiosity, or emotional reaction) manner

Sensibilities   sensitivities; awareness of and responsiveness to something

Sentient   finely sensitive in perception or feeling; aware

Sentiment   an attitude, thought, or judgment prompted by feeling

Serendipitously   obtained by serendipity (the faculty of finding valuable or agreeable things accidentally)

Serene   marked by or suggestive of utter calm and unruffled repose or quietude; peaceful

Sermonize   to preach to or on at length

Servile   of or befitting a slave or a menial person

Shroud   something that covers, screens, or guards

Shun   to avoid deliberately and especially habitually

Skirt   to avoid, especially because of difficulty or fear of controversy

Sleuth   detective

Slot   to place in or assign to a slot (a narrow opening or groove)

Solicitous   manifesting or expressing solicitude (attentive care and protectiveness)

Solidarity   unity (as of a group or class) that produces or is based on community of interests, objectives, and standards

Soluble   able to dissolve in a liquid

Sparsely   of few and scattered elements, especially not thickly grown or settled

Specter   something that haunts or perturbs the mind

Speculate   to review something idly or casually and often inconclusively

Spurious   outwardly similar or corresponding to something without having its genuine qualities; false

Squander   to spend extravagantly or foolishly

Squelch   to completely suppress

Stagnating   remaining stale (usually from lack of circulation or flow)

Statute   a law enacted by the legislative branch of a government

Staunch   steadfast in loyalty or principle

Stealthy   intended to escape observation; secret

Stifling   to withhold from circulation or expression; repressing

Stimulus   something that rouses or incites to activity

Stoic   not showing passion or feeling

Strife   an act of contention; fight, struggle

Stylistic   of or relating especially to literary or artistic style

Subject   to cause or force to undergo or endure

Subjective   modified or affected by personal views, experience, or background (a *subjective* account of the incident)

Submissive   to yield oneself to the authority or will of another

Subsequently   following in time, order, or place

Subsidize   to furnish with a subsidy (a grant or gift of money)

Subsist   to have or acquire the necessities of life (such as food and clothing)

Substantiate   to establish by proof or competent evidence; verify

Subversive   a cause of overthrow or destruction, esp. a systematic attempt to overthrow or undermine a government by persons working secretly within

Suffused   to spread over or through in the manner of fluid or light

Sully   to make soiled or tarnished

Superficial   presenting only an appearance without substance or significance

Supplant   to supersede (another), especially by force or treachery

Supple   readily adaptable or responsive to new situations

Supplement   something that completes or makes an addition

Suppress   to keep secret or to stop or prohibit the publication or revelation of

Surfeit   an overabundant supply; excess

Surmise   a thought or idea based on scanty evidence

Surmountable   able to prevail over; able to overcome

Surreal   having the intense irrational reality of a dream

Surreptitiously   done, made, or acquired by stealth; secretly, slyly

Susceptible   open to some stimulus, influence, or agency

Sycophant   a servile, self-serving flatterer

Symptomatic   characteristic, indicative

Synchronous   happening, existing, or arising at precisely the same time

Synonymous   having the same connotations, implications, or reference

Synthesize   to combine or produce by synthesis (the composition or combination of parts or elements so as to form a whole)

Synthetic   something resulting from synthesis rather than occurring naturally, esp. a product (as a drug or plastic) of chemical synthesis

Tabled   to remove from consideration indefinitely

Tacit   expressed or carried on without words or speech

Tactics   a device for accomplishing an end

Talisman   an object held as a charm to avert evil and bring good fortune

Taunting   to reproach or challenge in a mocking or insulting manner, jeer at

Temerity   nerve, boldness

Temperate   marked by moderation, not extreme or excessive; mild

Tenacious   persistent in maintaining or adhering to something valued or habitual

Tenacity   the quality or state of being tenacious (persistent in maintaining or adhering to something)

Tentatively   hesitantly

Tenuous   having little substance or strength

Theoretically   according to an ideal or assumed set of facts or principles, in theory

Theorized   to form a theory about; speculate

Therapeutic   providing or assisting in a cure

Throng   a multitude of assembled persons

Thwarted   to oppose successfully, to defeat the hopes or aspirations of

Toady   one who flatters in hope of gaining favors

Tonic   one who invigorates, restores, refreshes, or stimulates

Torpid   lacking in energy or vigor

Tractable   easily handled, managed, or wrought

Tranquility   the quality or state of being tranquil (free from disturbance or turmoil)

Transformation   the act, process, or instance of transforming (to change in composition or structure)

Transient   passing through or by a place with only a brief stay or sojourn

Translucent   clear, transparent

Transparent   fine or sheer enough to be seen through

Travesty   a debased, distorted, or grossly inferior imitation

Treacherous   marked by hidden dangers, hazards, or perils

Tremulous   characterized by or affected with trembling or tremors

Trepidation   apprehension, fear

Trivialize   to make trivial (of little worth or importance)

Trove   a valuable collection; treasure

Truculent   feeling or displaying ferocity; cruel, savage

Trump   a card of a suit any of whose cards will win over a card that is not of this suit

Ubiquitous   existing or being everywhere at the same time

Unalterable   not capable of being altered or changed

Unambiguously   without ambiguity or uncertainty; clearly, precisely

Uncanny   being beyond what is normal or expected, suggesting superhuman or supernatural powers

Uncensored   not examined for the purpose of deleting objectionable or sensitive information; unedited

Undermine   to weaken or ruin by degrees

Underscore   give emphasis to, highlight

Understate   to state or present with restraint, especially for effect

Unduly   in an undue manner; excessively

Unearthed   brought to light, discovered

Unfetter   emancipate, liberate

Unfounded   lacking a sound basis; groundless, unsupported

Unintelligible   incomprehensible, making no sense

Universal   worldwide, general, common

Unmitigated   not lessened; unrelieved

Unprecedented   having no precedent (previous example); novel

Unprepossessing   not attractive or tending to create a favorable impression

Unrelenting   not softening or yielding in determination

Unruffled   poised and serene, esp. in the face of setbacks or confusion

Unscrupulous   not scrupulous (having moral integrity); unprincipled

Unswerving   not swerving or turning aside; steady

Untenable   not able to be defended or occupied

Unutterable   being beyond the powers of description

Unyielding   not yielding (to surrender or relinquish to the control of another)

Uplifting   improving the spiritual, social, or intellectual condition of; inspiring, enriching

Upstart   unknown, insignificant person; low on the totem pole

Usurp   to take the place of by or as if by force; supplant

Utilitarian   no-frills, practical, and functional as opposed to decorative

Utopia   a place of ideal perfection

Utopian   of, relating to, or having the characteristics of a utopia, especially having impossibly ideal conditions, especially of social organization

Vacillating to waver in mind, will, or feeling hesitate in choice of opinions or courses

Vanity inflated pride in oneself or one's appearance

Vanquish to defeat in a conflict or contest

Variegated having discreet markings of different colors

Vast very great in size, amount, degree, or intensity, especially in extent or range

Vehemently marked by forceful energy

Veil to cover, provide, obscure, or conceal with or as if with a veil

Veneer a thin sheet of a material, finish, or coating

Venerable calling forth respect through age, character, and attainments

Venerate to regard with reverential respect or with admiring deference

Vengeance punishment inflicted in retaliation for an injury or offense

Venture an undertaking involving chance, risk, or danger

Verdant green with growing plants

Verifiable capable of being verified (to establish the truth, accuracy, or reality of)

Verity the quality or state of being true or real; esp. a fundamental and inevitably true value (such eternal verities as honor, love, and patriotism)

Vestige a trace, mark, or visible sign left by something (as an ancient city or a condition or practice) vanished or lost; relic

Vexed to bring trouble, stress, or agitation to

Vicarious experienced or realized through imaginative or sympathetic participation in the experience of another

Vigilant watchful, alert, and attentive

Vindictive disposed to seek revenge

Vindictive disposed to seek revenge; spiteful

Virtuoso expert, incredibly skillful and masterful

Visceral dealing with crude or elemental emotions; instinctive

Viscous   having or characterized by viscosity (the property of resistance to flow in a fluid or semifluid); a thick liquid

Vital   concerned with or necessary to the maintenance of life

Vitiate   to make faulty or defective, often by the addition of something that impairs

Vivacity   the quality or state of being vivacious (lively in temper, conduct, or spirit); enthusiasm

Vivid   producing a strong or clear impression on the senses; sharp, intense

Vocation   the work in which a person is regularly employed; career, occupation, profession

Vociferous   marked by or given to vehement insistent outcry

Volition   an act of making a choice or decision

Volubly   ready and rapid speech

Voluminous   having or marked by great volume or bulk

Warranted   sanctioned, authorized

Wary   marked by keen caution

Wavered   to weave or sway unsteadily to and fro

Whimsical   resulting from or characterized by whim or caprice; lightly fanciful

Wields   to exert one's authority by means of (*wield* influence)

Wily   full of wiles (a trick or a stratagem intended to ensnare or deceive); crafty

Wrath   strong vengeful anger or indignation

Yearning   to long persistently, wistfully, or sadly

Zealous   filled with or characterized by zeal (eagerness and ardent interest in pursuit of something)